Social Work Response to Examination Stress

Social Work Response to Examination Stress

Beena Antony Reji

KALPAZ

ISBN: 978-93-5128-180-1

Price: ₹ 890

First Published, 2016

Published by

Kalpaz Publications
C-30, Satyawati Nagar,
Delhi – 110052
E-mail: kalpaz@hotmail.com
Ph.: 9212142040

Printed at: G. Print Process, Delhi

Cataloging in Publication Data—DK
Courtesy: D.K. Agencies (P) Ltd. <docinfo@dkagencies.com>

Reji, Beena Antony, author.
Social work response to examination stress / Beena Antony Reji.
pages cm
Includes bibliographical references.
ISBN 9789351281801

1. Social service—India—Delhi—Psychological aspects. 2. Examinations—India—Delhi—Psychological aspects. 3. Students—India—Delhi—Psychology. 4. Stress (Psychology)— India—Delhi. I. Title.

LB1117.R45 2016 DDC 370.15095456 23

DEDICATION

I dedicate this book to my loving husband Reji and my dearest children- Divya and Rohan, And to all the children of the world-they are God's greatest gift to mankind.

Beena Antony Reji

Is this the Purpose of the School?

The first ray of sun kisses the earth, the birds are singing.
There goes the alarm clock, there's a hustle & bustle,
Amongst the chaos of brushing, bathing and dressing,
She is unaware of the glory of the morning.

Pack her up to school, in a dull grey uniform.
Hair in tight braids, with ribbon at the end.
Her freedom being tightened,
Just as the tie on her neck.

And there in school, no different.
Made to sit quietly, disciplining her with a bell.
Classes one after another, do not meander in the field.
Even her sports period is for her to do the drill.

Classes do nothing but box up her imagination, not allowing her to flow freely,
The battle of Panipat in 1526 and H_2SO_4 is Sulphuric acid.
She is being tested on her ability to memorize,
Not on what she thought or how she interpreted.

What if all roses were of the same colour?
And pruned to grow in the same way.
What if all fishes were to swim in straight rows?
What if all lions, tigers and snakes were tamed?

Is this the purpose of the school?
To make all children the same.
To create a breed of mediocre.
Killing their creativity and uniqueness.

Dr Beena Antony Reji

Contents

Preface

Stress is increasingly becoming a complex problem of our present times. It is very important that we understand this phenomena and how to deal with it. Stress management workshops and techniques are in vogue nowadays. Stress has infected every sections of our society in all age groups. School students are also affected by stress. School is considered another home for students. After family school is the most important socialising agent for a child. School plays an important role in making of an intellectual, mature and independent individual. School education is concerned with developing the body and mind, acquiring skills needed to mature into a self-reliant person with the right ideas, morals, balanced character and a behaviour which gives importance to discipline and sense of duty. But schools can also be a place of stress for the students. The school environment with its discipline, syllabus, school homework, and in some cases teachers are known to cause stress for the students. There is pressure on the students by the educational system.

Students, if exposed to optimal stress, are able to procure good results, but after certain point if the stress keeps on increasing, this stress becomes 'distress'. This brings in stress related disorders and decreased performance. If the stress continues behavioural, physical, emotional, cognitive problems may occur. Students are just like adults and are affected by stress but they are unable to comprehend stress and so are unable to control or deal with it. So they are more susceptible to the adversities of stress as what is most needed to gain control over stress is to control one's own life.

One of the most frightening events that cause stress in students is school examination. When students develop extreme apprehension of performing poorly in an examination, they experience examination related stresses. Researchers have shown that examination stress is a major factor contributing to a variety of negative outcomes like psychological distress, academic under achievement and academic failure. Many students have the mental capability to do well in examinations but are unable to do so because of extreme stress. Society also exerts pressure on students expecting students to do extremely well.

Over the last few years there has been an increase in examination stress among students in the higher classes of schools in India. This stress results in student's low academic performance and sometimes also causes suicidal ideations. Government and non-government organisations have initiated tele-counselling services to help students cope up with the examination stress. Helpline counsellors face an increasing number of anxious students and parents who are unable to handle stress due to examination. There is also an increase in the number of students suffering from traumatic disorders related to the fear of examinations.

Examination stress is the uneasiness, apprehensions or nervousness and extreme fear of performing poorly in the examination, and has now become a common form of stress among school students. Students suffering from examination stress may experience the association of academic performance with personal worth or fear of alienation from parents or friends or time pressure and feeling loss of control. An optimal level of arousal is necessary to best complete a task such as examination. However, when the stress or level of arousal exceeds that optimum, it results in a decline in performance.

This book is an attempt to understand examination stress, the extent of examination stress experienced by school students. What is the role played by familial environment, parental expectations and communication patterns on the aspirations of the students and how students respond to these demands created by the environment? It also explores the manifestation of examination stress by students and the coping strategies used by them. It is expected that the results of the study will help in the understanding of mental health needs of students and hence direct the nature of social work interventions in schools.

It is expected that the study will be beneficial to students, parents, teachers and school authorities also. The professionals like social workers, counsellors, psychologists, psychiatrists, school nurses and others interested in student's mental health can find this study useful in better understanding the phenomena of examination stress. The social work intervention model that emerges as the outcome of the study can be of significant importance in planning, organising and implementing school social work programmes to deal with examination stress.

Acknowledgements

Firstly, I thank JESUS for the bountiful blessings he has showered on me one of which is the completion of this research work. I express my feelings by these words from the Bible

"How precious, O God is your constant Love !
We find protection under the shadow of your wings"
(Psalms 36, 7)

I would like to acknowledge my heartfelt gratitude to Dr Tomy Philip who has been my guiding light. His intelligence, sense of logic, reasoning and hard work has inspired and helped in finally giving shape to this work.

I fondly thank my beloved parents, though far way in Kerala, their prayers and blessings has always shielded me in difficult times. I express my respectful gratitude to my supportive husband Reji, for adjusting to my demanding work schedule and always pushing me to achieve new heights.

My special thank to my patient children, Divya and Rohan I love you for always pepping me up with your pranks and melodious laughter. I thank my friends Archana Kaushik, Pooja Khanna, Sherry Joseph, R. Nalini, Neena Pandey and Reema Lamba who have been my pillars of strength. Their views, ideas and comments helped me to improve my work.

I dedicate my book to my student respondents and to all the school students may they bloom like flowers and be free from academic pressure to enjoy the light in learning and education.

Beena Antony Reji

Chapter I

Examination Stress: An Overview

Stress

Stress is an emotion consisting of fear and uncertainty that appears when an individual perceives an event as being a threat to him/her or to his/her ego or self-esteem. Stress in extreme cases produces unwarranted results. There is immense empirical support for the belief that stress has a negative impact on physiological and mental health (Bartlett, 1998). Stress is defined as a physiological non-specific reaction to external or internal demands (Selye, 1956). Alternately stress can be described as a relationship between individuals and their environment that is appraised as dangerous and evaluated as beyond their ability to deal with (Lazarus, 1966). Thus, more than the situation causing stress it is the person's perception and emotional response to it, that causes stress.

The modern world, which is considered to be a world of achievements, is also a world of stress. Stress is evident in every sphere of human life. Right from the time of birth till the last breath drawn, an individual is invariably exposed to various stressful situations (Pestonjee, 1999). The present age is often called the 'Age of Anxiety and Stress'. Stress is a term that did not originate in psychology or physiology, but was taken from the field of Physics. Selye introduced the concept of stress in Life Sciences. The word stress comes from the Latin word 'Stringere' implying force, pressure and strain on an object or person. In psychophysiology, stress refers to the environmental conditions that cause pressure on individuals, to which they cannot adjust- thereby affecting their behaviour and health.

The term stress is used to explain different negative feelings and reactions that accompany threatening or challenging situations. Not all responses to stress are negative. An optimum amount of stress is required for existence. The response to stress maximises the energy spent, thus, preparing the body to meet a threatening or challenging situation; the individual tends to mobilise enormous effort to deal with the event. While a certain amount of stress is necessary for survival, prolonged stress can affect health adversely (Bernard and Krupat, 1994). Different individuals react to situations in different ways. For example, a student who has forgotten his homework notebook at home is tensed, upset to go to the class and frightened to face his teacher, while another student in the same situation reacts in a way that is very relaxed and is not frightened to tell the teacher that he has forgotten the notebook home.

There are different kinds of stress- acute stress, episodic acute stress and chronic stress (Markle, 2006). These different kinds of stress have their own characteristics, symptoms, duration and treatment approaches. Acute stress is the most common form of stress. It occurs from demands and pressures of past and of future. Acute stress is exciting in small measures, but too much is exhausting. A student being caught for misconduct and sent to the principal's office or another not able to finish the school assignment on time are examples of this kind of stress. Acute stress symptoms are easy to recognise and the duration is short. Thus, it does not cause extensive harm. Acute stress could enter anyone's life but it is manageable. Episodic acute stress is reflected when people suffer from acute stress frequently. It is more frequent among people whose lives are disorderly and chaotic. Such people are always in a hurry but are always late. They take on too much of work and are unable to organise their work. Another form of episodic acute stress occurs due to endless worries and among people who are pessimistic about every situation. They are over aroused, short-tempered, anxious and tense. The third kind of stress, that is, chronic stress is neither thrilling nor exciting. In this type of stress, tension wears people away, day after day, and year after year. Chronic stress harms the body and causes long-term attrition. Examples of situations where chronic stress is experienced include stress of poverty, couple in conflict, person trapped in unhappy job or career and so forth. Chronic stress is a situation of total distress. Sometimes chronic stress stems from traumatic childhood experiences that get internalised as painful memories and then get reflected in their personality. Many a times in chronic stress people get used to the stress. Chronic stress leads to violence, heart attack, cancer and even suicide. People wear down due to prolonged stress till there is a final breakdown. As physical and mental resources exhausted through long time attrition, the symptoms of chronic stress are difficult to treat and require extended medical as well as behavioural treatment and stress management.

Conventionally, research on stress focuses on the physiological viewpoint it is oriented towards studies involving the body's responses to stressors. The cognitive processes that appraise the event as a stressor, explains the cognitive viewpoint. The various perspectives of the stress response have observed that different persons experiencing identical living environment are not necessarily affected in a similar way. There is an increasing concentration in the epidemiology of the diseases that are considered to be product of stress like hypertension, cardiovascular ailments, and depression. Research on the socio-economic factors of people suffering from these diseases reflects stressors that seemingly dispose persons toward these illnesses. These factors vary with race, gender, marital status and income.

The direction towards research on stress is shifting as consciousness of the social and cultural perspective involved in stress and coping are examined. Pearlin (1982) recommends that society, its value systems, the stratified populations, its institutions, and speed of transformation in these elements can be the sources of stress. Merton (1957) suggests that society can elicit stress by promoting values that conflict with the structures in which they are acted upon. As a consequence, many individuals who internalise these culturally prized goals are doomed to failure.

In history, we have seen that every age was known for a devastating disease. In the Middle Ages there were the plagues, then in the nineteenth century there were polio and pneumonia causing many deaths. These diseases were arrested with improved environmental conditions and advancements in medication. In the present times, stress is the major cause for various psychosomatic diseases like heart diseases, diabetes, gastrointestinal ulcers, cancer and respiratory diseases. In the beginning of nineteenth century the top killers in the world were infectious diseases and by the end of the century the top killer is stress-related diseases.

Stress among school students

School is the second home for a student. It is the second most important socialising agent after the family. An individual enters school as a child and by the time he finishes his schooling he becomes a young adult. School plays an important role in the making of an intelligent, responsible and independent individual. School education is concerned with developing the body and mind, acquiring special skills that require the use of the mind, developing appropriate values and attitudes, moulding character and behaviour with emphasis on discipline and sense of duty, acquiring information and learning how to apply them. But schools can also be a place of stress, fear and even pain for the students. The discipline, the timings of school, the curriculum, the homework and sometimes teachers are known to cause stress for students. There is an increasing pressure on the students by changes in the educational system. Schools burden the students by instigating them to excel. School management and the teachers want good results; they want their schools to be on the top and thus in turn pressurise the students. The schools strive for cent per cent results in board examination. Therefore, students who are not performing well in the school are often asked to leave school. Such actions increase the stresses among adolescent students. In the modern world, school environment is thought to be one of the major factors contributing to stress.

Ideally, school plays an important role in the development of cognitive, linguistic, social, emotional, moral and functional capacities in the students. Schools are increasingly restricting their roles in inculcating these positive attributes among students and compromising on their duty of guiding, supporting and promoting psychological and psychosocial developments of students. Students, generally, have to cope with expanded curriculum, syllabi, aloof teachers and very competitive examinations. The education department is reluctant to deal with the situation at macro level. Thus, schools for business purposes are mushrooming and education is getting highly commercialised. In the process, there is erosion of true meaning of education.

To procure good results students are exposed to optimal stress that they are able to cope with; but beyond a certain point, if the stress keeps on increasing, this stress becomes 'distress'. This brings in stress-related disorders and decreased performance. If the stress prolongs, behavioural, physical, emotional and cognitive effects set in. Stress regulates the activity of the central nervous system to fight the stressful situations and gets adapted to it. Students are like adults but they lack the ability to control or deal with stress.

One of the most threatening events that cause stress in students is academic examination. When students develop intense fear of performing poorly in an examination, they experience examination-related stress. Research reports have shown that examination stress is a major factor contributing to a variety of negative outcomes like psychological distress, academic under achievement and academic failure. Many students have the cognitive ability to do well in examinations but may not do so because of high levels of stress. There are high levels of societal expectation placed on academic examinations, which could potentially limit the student's educational and vocational opportunity (Zeidner, 1998).

Examination stress

The emotional reactions and physiological changes experienced by many students during examination have received increasing attention from physiologists and psychologists since the turn of the twentieth century. The emphasis has been on the physiological changes that were observed during examination situations. As early as in 1914 a study by Folin and his colleagues observed the presence of sugar in the urine of a group of medical students immediately after an examination.

Luria a renowned Russian physiologist in 1932 classified students as stable and unstable according to their behaviour before an examination. Luria found that examination situation evoked intense emotional reactions in the unstable students for whom these situations appeared to produce unmanageable stress (Spielberger, *et al.,* 1978).

Persons undertake important examinations either for getting promoted to the next level or for securing a seat in a particular educational institution or for a job. In India, good jobs are limited and seats in the best schools and colleges are limited; thereby creating an imbalance in the demand and supply. There is a huge demand for seats in educational institutions and jobs but only a few can obtain it. Thus, examination causes stress among students and their bodily and psychological reactions hinder their performance. Examination stress can be defined in terms of the fears and apprehensions of test situations and the consequences of the test results. In general the more difficult an examination is and the more important the consequences of an unsuccessful performance, the more likely the test situation will be perceived as threatening by most students.

Researchers who research anxiety phenomena often use the term stress and anxiety interchangeably. The term stress is used to denote different aspects of a temporal sequence of events that results in the state of anxiety (Spielberger, 1972). While stress is the adaptation of an individual to a situation or an event, anxiety refers to the complex emotional response that is induced in persons who translate situations as attacking. Anxiety is one of the most researched topic in psychology. Anxiety is understood as a reaction of an individual to an uncertain threat or a predictable danger. The anxiety reactions are more forceful and regular than is required by the apparent threat. Anxiety can be characterised by state anxiety and trait anxiety. State anxiety can be defined as an uncomfortable emotional state or situation that is differentiated by feelings of pressure and worry and the stimulation of the nervous system. Trait anxiety refers to the fairly constant personality nature. It mirrors individual diversity in anxiety proneness. Persons with high trait anxiety are more likely to risks when faced with difficult circumstances. Trait anxiety means that these persons have higher tendency for test anxiety than low anxious persons. General state anxiety and trait anxiety can further be subdivided into domain-specific anxieties such as social anxiety, sports anxiety, test (examination) anxiety, and mathematic anxiety (Sharma, 2002). Test anxiety refers to the anxiety by students in academic institutions because of examination.

A major source of confusion in research on stress has been due to the interchangeable use of the terms *stress* and *anxiety* (Sharma and Sud, 1990). The concepts can be viewed in the following lines.

> The term *stressor*...describes situations or stimuli that are objectively characterised by some degree of physical or psychological danger. The term *threat* refers to the individual's perception or appraisal of that situation or stimulus as potentially dangerous or harmful. People who see a stressful situation as threatening will experience an anxiety reaction. The term *state anxiety*...describe(s) an emotional reaction that consists of subjective feelings of tension, apprehension, nervousness and worry, and heightened activity of the autonomic nervous system. The overall process is referred to as stress. (Spielberger, 1972, p.17)

The two concepts 'test anxiety' and 'examination stress' are related and studies the same phenomenon. Test anxiety is the emotional response to the testing situation, that is, the flooding of fears, doubt and threats by the student when he/she is approaching examinations. Examination stress refers to the adaptations made by the student in the event of examination. In both the concepts test anxiety and examination stress, test or examination is the event or the stressor because of which the student suffers anxiety or stress.

Examination stress can be explained as "objective stimulus properties of the test situations" (Spielberger *et al.*, 1978; p.172). The term test anxiety is understood as "individual differences in anxiety proneness in examination situations" (Spielberger *et al.*, 1978, p.174). Test anxiety can, thus, be observed as a reaction to the stress experience. Test anxiety is induced when student's intellectual, motivational and social capabilities are strained by burdens from the person himself, from others or from the school environment. Spielberger *et al.* (1978)

in a chapter titled 'Examination stress and test anxiety' and Sharma and Sud (1990) have observed that examination stress and test anxiety are two related terms arising out of test/examination situations.

Kondas (1982) refers to 'Examination anxiety', another terminology used for the same phenomena. It refers to a mental state distinguishable by higher excitement, tension and fear in personally important and demanding condition. The situation comprises of conditions before and during examination. It is associated with cerebral stimulation and is considered a specific form of fear that disturbs performance. Test anxiety is sometimes subsumed under broader constructs such as examination stress of which it is a core feature (Stober and Pekrun, 2004). The terminology examination stress is of relatively recent origin. Based on the above review of literature, this study views test anxiety and examination stress as concepts studying similar phenomena. Examination stress can be considered a broader terminology, which arises out of a testing situation and the reactions are included in test anxiety.

Test anxiety has a long and rich history. Studies related to this concept began in 1914 and it was in 1952 that the concept began to be investigated under its own name. Mandler and Sarason (1952) published a series of studies on test anxiety and how it relates to performance. A sizable body of cumulative research findings has been published in different journals. It is also evident by the increasing number of scientific publications on test anxiety – more than 1000 since 1952 as summed up by Zeidner (1998). In the 1980s, test anxiety research reached its peak and started to decrease since then, though test anxiety remains an important factor in all disciplines of mental health and education.

To understand what is examination stress it is important to understand the theoretical perspective of stress and test anxiety.

Theoretical perspective on stress

Stressful situations are viewed as harmful, threatening, or challenging. According to Selye (1985) an important aspect of stress is that a wide variety of situations are capable of producing stress reactions, which come out in the form of fatigue, pain, fear and even success. This has led to different explanations of stress each of which highlights different facet of stress. One of the most comprehensive models of stress is the Biopsychosocial model of stress (Bernard and Krupat, 1994). According to this model, stress has three components, an external component, an internal component and the interaction between the external and internal components. The external component of the Biopsychosocial model of stress means environmental events that precede the recognition of stress and can cause a stress reaction. Stress reactions are caused by different psychosocial stimuli that are either physiologically or emotionally threatening and disturb the body's homeostasis.

The internal component of stress involves a set of neurological and physiological reactions to stress. Selye (1985) observed that a person subjected to prolonged stress goes through three stages: Alarm Reaction, Stage of Resistance and Exhaustion. He named this the General Adaptation Syndrome (GAS). This general response to stress is seen as a set of responses that activate the organism's resources to deal with an approaching threat. The alarm reaction is equal to fight-or-flight response and includes the different neurological and physiological responses when confronted with a stressor. When a threat is perceived the hypothalamus signals both the sympathetic nervous system and the pituitary system. The sympathetic nervous systems activate the adrenal glands. The adrenal glands release corticosteroids to increase metabolism, which provides instant energy. The pituitary gland releases adrenocorticotrophic hormone (ACTH), which also stimulates the adrenal glands. The adrenal glands then release epinephrine and norepinephrine, which prolong the fight-or-flight response. The stage of resistance is a continuous stage of arousal. If the stressful situation continues, the high levels of hormones in this resistance stage may disturb the homeostasis and damage the internal organs resulting in vulnerability of the organism to the disease. The exhaustion stage takes place after extended resistance. In this stage, the body's energy reserves are finally depleted and breakdown happens. Selye observed that in humans, many of the diseases caused by stress arise in the resistance stage and he calls these as "diseases of adaptation." The diseases of adaptation include headaches, insomnia, high blood pressure, cardiovascular and kidney diseases. The central nervous system and hormonal responses help in adaptation. This can also lead to diseases, especially when the stress is long-drawn-out or severe.

The third component of the biopsychosocial model of stress is the interaction between the external and internal components, related to the person's cognitive processes. Lazarus' cognitive theory of stress also talks of this interaction. He calls this interaction as a transaction between the individual and his environment. His theory places importance on the situation and its effect on the individual and not on the physiological responses. In this theory the manner in which a person appraises an event, plays an important role in influencing, not only the magnitude of the stress reaction, but also the kind of coping strategies that the individual can use in efforts to deal with the stress.

Dienstbier (1989) proposed another model of stress called Physiological Toughening, which concentrates on the duration of stressful events. He emphasises that stress differ in their duration. Acute stressors are the briefest and involve a tangible threat that is easily recognised as a stressor. Chronic stressors are those of a longer duration and are not easily identified as stressor as they are often ambiguous and intangible. Chronic stressors have become part and parcel of the present times thus they are taken for granted. They pose a serious health hazard if they are not recognised and appropriately managed. Physiological Toughening theory also talks of intermittent stressors that vary in duration, alternating from stress and calm. Intermitted stressor is viewed as a challenge. It could improve one's physiological resistance to stress by causing repeated, periodic increase in sympathetic arousal. This adapts the body to withstand other stressors better. For example, soldiers are trained and prepared for war, by creating war like situations, with resources, plans, and strategies and for all emergencies. Emergencies are, thus, altered into daily situations to decrease the intensity of the stressful situation.

Mandler's (1982) Interruption Theory of stress provides a transition between the internal component of stress and the interaction component. Mandler describes stress as a crisis indicating interruption. The fundamental basis is that autonomic activity results whenever some organised action or thought process is interrupted. The term interruption is used when any event, whether internal or external to the individual, avoids completion of some action, plans and is considered as interruption. Interruption can happen in the perpetual, cognitive, behavioural, or problem solving domains. The result of interruption will always be autonomic activity and will be interpreted emotionally in different ways, from most happy to most difficult.

According to the Transaction Theory of Stress proposed by Lazarus and Folkman the cognitive appraisal of stress is of two processes. This involves primary appraisal and secondary appraisal. Primary appraisal is the recognising of an event as stressful. At primary appraisal the event is classified as useless, useful, or stressful. If the event is appraised as stressful, the event is then assessed as a threat or a challenge. Lazarus is of the view that it is difficult to evaluate the source of stress by looking at the nature of the event, because stress is a process that occupies the interaction of the individual with the environment. Threatening stressors can create anxiety and challenging stressor can cause excitement. This theory helps to combine both the motivational aspects of stress and the different emotions that are linked with the experience of stress. Secondary appraisal arises after evaluating the event as a threat or a challenge. At the secondary appraisal the individual assesses his coping resources and alternatives. Stress arises, according to this theory only when a particular transaction is appraised by the individual as appropriate to his well being. Thus, in order for an event to be appraised as a stressor, it must be personally appropriate and there must be an apparent disparity between an event's demand and the individual's resources to cope with it.

Yet another theory explaining the phenomenon of stress is the cognitive activation theory of stress. The Cognitive Activation Theory of Stress is also called CATS. The term 'stress' is used for four aspects of stress, stress stimuli, stress experience, the non-specific general stress response, and experience of the stress response (Ursin *et al.*, 2004). The response to stress is an alarm in a homeostatic system, which produces broad and unspecific neurophysiological activation from different levels of arousal. The stress response occurs whenever there is something missing like a homeostatic imbalance, or a danger to homeostatsis and life of the living being. The alarm sounds when there is a difference between what should be and what is between the value a variable should have, and the real value of the same variable. The stress response, thus, is an important physiological response. If the alarm continues, the response may lead to illness and diseases by pathophysiological processes. The alarm calls for specific responses for coping, helplessness.

Test anxiety theories

There are specific theories on test anxiety that will help in the better understanding of the phenomenon of examination stress. Seymour Sarason who has worked for the development of the theory and research on test anxiety explained that we live in a test-conscious and test-giving society and our lives are determined by our performances in these tests. According to him, examination stress is a problem that is here to stay in the schools and colleges. Test anxiety is a widely studied personality variable, in part because it provides a measure of the personal salience of one important, definable class of threatening situations, those in which people are evaluated or assessed (Sarason, 1984).

According to the Test Anxiety Theory of Sarason and Mandler (1952), one of the leading theories in test anxiety, test anxiety is a "learned drive" and the testing situation evokes both, "learned task drives" and "learned anxiety drives". Some of the anxiety drives are "task relevant" while others are "task irrelevant". Both the drives are thought to be functionally alike as both add to the facilitation of efficient performance. The task irrelevant reaction induced by learned anxiety drives reduce the test performance. These reactions are evident by feelings of insufficiency, helplessness, and increased somatic responses, thoughts of penalty or loss of position and respect and efforts to abscond the testing situation. Individuals with high anxiety drives are driven to perform the task irrelevant behaviours that damage performance. Low-test anxious individuals less loaded by selfish inclination, can do easily the task-directed behaviours that promote achievement.

Later Sarason (1961) developed another test anxiety theory called Learning-Attentional Theory of Test Anxiety. His research has been associated with identifying situational aspect and personality features that add to the disparity in performance of high and low test anxious individuals in assessment situation. In a series of studies Sarason and his colleagues confirmed that when achievement features of performance are highlighted, high-test anxious individuals perform poorly than individual's who are low in test anxiety. By their study Sarason and his colleagues concluded that high-test anxious individuals are more selfish and self-critical than individuals low in test anxiety and are more probable to produce modified self-centred insulting reactions that hinder with task performance. Sarason depicts the behaviour of test anxious persons. The low-test anxious individual will head-on get involved with the task he is being assessed on. While the high test anxious moves inward, he ignores, misapprehends and experiences attentional blocks. Sarason observed that in anxiety disorders, precipitating proceedings bring out or enlarge fundamental individual concerns- like fears of harmful consequences. This gives rise to insecurity about result, hyper vigilance and apprehension over possible hazardous gestures. In looking for these gestures the individual may not give the required attention to the task at hand and so the performance goes down.

Lately, Sarason highlighted a cognitive perspective of anxiety that emphasised on the role of self-preoccupation in behaviour and physiological results. According to this perspective how the person thinks and feels in a particular circumstance and his stage of physiological stimulation at that time are strongly influenced by self-related thoughts. These thoughts have an important pressure over behaviour because they guide attention in particular manners.

For the test anxious student, there is a disparity in cognitive appraisal of test, self and results to objective elements of testing situation. Thus, individual disparities in test anxiety are a significant aspect of how an individual processes information. Evidences have shown the influence of high levels of test anxiety on information processing and performance. The negative pressure is heightened by examination stressors.

Wine (1971) proposed a cognitive attentional theory of test anxiety mentioning that individuals differ in the type of thoughts they develop during examination situation. The low anxious persons have a tendency to focus on the task while the high anxious persons mentally "wander off" to low self-esteem reflection and to the task, thereby affecting the performance results. Wine further observes that high-test anxious persons split their attention among the demand features of a task and task- irrelevant cognitive activities such as worry and self-criticism. This diverts the individual from task necessities thus effecting in lowering the performance. According to her, the highly test anxious individual reacts to the assessment testing situations with self-evaluative tension and so are unable to guide attention to task relevant alternatives.

Further research by Wine (1980) led to the development of a bi-directional model of anxiety in which she highlights the cognitive attentional features of persons scoring at two limits of test anxiety (high as well as low anxiety). Wine felt that the cognitive construction and self-reports of low-test anxious persons are just not reverse of the high test anxiety but vary qualitatively. The differences between low-test anxious and high-test anxious students as explained by Wine have been mentioned in the following table.

Low Test Anxious	***High Test Anxious***
Task oriented	Task avoidant
High belief in self efficacy	Low belief in self efficacy
Actor	Observer
Focused on task or situation	Focused on self and social evaluative cues
Active	Inactive
Current concerns-relevant cues in situation and appropriate actions	Current concern evaluation of others and anticipation of negative evaluation
Cognition situationally specific (wide range)	Cognition global and stereotypic (restricted range)
Arousal interpreted as energy	Arousal interpreted as distress
Behavioural, problem solving	Static cognitions
Kinesthetic imagery rehearsal of problem solving strategies	Visual imagery observes self negatively evaluated
In the present	Out of the situation

(Cited in Sanghvi, 1994)

Sarason (1975) put together the basic tenets of various theories on test anxiety of Sarason and Mandler (1952) and Wine (1971) and concluded that a person's level of test anxiety is to a significant degree, a product of experiences that influences what he attends to in himself and in the world. The highly test anxious individual is one who is prone to emit self-centred interfering responses when confronted with evaluating conditions.

All the theories of test anxiety reiterate that high test anxious individuals are prone to see examination situation as more hazardous and threatening than individuals with low anxiety. They experience worry cognitions and forceful state anxiety in circumstances in which they are assessed. These theories also highlights two components of test anxiety situation i.e. worry and emotionality. Liebert and Morris (1967) introduced the two components of worry and emotionality to test anxiety. According to them, two major components of test anxiety are worry and emotionality. Worry can be explained as the cognitive feature of the anxiety experience such as negative expectation and cognitive fears of themselves, the situation at hand and the possible consequences. Emotionality refers to individuals' perception of the physiological –affective features of the anxiety experience, that is indications of autonomic arousal and unpleasant feeling states such as tension and nervousness. Worry interferes with performance and results in decreased attention to intellectual and cognitive tasks. On the contrary, emotionality is not related to task performance except for individuals who are low on the worry factor. Worry and emotionality are correlated but worry items are more responsible for decrease in test performance.

Prevalence of examination stress

Over the last few years there has been an increase in examination stress among students in the higher classes of schools in India. As reported in a two-year prospective study by the department of mental health and behavioural sciences of Max Healthcare in New Delhi, over 70 per cent of the students appearing for board examinations, are experiencing more anxiety than they can handle (Kaul, 2005). Media reports indicate increased rate of suicide among students especially around the examination time. Government and non-government organisations have initiated telecounselling services to help students cope up with the examination stress a few years before. Helpline counsellors face an increasing number of anxious students and parents who are unable to handle stress due to examination. There is also an increase in the number of students suffering from traumatic disorders related to the fear of examinations (Chengappa, 2005).

Examination stress is the uneasiness, apprehensions or nervousness and extreme fear of performing poorly in the examination, and has now become a common form of stress among school students. Students suffering from examination stress may experience the association of academic performance with personal worth or fear of alienation from parents or friends or time pressure and feeling loss of control. An optimal level of arousal is necessary to best complete a task such as examination. However, when the stress or level of arousal exceeds that optimum, it results in a decline in performance. Examination stress has been reported to affect between thirty-four per cent to forty-one per cent of even third to sixth grade children (Beidel, 1991; Beidel *et al.*, 1998). The reasons for this apparent increase in prevalence of examination stress during the past years are unclear but may be related to parental or teacher pressure. Although the origin is unclear, it is clear that examination stress affects a substantial proportion of school age children. Sarason and Sarason (1990) explained that test anxiety is composed of three major components: cognitive, affective and behavioural. Students who experience test anxiety are worriers who lack self-confidence. They are preoccupied with negative thoughts, burdening their academic ability and intellectual competence. They feel helpless in an examination situation. Some negative thoughts are "I knew I was not going to pass this test", "I know I will get poor marks". The affective component causes test anxious students to experience physiological reactions such as increased heart rate, feeling nauseated, frequent urination, increased perspiration, cold hands, dry mouth and muscle pain (Zeidner, 1998). With these physiological reactions, emotions such as worry and panic may be present. When students are not able to control their emotions, they may experience higher levels of stress and low levels of concentration. Test anxious students express anxiety behaviourally by procrastinating and having inefficient study and test-taking skills. Zeidner (1998) contends that test anxious students have more difficult time interpreting information and organising it into larger patterns. Test anxiety affects children of all academic achievements and intellectual levels (Sarason *et al.*, 1960) and among various age groups.

Test anxiety is responsible for the student losing confidence in them and this lowers their self-esteem. The student feels he is a loser and is not able to cope with the examination situation. This in turn affects his personality and how he judges himself among his peer group and the society. Examination stress could be short-lived but in some cases it effects and scars the child's self-esteem permanently. The other effects of examination stress are negative influence on academic achievement (Sarason *et al.*, 1960). In its most extreme form, it can be a contributing factor to school refusal (Ollendick and Meyer, 1984). Children with test anxiety, in comparison to the non-test anxious, suffer from a broader pattern of psychological distress including higher general anxiety, more non-testing fears, and decreased estimates of their cognitive abilities. Studies of Beidel and Turner (1998); Beidel (1991) have shown that 50-60 per cent of children with test anxiety actually met the criteria for an anxiety disorder according to the Diagnostic and Statistical Manual of Mental Disorders (DSM). In majority of the cases, these children met the diagnostic criteria for social phobia or over anxious disorder. While most children may experience mild test anxiety at some time in their lives, there is an important subgroup, which is substantially large for whom test anxiety is a chronic and severe condition, and for them, the detrimental effect of test anxiety interferes with academic performance and social development too.

Researches have shown that stress is manifested in the body in as many as 1,200 ways (Gropper, 2005). Manifestations of examination stress are varied but they can be classified into four categories- physical, cognitive, emotional and behavioural. Physical manifestation include headache, dizziness, insomnia, clenching jaws, grinding teeth, facial twitching, nausea, vomiting, heartburn, indigestion, cramps, diarrhea, constipation, shaking, trembling, tremor of hands, clenching of fists, agitation, restlessness, feeling hyper, fatigue, weakness and appetite loss. Cognitive manifestations include decrease in concentration and increased forgetfulness, loss of decisiveness, decrease in sense of humour, mind racing, drawing blanks or confusions, indifference and loss of motivation. Emotional manifestations of examination stress include anxiousness, nervousness, depression, sadness or unhappiness, fear, worry, pessimism, irritability, impatience, anger and frustration, while behavioural manifestation are exhibited by fidgeting, pacing, restlessness, compulsive smoking, drinking, overeating, nail biting, foot tapping, jiggling knees, blaming, yelling, swearing, crying, weeping and feeling of always being on the verge of tears. There is a relation between stress and somatic symptoms.

Predisposing and precipitating factors of examination stress

Examination stress is on the rise because of the overemphasis on performance and perfectionism. Individuals are born with different talents and are not the same in intelligence, skills, capacities and abilities. But performance and perfectionism in education is gauged by achieving the first position in the examination, not realising that only one can hold the first position. The competition for highest marks also has its adverse effects. The emphasis is not on developing competency or performance, but on the marks obtained in the examination. The evaluation by percentages has created an unhealthy competitive environment in the educational system. There is cut-throat competition, which considers marks to decimal points. These pressures contribute to high examination stress among students especially for those appearing in the board examination or the school leaving examinations.

With families becoming more and more nuclear, parents have higher aspirations and expectations from their limited number of children. They want a super child who should excel in all spheres of life. The parents, many a time, wants their own ambitions to be fulfilled by their children. Children are also seen as a status symbol. All these put unwarranted pressure on the children. Lot of emphasis is given on the Board examination (Board examinations are the X and XII class examination that are conducted by the government examination boards) by parents, peer group as well as teachers and the school, as though this is the most important examination of life that will determine the child's future. The child sees everyone around over-concerned and over-conscious about his/her examination, further putting more pressure on him/her. The school environment also exerts pressure on the students for better results, as the school also has to perform better at the national/ state level in the board examination to keep its name high. Some schools in an attempt to keep the pressure on the students retain students who are not performing well in preboards (an examination held in schools before the board examination in X and XII classes). Schools don't want to give a chance to the students, as such school fears that if the students fail in the board examination, the name of the school will be tarnished. Thus, many students are forced to leave the schools, if they are not up to the standard of the school.

The higher educational scenario too is also very competitive in India. The seats available in professional and non-professional courses at the college level are limited and cannot accommodate the large number of students passing from the schools every year. In order to get admission to professional courses, students have to clear entrance examination, further increasing the examination anxiety at the secondary level. The employment opportunities, especially in the public sector are also decreasing. There is a situation of very high demand for admission to higher studies and employment but lesser opportunities. Privatisation has added to the problem. There has been a decrease in jobs available and there is a culture of 'hire and fire' in the public sector. Permanent jobs are replaced by contracts. Even today medical (MBBS) and engineering (BE) courses are considered as the best professional courses and students accord the highest priority to these courses. Management degree is a recent addition to this along with other professional courses like computers, biotechnology etc. The students even without getting an opportunity to realise their interest and capability are pushed towards these professions.

Need for social intervention

The consequence of examination stress adversely affects the future of the students by affecting their performance in the examination. This could also be the cause for suicides among students. Students who have been suffering on account of examination stress, endure everything with the hope that he/she will realise his expectations but when results are declared, realising the loses, take the extreme step towards self-destruction. The National Crime Record Bureau, in 2000 reported a total of 2320 people (1271 males and 1049 females) who committed suicide due to failure in different examinations. The extent of suicide due to examination failure accounts for 2.14 per cent of the total suicides in the country (Handbook on Social Welfare Statistics, 2004). These figures show that examination stress has emerged as a major concern for social work interventions in schools. The increasing trend in the suicide deaths due to the examination failure from 1380 persons in 1990 to 2320 persons in 2000 is also a matter of concern.

There is a growing awareness of the situation among various sections of society and they are helping out in their own ways to help students face this problem. Media for example, have been spreading the message on ways to cope with examination stress through talk shows with experts. Counsellors, psychologists and social workers are addressing this problem at schools and counselling centres. There has been a rise in the number of cases seeking help due to examination stress. Alarm bells are ringing across the educational campuses and examination boards as reports of students loosing their lives and suffering from nervous disorders are gaining visibility.

To a student, the prospect of sitting for an examination is a stressor and the resulting emotional and physiological state is often discomforting. It is essential that students cope effectively with examination stress so that the outcome of examination provide them happiness and success. Coping is to adjust oneself to the stress in our life. Lazarus and Folkman (1984) put forth eight separate coping strategies that help individuals in stressful situations including confrontation, seeking social support, planned problem-solving; self-control; accepting and escape/avoidance. Posen (1995) have listed different coping strategies to counter examination stress that include change in life style by taking well-balanced diet, regular exercise, adequate sleep, adequate leisure, involvement in relaxation exercise like deep breathing, meditation or change in stressful situations by time management, assertiveness, problem-solving or change in thinking by having a positive attitude, seeing problems as opportunities and by keeping a sense of humour.

Students cope with examination stress in ways they think are right; many a times they are not consciously aware of the stress and strain and may also resort to negative coping mechanisms. These affect them adversely and cause further problems. For example, students may resort to medicines to increase concentration and reduce sleep and stress. The abuse of drugs causes short-term and long-term problems in them and finally they are not able to accomplish their targets of getting good results in school. The well being of students is of prime importance to the school and preparing for examinations is only one of the objectives of the school. Stress cannot be totally eliminated but has to be reduced and appropriately managed. Students need to be introduced to intervention techniques to understand the phenomenon, so that they are empowered to handle this situation. Hathie *et al.* (1996) via a meta-analysis examined fifty-one studies of intervention to reduce examination stress. These interventions aimed at enhancing student learning by improving the students' use of either one or a combination of learning or study skills. Such interventions typically focus on task-related skills, self-management of learning or affective components such as motivation and self-concept.

Issues concerning the welfare of children are of paramount importance to the society as children are the future of the nation. As a nation that is thriving towards compulsory education till 14 years, the children should be adequately supported with resources to overcome all obstacles in learning at home, school or broader societal environment. Services by counsellors, psychologists and social workers can enhance children's well being through interventions to assess and rectify learning and behaviour problems of students to improve their mental health and academic achievement.

Society recognises the presence of examination stress of school students and various government and non-government organisations are incorporating measures in their working with school students to address this problem. Services like telephonic counselling, face to face counselling, talks, seminars are being provided to help students and parents to face the problem of examination stress. CBSE, Directorate of Education, NCERT, Snehi, Sumaitri Berfrienders India, Sanjeevani Society for Mental Health, VIMHANS, Max Health Clinic and Sarthak are some of the organisations that have planned measures to improve the situation in the city of Delhi. Central Board of Secondary Education, the examination board of the country has brought in examination reforms to arrest the problem. From 2006, CBSE examination has given an extra 15 minutes to read the question paper, giving time to de-stress the students before the examination. In 2008, CBSE has changed to Cumulative Grade Point Average (CGPA) system for classes IX and X. The grading has helped to reduce the examination stress without blurring the lines between good and mediocre students. The system of continuous and comprehensive evaluation (CCE) has also reduced examination stress among school students. This lays emphasis on school-based assessment. Primary classes also have CCE in place. The National Progressive Schools Conference (NPSC), an association of more than 100 prominent independent schools of Delhi along with an NGO have introduced a comprehensive mental health programme into their curriculum so that the mental health issues of the students can be taken up, of which one of issues being taken up is examination stress.

In conclude, examination stress is a major factor contributing to a variety of negative outcomes like psychological distress and academic underachievement. Some students have the cognitive ability to do well in examinations but examination stress cripples their performance and this adversely affects their personality. This study is an attempt to understand the extent of examination stress and develop measures to control the problem.

Chapter II

Examination Stress: Retrospect and Prospects

Research on examination stress and test anxiety is little short of a century old. In the 1930s and 1940s there was an increase in experimental research to understand the problem of anxiety. Since the turn of the twentyfirst century there is an emphasis on specific forms of anxiety, like sports anxiety, social anxiety and test anxiety. The earliest study in research on test anxiety was first reported in 1914. In 1930s, Luria a Russian physiologist drew the attention to individual differences in emotions experienced by students in an examination situation. In 1950s, there was again an increase in research work on this issue. By now test anxiety became the widely studied anxiety. This led to the development of instruments to measure the test anxiety of individuals, Test anxiety questionnaire and Test anxiety scale for children by Sarason and colleagues in 1960 resulted in an increase in research studies which continued till 1980s. Here we observe the contribution of Spielberger (1966, 1972, 1978), Liebert and Morris (1967), Wine (1971) and Sarason (1961, 1972, 1984) in the advancement of the conceptual framework of the phenomena. Zeidner (1988) had observed that the period between 1950s and 1980s contributed to enormous collection of research studies in the area of test anxiety. After a peak in 1980s there has been a decline in the trend of scientific publications in test anxiety but this is because test anxiety has been covered under a broader construct that is examination stress

(Stober, and Pekrun, 2004) and research work has been appearing in different name like performance anxiety relating to artists, or competitive anxiety relating to sportsmen, maths anxiety or statistic anxiety (Hembree 1990; Birenbaum and Gutvirtyz, 1993; Cate and Rhymer, 2003). Examination stress was studied worldwide; Nijhawan conducted the first study in India in 1972. This chapter will cover the review of literature on examination stress and related works that will help in the understanding of the phenomena of examination stress.

The Research studies included for the review are from published and unpublished sources. Research studies were procured from books, articles from journals and from the Internet. PhD, M.Phil thesis were also consulted in the concerned and related topics.

The researcher also collected literature from the Resource centre of Indian Council of Social Science Research, New Delhi. This resource centre has access to various databases and also subscribes to various online journals. The data base which were useful for the present review of literature were Psyc Lit (1991-1997), Psyc INFO (1999), Educational Resources Information Center (ERIC) 1983-2003, CSA Multiple Databases, Sociological Abstracts and Social Services Abstracts.

Literature on empirical studies has been thematically reviewed under five subheadings according to the objective of the present study. The themes include:

- Extent of examination stress among students
- Factors contributing to examination stress
- Manifestations of examination stress
- Strategies of coping with examination stress
- Evidence-based interventions

Extent of examination stress among school students

Examination stress is a universal phenomenon. Research studies conducted in different countries observe the presence of examination stress among students. The students of the different cultures studied include Singapore primary school students (Parker *et al.*, 2003), Sydney High school students (Hannah, 2006), Canadian high school students

(Gierl and Roger, 1996), Japanese students (Araki, 1992; Shioya, 1995), Australian high school students (King *et al.*, 1995; Kouzma and Kennedy, 2004), Arab students in Israel (Birenbaum *et al.*, 1994), Ecuador students (Ayora, 1993), Italian students (Comumian, 1993), German students (Kirshmann and Rohm, 1991), South African students (Mwamwenda, 1994) and Brazilian students (Coes, 1991).

Reports of few cross-cultural studies published during the last two decades have brought out the differences in examination stress across cultures. El-Zahhar and Hocevar (1991) found high levels of test anxiety among students in Egypt and Brazil as compared to the students in America. Sharma and Sud (1990) studied four Asian (Indian, Jordanian, Chinese and Korean) and five Euro-American (Hungarian, Turkish, Italian, German and American) cultures and observed that students from Korea, Jordan and America lie in the upper range of test anxiety and those students belonging to Germany, Hungary and China lie in the lower range of test anxiety. El-Safly (1995) also observed negative correlation between test anxiety and achievement motivation among students in Egypt and UAE. In a research study by Yue (1994) it was found that Chinese students were more appreciative of the role of examination stress in learning than American students. Sud (1990; 1991) conducted two studies observed the cross-cultural difference in test anxiety, in the first study he compared Indian students with Italian students and in the second study he compared the Indian students with the American students. Results of the two studies found that higher levels of examination stress was observed among Indian students as compared to their Italian and American counterparts. Similarly Son and Matubara (1991) found that students in China have higher test anxiety than students in Japan.

Gender difference has been observed on examination stress in different research studies. Higher score of test anxiety among female students are reported in different countries. El-Zahhar and Hocevar (1991) found female high school students with high levels of test anxiety in Egypt, Brazil and America. Similar results were observed in a study by Sharma and Sud (1990) across nine cultures viz. Indian, Jordanian, Chinese, Korean, American, Hungarian, Turkish, Italian and German that reported girls with high examination stress. Some studies stated that female students are more test anxious, more worrisome and more emotional compared to male students. (Nijhawan, 1972; Singh and Broota, 1992; Araki, 1992; Birenbaun and Gutvirtz, 1993; Grover, 1996; Besharat, 2003). Higher test anxiety in females was traced to their greater role expectation conflict as compared to male students. Indian high school female students reported greater worry than the college female students in a study by Sud, (1991). In another study Higgins, (2000) reported that male students have higher achievement scores, as female students recorded higher test anxiety. However, Jeanell (1984) found that the absence of fear of success among female students resulted in lower examination stress and the study concluded that gender had no modulating influence on stress response.

The research studies reviewed on examination stress and test anxiety had studied these phenomena among students at various educational levels. Among the school levels itself various research studies reported examination stress in primary school class (Cox, 1971; Araki, 1992), among middle school students by Schimitt and Crocker (1982), Davis (1986), Arkai (1992) and Stanton (1992). High school students were also reported with examination stress (Volkmer and Feather, 1991; Gupta and Sharma, 1991; Singh and Broota, 1992; Newbegin and Owens, 1996; William, 1996; Zeidner, 1996; Sood, 1998; Krishnamurthy, 2000; Katyal *et al.*, 2001; Lata and Dwivedi, 2001).

Various research studies have found high examination stress among students of different countries appearing for the school leaving examination. The school leaving year examination is given too much of emphasis, this results in high stress levels among the students. (Volkmer and Feather, 1991; Gupta and Sharma, 1996; William, 1996; Zeidner, 1996; Soric, 1999; Krishnamurthy, 2000). El-Zahhar and Hocevar (1991) also found high scores of test anxiety were reported by Egyptian high school students in the school leaving examination. The performance in this final year schooling examination is important as admission into college and higher professional courses (medicine, engineering) depend on the marks obtained in these examination.

Gadry and Bradshaw (2000) also observed that formal examination places high anxious pupil at a disadvantage to the less anxious and the introduction of progressive assessment favours the high anxious. However, the low-anxious students performed better than the high anxious students under both terminal and progressive examining.

Research studies on college students also have reported high examination stress among them (Brown and Nelson, 1983; Rao *et al.*, 2000; Lata and Dwivedi, 2001; Cates and Rhymer, 2003). High examination stress level has been observed among postgraduate students (Semple *et al.*, 1988; Sarladevi, 2004), among medical students (Leo, 1986; Lewis *et al.*, 2000; Sarikay *et al.*, 2006) and among Ph.D. students (Fortuyn, 2004).

Examination stress is the stress occurring because of the pressures of examination. Examination stress starts much before the examination, continues during examination and sometimes continues after the results of the examination are declared. At all phases of examination i.e. in pre-examination period, during examination and post-examination physiological changes on account of stress has been reported by Strelets and his colleagues (1998);Govorkian (2003); Simic (2006); Koul and Bhadwal (1991); Grina (1987) and Soric (1999). In a study by Jemmoth (1983) and his colleagues, at different phase examination stress was studied using salivary secretor immunoglobulin A (s-IgA) as an indicator of stress. The s-IgA secretion rate was measured five times, during initial low-stress period, three high stress periods coinciding with major examination and a final low-stress period. The results showed s-IgA secretion rate was significantly lowered in high-stress than low-stress periods for all students.

Few researchers have examined the influence of socio-economic environmental factors on examination stress. Akanda (1990) examined the influence of urban-rural upbringing on Nigerian student's test anxiety levels and observed that younger urban groups scored higher than older rural groups in academic performance. In India, a study by Nijhawan (1972) observed that rural children from upper class of society were more test anxious. Bhadwal and Panda (1992) found a package of curricular strategies on cognitive and non-cognitive characteristics decreased levels of test anxiety among rural primary school students. In another research by Krishnamurthy (2000) that studied the relationship in test anxiety and achievement in history among rural and urban students, results revealed no significant difference on the basis of gender, locality, parent's education, income and test anxiety or achievement in history.

Indian research studies have examined difference in examination stress among students due to difference in the type of schools. Grover (1996) in her study in Delhi observed that government and aided school students had high levels of test anxiety and low academic performance. Central school students had average test anxiety, while public school students exhibited low-test anxiety and high performance. On the contrary a study by Chatrath (2004) reported high mental stress experienced by public school students during examination.

Factors contributing to examination stress

This section deals with various studies to understand the role played by family environment, personality and aspirations of the student, skill deficit, school environment and other factors in inducing examination stress.

Family environment of the students and its relationship with examination stress was examined by various research studies. Singh and Broota (1992) found that parental pressure increased test anxiety among students. The parents' occupational and educational background also affected test anxiety, while in a study by Besharat (2003) results showed maternal perfectionist attitude increased examination anxiety among students. Nijhawan (1972) examined the association between examination stress and parent-child relationship as well as early childhood experience. It was observed that high anxious children showed higher incidence of illnesses and traumatic experiences. Low anxious children's mothers were found to be warm and permissive. Parents of low anxious students less beat their children and are more democratic in their behaviour towards children. Greater discrepancy was found in the attitudes of mothers and fathers of high anxious children. Parents of high anxious children were more rigid and children from autocratic families and families with high degree of tension on various household issues were found to be more prone to high anxiety.

Anand (2002) observed that well-adjusted adolescents show better perception of family environment than maladjusted adolescents on three dimensions of family environment that is cohesion, expressiveness and recreational orientation. Well-adjusted adolescents showed lower levels of anxiety as compared to maladjusted adolescents. Another study by Peleng-Popko (2002) found similar results indicating that there was an inverse relationship between children's test anxiety and family interaction on factors like communication and encouragement of personal growth. Palmer (1999) in his research study found that family responsibilities and family commitments increased examination stress.

Some research studies attributed high examination stress to the individual personality of the students. In a study by Sharma (1986) it was observed that high anxious individuals and emotionally less matured (unstable) persons were found to exhibit high-test anxiety, while low anxious and emotionally more matured (stable) individuals tended to be less test anxious. Osterhouse (1975) found that test anxious students have a tendency to respond to the examination stress with self-evaluation and task-irrelevant response that interferes with examination performance. While the low-test anxious students have lesser interfering response, they focus more of their energy and attention on the examination. Similar results were found by Brush *et al.* (1983) where they reported that the anxious students, when under evaluative threat, engage in more negative thinking that interfere with task accomplishment. Carver *et al.* (1983) also found similar results indicating that self-directed attention impairs the performance of test-anxious persons in an examination situation, while it improves the performance of low-test anxious students.

Sud and Prabha (2003) reported a new dimension to the findings on examination stress where they found that academic performance was negatively related to self-oriented perfectionism, procrastination, test anxiety, worry and emotionality of the students. However, Rajendran and Kaliappan (1991) reported that personal inadequacy, fear of failure, inter personal difficulties and lack of study facilities are the main factors causing examination stress.

Few studies reported students' aspirations as one of the major factors causing examination stress. In a study by Sharma (1986) the results observed students with high aspiration level, low intelligence and high academic achievement exhibited higher level of test anxiety as compared to those having low aspiration level, high intelligence and low academic achievement. Dendato and Diener (1986) also observed that test anxiety is the result of past failures and the student knowledge that he is unprepared for the examination. Study practices of students have been a key variable in explaining the etiology of examination stress. Studies have stated that lack of study skills in students contribute to examination stress. Musch and Broder (1999) have reported that test anxious students have skill deficits thus low in performance. Study habits and examination-taking skills of high test-anxious students have been found to be poor and inadequate (Culler and Holahan, 1980; Benjamin *et al.*, 1981; Tobias, 1985; Dendato and Diner, 1986). Paulman and Kennelly (1984) stated that good examination skills can compensate for anxiety-induced deficits in working memory capacity by refocusing attention toward the task. They also stated that test anxiety and examination taking ability independently influence cognitive problem solving in the examination setting. Similar findings have been reported by Benjamin *et al.* (1981) and Benjamin (1991) where they reported that high-test anxious students also have problem encoding, organising information and in retrieval of information in an examination situation. Culler and Holahan (1980) also attributed quality of study habits and amount of study time were positively related to academic performance for high test-anxious students, while missing classes and delaying examination were inversely related to their performance.

Another study that repatriated the importance of study habits was by Wittmainer (1972). The study examined the relationship between facilitating test anxiety and debilitating test anxiety and study habits. It was observed that students with low debilitating test anxiety scores have more effective study habits and avoid delaying academic tasks indicating that test anxious student's test performance is affected by ineffective pre-examination behaviour.

Research studies have also reported the effect of school environment on students test anxiety. Osterhouse (1975) found that a high level of classroom anxiety debilitate the examination performance of high-test anxiety students. Torsheim and Wold (2001) reinforced the earlier study and reported that students with high level of stress had higher somatic complaints. A study by Honnah (2006) attributed hefty homework to extreme stress among senior school students who have been identified with worrying levels of anxiety and depression and a tendency to inflict self-harm. Crocker and Schmitt (1987) have established the link between nature of question in examinations and examination stress. Multiple-choice items in the examination paper can reduce test anxiety.

Manifestations of examination stress

There are various research studies that have examined the manifestations of examination stress among students. These studies have been broadly classified and arranged according to physiological, cognitive, behavioural and emotional manifestations.

It is perfectly normal to experience symptoms of anxiety or stress before and during an examination. These feelings are caused by the release of adrenaline, which is the body's normal reaction to fear. The release of adrenaline causes a series of physiological reactions. This causes heart to beat faster so that blood can be carried to where it is most needed. Breathing becomes rapid in order to provide more oxygen, which provides more energy. Digestive system slows down allowing more blood to reach the muscles, and as a result the mouth may feel dry. The need to go to the toilet is the body's response to rid itself of waste products, thus making the body lighter. Brain becomes alert as senses are heightened.

Examination stress alters the salivary immunoglobulin A (s Ig A) in students facing examination (McCleeland *et al.*,1985; Mouton *et al.*, 1989; Deinzer and Schullar, 1998; Deinzer *et al.*, 2000; Bosch *et al.*, 2004). Research report of Bosch (2004) and his colleagues found that acute stress of important examination is associated with enhanced salivary Ig A levels, while extended examination period is associated with lowered salivary Ig A. These research results were supported by Jemmott's (1988) study that found salivary Ig A level lowered during examination. Students reporting more social support had consistently higher salivary Ig A than others with less social support. Spangler (1997) also studied different emotional and physiological response patterns during examination, and observed that heightened anxiety was observed only before the examination, while during examination the physiological responses like heart rates and cortisol and salivary IgA levels were higher.

Examination stress alters the white blood cells and platelets in the blood during examination. (Karp *et al.*, 1989; Shukla *et al.*, 1993; McCann *et al.*, 1996; Qureshi *et al.*, 2002; Saraladevi and Devraj, 2003; Fortuyn, 2004). Pramanik (2005) and colleagues reported significant rise in mean blood pressure during the period of preparation for examination.

Another physiological change found due to examination stress was increased nervous system activity during examination, which caused alterations in the structure and functions of heart and body (Shcherbatykh, 2000; Gevorkian *et al.*, 2003; Makarenko *et al.*, 2003). Shenkin (2004) and his colleagues reported increased urine cortisol excretion during and before examination. The study detected only small changes in immune function related to examination stress but micronutrient supplementation limited the reduction in T lymphocyte numbers associated with severity of depression.

According to Johansson (1988) and his colleagues, the psychological stress is associated with different hormonal effects in males and females, and the male Luteininzing hormone (LH) values were lower than their control levels, but there was no such difference in the females. Another aspect of physiological manifestations of examination stress includes adverse consequences for immune function. Students took an average of three days longer to completely heal the wound during examination (Marcuha *et al.*, 1998).

Cognitive manifestations of examination stress include negative thinking, tears, worries and ideas of helplessness and worthlessness. While approaching examinations most students are worried and experience problem in concentration (Keogh *et al.*, 2004). Lee (1999) reported that during examination, highly anxious students have less available working memory capacity for task solution than their low-anxious counterparts. Yet another study on cognitive manifestations by Galassi *et al.* (1981) reported that behaviour of high, moderate and low-test anxious students significantly differed from high-test anxious students on eight dependent variables that are positive thoughts, negative thoughts, evaluation, potency, activity sematic differentials, history test grade, bodily sensation and subjective units of disturbance scale score. Students with high grade point averages received significantly higher test grades and reported more bodily sensation indicative of arousal than students with low grade point averages. Students assessed towards the end of the test (in the last 10 minutes) reported significantly more negative thoughts and bodily sensations.

Few researchers have studied the emotional manifestations of students during examination. According to Spangler *et al.* (2002) negative emotions are highest before, and at the beginning of the examinations and positive emotions increase during the examination and reach the highest after the examination. Students with extreme test anxiety score experience anxiety disorders, high levels of self-reported fear, anxiety, depression, hopelessness and dysfunctional thinking (King *et al.*, 1995).

Duke and Davidson (2002) compared the emotional feeling state of students before, during and after examination. According to them a week before examination, anxiety and its negative effects are high. Recurrent dreams are significantly higher in nights before the examination than after the examination.

Examination stress also influences the behaviour patterns of students. In a study by Palmer (1999) behavioural manifestations like disturbed sleep patterns, tiredness and irregular eating habits. Examination stressed student's group reported significant increase in perceived stress and deterioration in emotional well being at the examination periods. Those with high examination stress had high trait anxiety, low social support and showed significant increase in total energy intake and high amount of fat consumed. Students with low trait anxiety and high social support showed a reduction in energy intake. Some of these results were replicated in a study by Oaten and Cheng (2005) who reported caffeine consumption and reduction in healthy eating habits, poor emotional control, reduction in exercise, deterioration in sleep pattern and study habits during examination.

There are disparate views on the components of test anxiety. Minor and Gold (1985) and Liebert and Morris (1967) mentioned worry and emotionality as two components of test anxiety. Minor and Gold (1985) found worry to be correlated with measures of internal dialogue and emotionality was found to be correlated with the self-reported arousal measures. Liebert and Morris (1967) found worry was inversely related to performance and emotionality had no relationship with performance. Another component of test anxiety comprise task-generated interference to performance. Research studies indicate that all three components affect examination performance (Spiegler *et al.*, 1968; Doctor and Attman, 1969; Morris *et al.*, 1981).

Deffenbacher (1977, 1986) studied cognitive and physiological components of test anxiety in real-life examination and observed that worry, emotionality and task-generated interference correlated positively with each other and negatively with performance. High-anxious subjects performed poorer, had higher pulse rate and reported more worry, emotionality and task-generated interference. High worriers performed less well than low worriers. Sarason (1984) also examined worry, tension, test-irrelevant thinking and bodily symptoms to performance and cognitive interference and found that anxiety is a problem of intrusive thoughts that interfere with task-focused thinking. The relation between the emotionality component of test anxiety and performance in Cassady and Johnson (2002) study revealed that moderate levels of physiological arousal were associated with higher examination performance. Cognitive test anxiety exerts a significant negative impact on academic performance measures.

Coping with examination stress

Coping means a characteristic or typical manner of approaching a stressful situation and dealing with it. Coping with examination stress is related to a reduction in psychological distress and physical symptoms, as experienced by students while enduring highly demanding examinations. Research studies on coping with examination stress highlight various adaptive coping strategies that are beneficial in reducing examination stress and in improving academic performance.

Students can be helped to cope with the examination situation by successful task strategies and varying the situational parameters that surround testing conditions. Modeling can be used to teach coping response to students (Sarason, 1973; Dusek and Dusek, 1978). Roy (n.d.) investigated wishful thinking and problem-focused coping and found that wishful thinkers are also more likely to be anxious while problem-focused copers are not anxious, depressed or stressed as they focus on the problem and finding ways to get out of the situation.

Spangler and colleagues (2002) reported that the influence of coping on emotional regulation is significant both on the emotional and adrenocortical level. Emotion-focused coping is related to low anxiety and cortisol response. Emotional as well as adrenocortical response depend on the situation and are co-regulated by stable psychological characteristics, emotional disposition and coping abilities. Students with high ego-resiliency show better coping than subjects with low ego-resiliency both on emotional level and on the physiological level.

Research study of Lee and Larson (1996) reported that problem-solving and information-seeking coping styles were related to reduction in depression while emotional coping was related to increase in physical symptoms. Coping with examination stress is related to adjustment and independent of the level of additional life event stress. Students with poor coping strategies do not perform well in their examinations. Examination-taking coping strategies and study coping strategies reduce test anxiety and improve test performance (Onwuegbuzie and Daley, 1996).

Palmer (1999) reported that in an examination room student, who is intelligent and well schooled in subjects, could fail an examination due to examination nervousness. Thus, examination is not a test of knowledge or educational ability but a test of stress coping ability. Palmer (1999) then formulated three styles of coping with examination stress that are operational. Style A is used when examination pressure creates the motivation to study leading to better performance. Style B corresponds to resignation when not enough revision has been done. Style C is adoption of an attitude that studying will help in dealing with other external stressors. Because of studying the student is away from other stressors. Those with type C style of coping do not face examination stress but they may experience difficult symptoms during the post-examination phase.

Sood (1998) in his study on coping strategies of high school students, the researcher observed that students low on stress used more direct coping strategies. Fear of failure as a source of stress was highly correlated with general coping. Personal inadequacy and direct coping were significantly correlated. Girls more often used direct coping and suppression as coping strategies and exhibited a higher degree of fear of failure than boys. Gender differences were noted in the use of emotion focused coping, females preferred distress reducing strategies and social support while males preferred high risk coping behaviours (Rao *et al.*, 2000).

Ramya (2002) found junior college students used a variety of coping strategies like problem-focused coping, emotion-focused coping, avoidance, acceptance, denial, mental behavioural disengagement, cognitive restructuring, seeking social support and so forth. Students also resorted to maladaptive coping strategies like taking alcohol, smoking, taking minor tranquilizers, taking mood-elevating drugs and seeking sexual comfort.

Some of the adaptive coping strategies used by students at examination time include cognitive appraising, task focusing, emotion focusing, maintenance of household chores and self-care habits (Schutz *et al.*, 2004 ; Oaten and Cheng, 2005). Time management, help seeking, uncontrolled relaxations, positive reappraisal in waking, active problem-solving in dreams and rest (Duke and Davidson, 2002). Maladaptation style of coping includes excessive sleeping, smoking and substance abuse.

Evidence based interventions

A number of research studies have examined the impact of examination stress management using professional nature of intervention. Different interventions experimented in these studies throw light on the intervention and its effect on students' examination stress.

Examination stress is a serious problem among students as it is negatively associated with performance, achievement, and selection of a course or an occupation. Students react to examination stress with fear and threat, reduced feeling of self-efficacy, self-derogatory feeling, anticipating failure and intense emotional response and arousal at the first sign of failure making of an important cause of concern in the present times.

There are different ways of understanding this problem and there are different ways of approaching for interventions. Earlier examination stress was understood as was a physiological and emotional phenomenon and hence treatment was aimed at reducing the physiological arousal through behavioural methods. Recently there has been a renewed focus on cognitive approaches.

For the examination stress different approaches have emerged over a period of time. These approaches are the behavioural approaches include specific interventions like systematic desensitisation, relaxation training, anxiety management training and various behavioural adjuncts such as yoga and transcendental mediation. Cognitive approaches include rational emotive therapy, cognitive restructuring, and cognitive modeling. Cognitive-behavioural approaches (Wessel and Mersch, 1994; Sud and Prabha, 1995; Elia, 1998; Wachelka and Katz, 1999) includes cognitive-behavioural modification, stress-inoculation training. Skill-deficit approaches include study skills training, attentional skill training. The eclectic approaches combining cognitive, behavioural and skill-focused approaches have also been used as programme intervention for most of examination stress.

Some of the research results that are worth mentioning are the study on desensitisation and study skills training by Osterhouse (1972). His findings indicated that desensitisation offers more promise as a treatment method for test anxiety than did training in study skills. Richardson and Suinn (1974) examined desensitisation and anxiety management training and observed that, the desensitisation procedure was significantly more effective than anxiety management training. Anxiety management training reduced test anxiety with just one hour of direct training but however did not reduce other salient fears as measured by a fear survey schedule.

Sud (1994) examined the efficacy of attentional skills training and cognitive modeling as short-term cognitive interventions and results revealed that attentional skills training was effective in worry state, emotionality state, anxiety interference and task generated interference and cognitive modeling was effective in the worry state and task generated interference. Harris (1987) observed that individual treatment was more effective than group treatment and live treatment more effective than automated treatment.

Juster (1985) developed a model to reduce examination stress and increase academic performance. The components of the model included facilitating academic belief, ability level, internal dialogue, study skills and test taking skills and strategies. Carver and colleagues (1983) proposed that self-directed attention impairs the performance of test-anxious persons in evaluative situation. Self-focus is sometimes facilitating and sometime debilitating depending upon the person's expectancies of being able to perform adequately. It was observed that self-directed attention interacted with level of test anxiety to increase persistence among low-anxious subjects and to decrease it among the test anxious subjects.

Few research studies made comparison of the interventions, stating which intervention was more effective. Cornish and Dilley, (1973) compared systematic desensitisation, implosive therapy and study counselling. All three have been effective in reducing test anxiety while systematic desensitisation was more effective than the other two methods of reducing anxiety.

Lent and Russell (1978) compared the effectiveness of two multi-component strategy in treatment of test anxiety. Systematic desensitisation in combination with a study-skill course was combined with cue-controlled desensitisation study-skill programme. Both multi-component groups significantly improved grade point averages and reduced anxiety more effectively than just a study skill programme.

Harris and Johnson (1980) compared three intervention programmes on test anxious students to find which programme reduced test anxiety and improved academic performance. Individualised covert modeling combined with study skills training and self-control desensitisation combined with study skill training were compared and both intervention were found to have substantially reduced self-reported test anxiety. However, the individualised covert modeling group was the only treatment group that showed significant improvement in academic performance.

Kirkland and colleagues (1980) reported that an intervention aimed at skills acquisition was superior to cue-controlled relaxation and meditation in increasing academic performance.

Bradely (1987) compared three multi-modal treatment packages for test anxiety. Individualised covert modeling plus study skills and relaxation training, systematic desensitisation plus study skills and relaxation training and study skills plus relaxation training. It was found all three packages reduced test anxiety but systematic desensitisation plus study skills and relaxation training package proved better than the other two in lowering test anxiety.

There is abundant literature that exists on intervention in examination stress. They describe the process and outcome of stress and anxiety reduction programmes. This shows that examination stress as a problem is on the rise and examination stress reduction programmes have gained widespread acceptance among students.

Conclusion

The review of various research studies and related topics has provided deeper insight on the complex phenomenon of examination stress. This chapter categorised the finding thematically into subheadings. The first section shows that examination stress is a universal phenomenon as research studies have indicated its presence world over. Finding indicates that examination stress is widespread and is observed among students of all age groups, including even the primary school students. Female students have higher examination stress as compared to boys. An understanding into the contributory factors of examination stress enlightens what are the issues, problem that need to be taken up to manage examination stress. Various studies on changes in individual during examination give information of the different manifestation of examination stress observed among students.

The studies on coping strategies elaborates on coping strategies taken up by students and throws light on the different kinds of coping strategies both adaptive and maladaptive. The studies on intervention in examination stress broaden the choices of how to manage examination stress. This exercise of review of empirical studies on examination stress was beneficial to the researcher in understanding the phenomenon holistically and in planning the present research work.

Chapter III

Research Methodology

This chapter presents the research methodology that has been used in the study. Review of literature of empirical studies on examination stress highlights the universality of the problem. Examination stress cuts across the globe and is widespread among students of various groups. There is enormous number of research studies showing the intensity of the problem and the growing concern to intervene and manage the problem.

Statement of the problem

Stress is a scourge of the modern day living. We are in a phase of tremendous growth of knowledge, rapid social change and technical innovation. For many people, the pace of change is too fast, resulting in stress. Stressful events as cause of illness have a long tradition in human history. In contemporary societies, stresses of one or the other kind have become a common source of threat to mental and physical health and well being of the people. This situation has emerged in the context of unprecedented technological change accompanied by industrialisation and increasing attraction to consumerism as an ideal or functional form of life. The life of an average urban person has become a constant struggle with pressures, conflicts and limits. The stresses are continuously evoked and escape from them has become difficult (Misra, 1991).

The idyllic world of students is under attack by the stresses of modern life and students are ill-prepared to cope with them.

Even though students can feel the same psychological pains that adults feel, they differ in the intellectual ability to understand the pain and ability to control and manage it. They are more vulnerable than adults because they have not developed skills necessary to understand what is happening to them and the reasons for it. What is necessary to conquer stress is to gain control over one's own life and students are too young to control.

Schools play an important role in the life of a child. Schools are often place of stress, anxiety, fear and even pain for children. The discipline, the timing, the curriculum, the homework and the teachers cause stress for students. There is an increasing pressure on students to academically do well. There are pressures to read and to learn, very early in the students' life. Unfortunately a growing number of students are unable to cope up with the increasing stress created by the educational system and taking to harmful coping habits. These habits affect the personality of the individual. Therefore, it is very important to identify the stress symptoms and seek help to overcome them as early as possible.

Stress is a universal phenomenon. It can be a stimulant to growth. Optimum amount of stress is necessary to achieve the best results. However, for some individual it could be a disabling phenomenon. A high degree of stress persisting for relatively longer periods damages the physical and mental health. For instance, imagine a student who is being totally cool about a forthcoming examination. It is likely that the student is not alert and motivated to work towards the examination. On the other hand, if a student is succumbed under too much stress it can cause confusion, disturbed thinking, distorted perception, insomnia and such other symptoms that would result in poor performance.

Taking examinations can be very worrying and stressful. The worry of not doing well in itself can cause stress, that impact the performance of the examination. The fear associated with examination is largely due to anxiety about the outcome. There are worries that the student will be disgraced and embarrassed about how the family and friends will react and about letting them down. In extreme cases the student reacts as if the whole life depends on the results of the examination.

While performing well in the examinations is important, life does not entirely depend on the results of the examination and there is an opportunity to improve the results in the next or another examination.

Even if students are very hardworking and intelligent there is no guarantee of getting a seat of their choice in higher education. As the examination time comes closer many students approach the school counsellors with certain uneasy symptoms like lack of sleep, hunger, anxiety, depression or a strong unknown fear. Attribution of all such symptoms to examinations may not be justified. A strong combination of factors such as family environment, parental attitudes/expectation, friends, social circle, individual and their aspirations play a crucial role in causing examination stress. Fear of failure too, adds up and multiplies their tensions related to examination.

Examination stress causes depression, forgetfulness, irritability and many other behavioural and emotional disturbances. The sufferer of stress is always tired and is less efficient in every way than he should be normally. Examination stress can influence both the personality and performance of the students. Every year media reports stories of children suffering from stress of examination and in extreme cases taking their own lives. Stress among children as a phenomenon is on the rise and has dangerous manifestations both psychologically and physically.

In the recent years we have seen the emergence of NGOs providing counselling services for students during school examinations and at the time of declaration of results. The increase in the number of helpline services for students in itself is an indication that stress is on the increase, and it has a long lasting effect on students in the form of their performance in their examination.

Rational of the study

This research is an attempt to understand the phenomenon of examination stress, which is on the rise and has serious ramifications. The study examines various factors contributing to examination stress, how family environment, study habits, parental expectations and aspiration of individual students effect the students, making them very conscious and instilling a feeling of 'do-or-die' towards their examination. Students are made to feel that their entire life depends on these examinations and they have to prove themselves worthy through these examinations to their parents, peer group, teachers, school and society at large.

Examination stress causes various physical, emotional, cognitive and behavioural manifestations on students, which they are unable to comprehend. Students develop their own coping mechanisms to adjust to these manifestations and demands from the environment. Some of these coping strategies are effective in reducing the stress but some maladaptive coping strategies like substance abuse could damage the situation even further. Examination stress results in lack of confidence and low self-esteem that adversely affect the academic performance of the students. They are often unable to understand what is happening within, ramifications of which leads to inferiority complex among the students.

Social work is a helping profession. Social work has entered the area of school setting since a hundred years. In India, as early as 1958 school social work was introduced as a setting in Kashi Vidyapeth, Varanasi. Gandhi (1990) has formulated models of school social work in India with main thrust points being helping the child cope with behavioural, learning and interpersonal problems within the systems of school, home and larger community through vocational guidance, leadership training programmes, family life education and the like. The key to help students learn and grow is in a way problem prevention and intervention. School social worker can prevent or minimise the effect of various emotional and behavioural problems that students suffer from (Antony, 2006). In school social work, students are helped to cope up with their personal, academic and school issues and problems. Since the emergence of examination stress as a serious problem, it has become all the more important, to better understand the phenomenon so that school social workers can help students cope up with this problem in a proper and scientific manner.

One of the objectives of the present research is designing a suitable social work intervention for schools in preventing and reducing examination stress. Schools can adopt this social work intervention model to sensitise and promote the students, parents, peers and teachers, to help students handle examination stress effectively. Students can be helped to prevent the adverse effects of examination stress and help to focus on their academic pursuits and performance. Students who have been identified with stress can also be helped by parents, peer group, teachers and by professionals to reduce the examination stress and prevent further psychological problems.

The present study also highlights the role played by the familial environment, parental expectation, and communication patterns on the aspirations of the students and how students respond to these demands created by the environment. It also explores the manifestation of examination stress by students and the coping strategies used by them. It is expected that the results of the study will help in the understanding of mental health needs of students and hence direct the nature of social work interventions in schools.

It is expected that the study will be beneficial to students, parents, teachers and school authorities also. The professionals like social workers, counsellors, psychologists, psychiatrists, school nurses and others interested in student's mental health can find this study useful in better understanding the phenomena of examination stress. The social work intervention model that emerges as the outcome of the study can be of significant importance in planning, organising and implementing school social work programmes to deal with examination stress.

Aim and specific objectives of the study

The study aims at measuring the extent of examination stress and its behavioural manifestations among students of senior classes.

The specific objectives of the study are:

- To measure the extent of examination stress experienced by students as they approach examinations.
- To understand the role-played by study habits, parental expectations, family environment and aspirations of the individual students in inducing examination stress.
- To study behavioural manifestations of examination stress seen among students.

- To explore the coping strategies used by students in dealing with stress generated by examinations.
- To suggest a model of social work intervention to deal with examination stress of students.

Operational definition of concepts

Stress is defined as a negative feeling state experienced by an individual that adversely affects his/her task performance as well as mental and physical health.

Examination stress is defined as experiences of a continuum of negative feelings states, which are induced by an examination. Such negative feeling states are considered examination stress because of the temporal relationship between onset of negative feeling states and the commencement of examination.

Coping strategies are defined as mechanisms used by students to deal with the stress generated by an examination.

Study habit refers to all study practices followed by students to assist them in their various scholastic assignments.

Behaviour manifestations are the emotional, cognitive and physiological changes experienced by students as a result of and in response to examination stress.

Parental expectations are the nature of demands placed on the students by their parents and their eagerness about the outcome of academic exercise.

Social work intervention refers to the use of appropriate social work methods and skills to effectively address the mental health needs of students with special reference to examination stress.

Family environment refers to the general social and psychological situation that prevails in a family.

Aspiration is defined as the goal set by the individual for achievement in his/her life.

Senior classes: A student is considered to be in senior classes if, he is enrolled in school for studies in 9th to 12th classes.

Research design

The research design is the 'blueprint' of the study. It is the framework on which the study is built up. The present study is an investigation into the phenomenon of examination stress and its manifestations. In the process it purports to describe the extent of examination stress among students in senior classes in the National Capital Territory of Delhi and its emotional, cognitive and physiological manifestations. The study also intends to describe the role played by study habits, parental expectations, family environment and aspirations of the individual students in inducing examination stress. In order to realise the objectives of the study, a descriptive research design has been used for this scientific endeavour. The descriptive design used in the study allows inter-group comparisons, and facilitates understanding of the factors that are responsible for its causation.

Universe

The complete set of units that the researcher wants to study is the universe of the study. The primary data for the study is collected from two sources; the students and the other source are professionals working in the field of student welfare.

The universe of the study for the first source comprises all students in senior classes (9th to 12th) in the National Capital Territory of Delhi. As per the Central Board of Secondary Education there are 1216 schools with secondary level education in the locale of the study. The universe for the second source included all professionals, working in the area of student welfare in the National Capital Territory of Delhi.

Sampling method and process

Sampling is the process of selecting units (e.g., people, organisation) from a universe of interest so that by studying the sample, we may fairly generalise our results back to the universe from which they are selected. In the present study, a sample of 640 students was drawn from the universe, to study the extent of examination stress, its manifestation, contributory factors and the coping strategies adopted. To identify the units to be studied a multistage stratified random sampling method was used. The sampling process followed for the study is explained below.

At the first stage of the sampling, schools were selected from the NCT of Delhi through stratified sampling. Since most of the schools in NCT of Delhi follow the Central Board of Secondary Education (CBSE) system, the study was confined to schools under the CBSE Board. There were 1216 schools that offered education up to the Senior Secondary Level under the CBSE Board in Delhi in 2003. The CBSE has classified schools into Kendriya Vidyalayas, Government Schools, Independent Schools and Jawahar Navodaya Vidyalaya based on the type of management of the institutions. The researcher used this criterion for stratifying the schools.

A comprehensive list of all the schools of Delhi, were procured from Central Board of Secondary Education.

Kendriya Vidyalayas are managed by the Kendriya Vidyalaya Sangathan, an autonomous organisation under the Ministry of Human Resource Development, Government of India. The Directorate of Education, Government of the National Capital Territory (NCT) of Delhi or the New Delhi Municipal Council (NDMC) manages the Government Schools. In Delhi, pre-primary and primary education is the responsibility of the local bodies namely, the Municipal Corporation of Delhi (MCD), the New Delhi Municipal Council (NDMC) and the Delhi Cantonment Board (DCB).

The middle, secondary and senior secondary education is primarily looked after by Directorate of Education, Government of National Capital Territory (NCT) of Delhi. The Directorate of Education has introduced primary classes in existing secondary/senior secondary schools and converted them into composite schools. They are called Sarvodaya Vidyalayas and now have classes I to XII. The New Delhi Municipal Council (NDMC) is mainly running primary education but is also running few middle, secondary and senior secondary schools. Pratibha Vikas Vidyalayas another type of schools under the Directorate of Education are schools for the students performing well in studies.

Jawahar Navodaya Vidyalayas are residential schools set up in rural areas based on the direction of the National Policy on

Education, 1986. These residential schools are to bring out the talent of rural students. The name, Navodaya mean "Nav-Uday" or New Dawn. These schools are run by the Navodaya Samiti, an autonomous organisation under the Ministry of Human Resource Development.

The independent schools are the private educational institutions, which are run by an individual or a private organisation including religious bodies, private trusts and philanthropic institutions.

In order to select the schools from the total of 1216 schools in Delhi, the schools were stratified based on the above criterion followed by CBSE. As per the list available with CBSE, there were 681 government schools, 498 independent schools, 35 Kendriya Vidyalayas and two Jawahar Navodaya Vidyalayas in Delhi. Since there are only two Jawahar Navodaya Vidyalayas in Delhi, they were merged with the Kendriya Vidyalayas for sampling purpose, as there was similarity in their curriculum and because the size was less compared to others. It was decided to select one per cent of schools from the three types of schools at the first stage of sampling for schools. Accordingly the size of the schools to be selected was arrived at, 6, 4 and 1 school respectively.

Table 3.1: Universe and Sample of the Study

Types of schools/ stratum	*Total no. of schools*	*Sample no. of schools*	*Name of the institutions*
Government School	681	6	Government boys senior secondary school No.1, West Patel Nagar.
			Government boys senior secondary school No. 2, Kalkaji.
			Government Sarvodaya boys senior secondary school, Shastri Park.
			Government Sarvodaya kanya senior secondary school, Mayur Vihar.
			Pratibha Vikas Vidyalaya, Surajmal Vihar.
			Government girls senior secondary school No.1, Janakpuri.

(*contd...*)

Independent School	498	4	Delhi public school, Dwarka. Vidya Bharti school, Rohini. Fr. Agnel school, Gautam Nagar. Kerala education society senior secondary school, Canning Road.
Kendriya Vidyalaya + Jawahar Navodaya Vidyalayas	37	1	Kendriya Vidyalaya, Janakpuri.
Total	**1216**	**11**	

The selection of schools under each stratum was selected using simple random method. The list of schools was available from CBSE. Using Tippett's table of random numbers the schools were selected by reading the table horizontally, taking the last digit.

In the second stage of sampling sections were to be selected from 9th to 12th classes from which respondents were to be finally selected. From the different sections in each selected school one section was randomly selected from classes 9th and 10th. For 11th and 12th classes, one section from each of the streams offered was chosen (science, humanities, commerce) to have a better representation of the whole.

In the third stage of sampling students were selected. It was decided to select twenty per cent of students on a random basis from each of the selected sections in the selected schools. For selection of students at this stage, the attendance register of the selected section of the school was used as the source list. Here again Tippett's table of random sampling was used to select the students. The total sample numbers of students thus selected were 640.

In addition to this, interviews were conducted with 16 professionals that helped in designing a model of school social work intervention. The selection of professionals was done using a purposive method of sampling. Four different groups of professionals who are directly involved with students were identified as

- Teachers/Principals
- Counsellors/School social worker

- Professionals and NGO personnel in the field of student welfare.
- Social work educators.

From these four different areas of professionals in the NCT of Delhi, four professionals from each area were selected, which totalled to 16.

To ascertain the feasibility of data collection a pilot study was conducted and permission was sought from authorities of the selected schools. The timing and mode of collection of data were also finalised in discussion with the school authorities.

Tools of data collection

The primary data for the study were collected from the school students and professionals working in the field of student welfare. During the pilot study it was clear that the schools will allow students to meet the researcher in groups for a limited time ranging from one to two school periods (about one to two hours). Hence, it was decided to administer the tool of data collection as a self-reporting inventory.

A self-administered questionnaire was developed in English with multiple-choice answers including the Test Anxiety Inventory (TAI) developed by Spielberger and colleagues in 1980. In addition to the TAI three Likert type scales were developed by the researcher for studying study habits, behavioural manifestations and coping strategies (Appendix I).

The Test anxiety inventory is a psychometric scale, that measures students' differences in test anxiety. This inventory includes 20 items, which the students respond to according to their own experiences at examination time. The TAI subscales measure worry and emotionality components of test anxiety. TAI is developed on the assumption that students who are test anxious perceive the examinations as threatening, so they are tense, apprehensive, nervous and emotionally sensitive during examination. The adverse self-conscious, worry cognitions distract their attention and interrupt with their preparation and concentration in examinations leading to low performance of test anxious students. Emotionality is the reactions of the autonomic nervous system that are stimulated due to the examination stress. TAI have been developed on these concepts of worry and emotionality.

The Test Anxiety Inventory forms were administered at college level to college students. There were 1449 undergraduates out of which 654 were males, and 795 were females, and 1129 in coming freshman, out of which 533 were males and 596 were females from the University of South Florida. The norms for high school students are based on 1118 ninth to twelfth class students of which 527 were males and 591 were females. These students were enrolled in public high schools in Jacksonville and Pinellas County, St. Petersburg and Clear Water, Florida. For the shorter period, the reliability (test-retest) coefficients were 0.80 or higher, but dropped to 0.62 for the group of higher, school students who were retested after six months. The research results indicate that the Test Anxiety Inventory and its subscales provide reliable and valid measure of test anxiety as situation specific personality trait. The relationship between the Test Anxiety Inventory and its subscales with other anxiety measures like Sarason's Test Anxiety Scale (TAS), Liebert & Morris' Worry and Emotionality Questionnaire (WEQ), the STAI State and Trait Anxiety scales, and the STAI State Anxiety scale administered under examination stress conditions all provide evidence of convergent validity. The correlation between the TAI score and the TAS was sufficiently high (0.82 to 0.83) to suggest that the two scales measure essentially the same construct. This TAI has been administered in Indian settings (Sanghvi, 1995; Grover, 1996) and is reported to be culture relevant.

TAI Scores

The scoring of TAI ranges from a minimum score of 20 to maximum score of 80. The respondents select the response, which is rated on a four point rating scale. The first item is framed in a way that rating '4' indicates low anxiety and other items are worded to mean a rating of '4' indicates high level of anxiety. For the first item the scoring is reversed. The weight scores of the response marked 1, 2, 3, 4, for the reverse scoring are 4, 3, 2, 1. Total score is arrived by adding the ticked rating. The students are classified as high test anxious by calculating the high test anxious as mean plus standard deviation (X + 1SD) and the low test anxious as mean minus standard deviation (X – 1SD).

The researcher developed scales for understanding study habits, behavioural manifestations and coping strategies of the students.

The study habits scale

The study habits scale was constructed keeping various points in mind. Carefully progressing from one step to another, this has ensured that the scale is appropriate to what it has to study. The first step of the scale construction was that the definition of study habits was viewed. The researcher gathered statements on study habits through library work. Initially 62 statements covering different dimensions of study habits were framed. At the second step, these statements were carefully viewed and edited according to Edwards procedures (1957). From a range of 62 statements, 44 statements were selected.

At the third step of scale construction, the 44 selected items of the scale was administered on 60 students from the three different types of schools. (Government School, Kendriya Vidyalaya and Independent School) The statements were assigned four-point response categories – "Often, sometime, rarely and never". Following this, the responses to the statements were tabulated with a view to ascertain the distribution. The statements having a concentration or near concentration on any of the four response categories were taken as having low discriminal power. As a result, 12 statements with low discriminal power were rejected.

The responses were assigned weight '4' to often, '3' to sometimes, '2' to rarely and '1' to never. Negatively worded statements were given reverse weights. The weights of the items were summated across the 32 statements. This was followed by statistical analysis using t-test. Again 22 items having low t-test values were eliminated from the scale. Finally 10 statements having the maximum discriminatory power have been retained on the scale.

To calculate the reliability of the scale, the test-retest method was used. The test-retest of the study habit scale done at a gap of 15 days measured 0.74. The scale validity was examined by face-validity by the researcher. The validity of the scale would become more apparent when tests are carried out in different settings. The content validity of the scale was examined by getting experts from the field of education, mental health and social work to study the different items of the scale and the relevance of these items to study the study habits of the students.

The Behavioural Manifestation Scale was constructed to measure the behaviour manifestations of school students on account of examination stress.

At the initial step the researcher gathered 103 statements from research articles, newspaper and articles from the Internet to measure the two dimensions of behaviour manifestations that are physiological and psychological in nature. These statements were changed, reworded and some rejected according to Edwards (1957) procedures for editing items. From the 103 statements, 73 statements were selected.

These 73 statements were administered on 60 students. The responses to the statements were tabulated to ascertain the distribution. The statements having a concentration or near concentration on any of the four response categories were taken as having low discriminatory power. As a result 16 statements with low discriminatory power were rejected. The responses were assigned weights '4' to often, '3' to sometimes, '2' to rarely and '1' to never. The weights of the items were summated across 57 statements. This was statistically analysed using student's t-test. Again, 28 items having low t-test values were eliminated. Finally 29 statements having the maximum discriminatory power have been retained on the scale. The scale reliability was measured by test-retest method on a group of 30 students at a gap of 15 days measured 0.82. The content validity of the scale was determined by experts from the field of education, mental health and social work to examine the different items of the scale to observe if these items measure the behaviour manifestations of students due to examination stress.

The scale on coping strategies by students experiencing examination stress was constructed based on the operational definition of the concept in the present study.

The researcher after review of literature and Internet search gathered 71 statements on different dimensions of coping strategies. These statements were edited according to Edward (1957) procedures of item selection. Thus, 25 statements were rejected and 46 statements were retained.

These 46 statements were administered on 60 students in three schools. The statements were assigned 4-point response categories – "Often, sometime, rarely and never". Their responses were recorded. Those statements, which had similar responses, were rejected and those with different responses were accepted. So 18 statements were rejected and 28 statements retained. The students' responses were given scores, '4' to often, '3' to sometimes, '2' to rarely and '1' to never. The maladaptive coping strategies were given reverse scores. These scores were totalled and t-test applied. The 18 statements with higher t-values were retained in the scale. The reliability of the coping strategies scale was 0.73, measured by test-retest on 30 students in the gap of 15 days. The content validity of the coping scale was assessed by experts from education, mental health and social work fields to examine the relevance of the scale in studying the coping strategies of students when faced by examination stress.

Data were collected from the professionals with the help of a semi-structured interview guide, so that they could give in-depth information on the social work intervention model (Appendix II).

Pretesting

The questionnaire was pretested on 20 students each from the three different types of schools and necessary modifications made to make them simple for students to understand and respond.

Time period of the study

Examination stress is the anxiety experienced by students due to the approaching examination where they are evaluated. Examination stress may begin few weeks to months before the examination, continue to persist during examination and may even last till the declaration of results. Before the results are declared there is uncertainty and negative feeling of insecurity and if the results are not according to their expectations they are ashamed and unable to face parents and the society. All these different time periods are a matter of concern. Research into these different time periods may bring out different issues that need to be addressed to.

The researcher in the present study has investigated the period before the examination. The review of literature also lays emphasis on this period highlighting that stress is maximum just before the examination. The period before examination is of great importance as it is at this time period prevention measures can be introduced to control the problem. Various measures can be taken to help students, peer groups, teachers and parents to make an environment conducive for the affected students. Students can be helped specifically to become aware of the task at hand and to manage without experiencing stress. Before the examination preventive measures are important and if students of high stress are identified they can be helped by curative measures. The social work intervention model designed in this study can be introduced in schools at the pre-examination stage, which will help the students to tackle examination stress. Thus, the researcher is examining the first phase of examination stress that is before the examination, which is of most importance, in any meaningful intervention programme.

Data collection

Data for the study was collected from primary and secondary sources. The secondary data was gathered from various libraries in and outside Delhi. These libraries were National Council of Educational Research and Training, New Delhi; Department of Social Work, New Delhi; Jamia Milia Islamia University, Delhi; Indian Council of Social Science Research, New Delhi; Tata Institute of Social Sciences, Mumbai; National Institute Mental Health and Neuro Sciences, Bangalore; NIPA, New Delhi; Central Reference Library, New Delhi; National Institute of Public Co-operation Child Development, New Delhi.

Primary data were collected from students and professionals.

Firstly, the researcher contacted the selected school principals, after taking prior appointment and seeking for permission to collect data from the students. Some of the principals were forthcoming, few asked what the school will get in return, the researcher agreed to conduct sessions on 'Tips to control examination stress', before the data collection from the students. These sessions proved beneficial for the researcher in rapport formation also. One of the Principals was very defensive with the idea of a researcher in the school, however she agreed for data collection. The researcher before distributing the self-reporting questionnaire interacted with the students explaining the researcher's purpose of visit to their school, taking the students oral consent for the research, informing them their importance as the sample. The researcher also made them comfortable by saying that confidentiality will be strictly maintained of the information revealed as data. The researcher administered the questionnaire in the allotted time period in selected sections of the universe.

Data were also collected from professionals in the field of education and child welfare. The researcher fixed prior appointment and collected data from the professional.

Data analysis

The primary and secondary data collected were organised edited and processed. The data was edited at the time of data collection so that no questions were left incomplete. The primary data was coded and fed into SPSS spreadsheet. Different descriptive and inferential statistical applications were performed in order to realise the objectives of the study.

The data collected from the professionals through interview guide, were separately analysed.

Chapterisation

The chaperisation followed in the research study was

Chapter One	–	Examination stress: An overview
Chapter Two	–	Examination stress: Retrospect and prospects
Chapter Three	–	Research methodology

Chapter Four	–	Factors involved in examination stress
Chapter Five	–	Manifestations and coping strategies for examination stress
Chapter Six	–	Social work intervention
Chapter Seven	–	Summary of findings and suggestions

Limitations of the study

Examination stress is spread over a long and continuous period, which may vary from student to student. The nature of examination stress may vary according to the phase of examination i.e. before the examination, during the examination, and after the examination. The researcher has investigated the period before the examination. It would have been of interest to examine students and their reactions in all these three phases of examination stress. The researcher would have gathered important information about the problem but was unable to do this because of time constraint. A longitudinal study would have highlighted the difference in all these three phases, but this was not done due to time constraint.

The researcher has only studied students and their views. The other important people around the students, who would have been able to give more information about the students' activities and performance, are teachers and parents. A study of teachers and parents of these students may have given a holistic view of the phenomenon of examination stress.

The researcher had wanted to interview the students to understand the different causes of examination pressures from the students' experience and viewpoint. To gain in-depth information from the students but due to the school curriculum and syllabus of the students, the students being in the senior classes had no free time within the school schedule, even their extra-curricular activities were minimised. Thus, the present research was a quantitative study with the total sample of 640 students. Qualitative aspects of the data could not be taken up.

The sample at the first stage of sampling was stratified into three different types of school. Jawahar Navodaya Vidyalayas were combined with Kendriya Vidyalaya. Though these two schools come under the ministry of human resource development, Government of India, there are certain differences between the two. Jawahar Navodaya Vidyalayas are residential school for the talented students, while Kendriya Vidyalaya are non-residential schools for all students. It would have been informative to study the students of Jawahar Navodaya Vidyalayas also.

The scales constructed to measure, study habits, coping strategies and behavioural manifestation of students have not been standardised in terms of construct or criterion validity. Similarly, norms for interpretation of the scores were also not developed as this study did not aim at classifying students based on study habits, behavioural manifestations or coping strategies.

The social work intervention model designed in this study has not been tested in schools. It would have been more scientific to administer the social work intervention and test its efficacy in different types of schools to establish its suitability as a model of social work intervention.

Chapter IV

Factors Involved in Examination Stress

Analysis and interpretation of data on examination stress collected for the purpose of this study are presented in chapters four and five. This chapter presents the personal details of the student respondents, their socio-economic background, the extent of examination stress among students, and an enquiry into the factors contributing to examination stress.

Extent of examination stress

Examination stress is the experience of unpleasant feeling states like fear, worry, sadness and the like manifested by students through physiological and psychological changes during examinations. As examinations approach or during examinations students experience a range of negative emotions. These feeling states interfere with students' mental state thus affecting their performance and self-confidence. Test anxiety is also understood as a stress phenomenon and a situation-bound stress reaction. As like other emotional states it has encompassing cognitive, affective, physiological and behavioural components. Actually test anxiety is debilitative anxiety as it interferes with test taking behaviour of an individual. Stress is not supportive to the testing situation as it pulls the student down farther from accomplishment. Sarason (1984) reported that high test-anxious students are more self-centred and self-critical and are likely to be personalised and derogatory in their response to themselves in testing situation.

In this study, examination stress of senior class students was tested using the Test Anxiety Inventory (TAI) which has excellent potential for use in the assessment of test anxiety as a situation-specific personality trait, as highlighted by Spielberger *et al.* (1978). The inventory has 20 items measuring two dimensions of stress namely, worry and emotionality. The scores of the responses were 1, 2, 3, and 4 for the responses, except for the first item where the score is reversed. Thus, the minimum score a student can get is 20 and the maximum 80. In order to classify students into low, medium and high test anxious categories, respondent's total score is grouped into three. By adding standard deviation of the group with group mean one gets the cut off point for the high test anxious group and by subtracting standard deviation from the group mean one gets the cut off point for the low test anxious group. The value of mean test anxiety scores in this study is 46.37 and the standard deviation is 11.8. Thus, the low-test anxious respondents were those with scores 35 and below, high test anxiety were respondents were those with scores 59 and above. The medium test anxious respondents were those falling between 36 and 58.

Table 4.1 : Examination stress of students

No.	*Level of stress*	*Number*	*Per cent*
1.	Low	139	21.7
2.	Medium	363	56.7
3.	High	138	21.6
	Total	**640**	**100.0**

The extent of test anxiety among the school students observed in this study indicate that 21.7 per cent students belong to the low test anxious group and same per cent of respondents fall in the high test anxious group. Little more than half (56.7 per cent) of the respondents fell in between and belonged to the medium test anxious group.

The test anxiety inventory also studied the two components of test anxiety i.e. worry and emotionality. The subscales were called test anxiety inventory-worry (tai-w) and test anxiety-emotionality (tai-e). Worry refers to the cognitive concern about performance and the consequence of failure, tendency to compare one's ability to others, and negative thinking. Emotionality refers to self-perceived physiological arousal and upsets like heart racing and an upset stomach, and unpleasant feeling states such as nervousness and tension. The worry component of test anxiety (tai-w) was calculated by eight items on the test anxiety inventory. In the present study the tai-w was calculated with a mean of 18.48 and standard deviation of 5.08. The emotionality component (tai-e) was calculated with the mean of 18.18 and standard deviation of 5.52.

The students exhibit high levels of worry for their examination. The examination is seen as a threat to them. Students feel that examination is taken too seriously by teachers and parents which is cause for extra burden on them. The emotions at the time of examination is very heightened, the students are very sensitive, they get angry and can cry at the smallest reason.

Profile of the students

Many studies on examination stress have indicated that sex of students have a significant bearing on anxiety experienced during examinations. In order to understand the association between examination stress and gender of students, data on sex was analysed and the findings are as given below. The table below shows that both female and male students experience stress for their own reasons. Male students shared that they want to get high marks so that they can get into good colleges and good professions. They expressed that Delhi had fewer colleges for males as compared to females, thus, the male students require to get higher percentages to secure a seat in Delhi colleges. Female students said if they didn't perform well in examinations they may not get the opportunity to study further. They had to do well to continue education.

Table 4.2: Gender of the students

No.	*Gender*	*Number*	*Per cent*
1.	Female	323	50.5
2.	Male	317	49.5
	Total	**640**	**100.0**

In the present study undertaken in six government schools, four independent schools and one Kendriya Vidyalaya, the female respondents constituted 323 (50.5 per cent) of the sample and the male respondents were 317 (49.5 per cent). An enquiry was made into the difference in examination stress within the different groups of the sample. Examination stress, the dependent variable in this study, would be affected by the independent variables like gender, type of school, examination board and others.

Difference between boys and girls on test anxiety

The results showed that the female students reported a higher mean test anxiety score of 49.06, while the mean test anxiety score of male students was 43.64. To find out significance of difference in mean scores test anxiety of boys and girls student's *t*-test was done. The null hypothesis formulated for the purpose stated that there was no difference in test anxiety due to gender. The alternate hypothesis stated there was difference in test anxiety due to the difference in gender of the students. The *t*-test result ($t = 5.926$, df $= 638$, $p = 0.000$) indicated that there is significant difference in the test anxiety scores of female students and male students. Thus, the null hypothesis was rejected and the alternate hypothesis was accepted. Gender difference has also been reported in other studies. Nijhawan (1972), Araki (1992), and Singh and Broota (1992) have also found that female students were more worrisome, anxious and emotional than male students. This difference in the test anxiety of female and males can be attributed to the patriarchal family system that is followed in India. There is preference given to the male child over the female child. There is more importance given to the educational status of the male child also.

Student's *t*-test was also done to find out if gender difference has any effect on the worry (tai-w) component of test anxiety.

Difference between boys and girls on worry regarding examination

It was observed that the mean worry score among female students was 19.53 and among male students the mean was 17.41. The test of difference was found to be ($t = 5.38$, $p = 0.000$) significant and hence the null hypothesis stating there is no difference in worry score of boys and girls was rejected. The result shows that female students are reported with more worry than male students. Female students tend to think more negatively and are more worrisome as compared to their male counterparts.

An attempt was made to find out if gender difference has any effect on the emotionality (tai-e) component of test anxiety.

Difference between boys and girls on emotionality dimension

It was observed that the mean emotionality score among female students was 19.47 and among male students the mean emotionality score was 16.88. The result of the test of difference was found to be (t = 6.10, p= 0.000) significant and hence the null hypothesis stating there is no difference in emotionality based on the gender of students was rejected. Thus, the result shows that female students are more emotional than male students.

Age of the student

In Delhi, students are admitted to schools at lower kindergarten class at the age of minimum three plus years or in the first standard at a minimum age of five plus years. So by the time the student finishes schooling 10+2, the student completes a minimum of 17 years in school.

Table 4.3: Age of the students

No.	*Age of respondents*	*Number*	*Per cent*
1.	Less than 15	222	34.7
2.	16-18	406	63.4
3.	Above 18	12	1.9
	Total	**640**	**100.0**

The age of the respondents of the sample was a minimum of 13 years and a maximum of 20 years. The mean age was found to be 15 years.

Class of the students

According to Central Board of Secondary Examination (2003) 2,04,505 students had registered for the Secondary School Examination

(X class) in Delhi and 2,00,232 students appeared for the examination. At the Senior School Certificate Examination (Class XII) 1,34,885 students had registered and 1,32,300 students had appeared for the examination.

Table 4.4: Class of the students

No.	*Class of the Respondent*	*Number*	*Per cent*
1.	Ninth	109	17.0
2.	Tenth	123	19.2
3.	Eleventh	202	31.6
4.	Twelfth	206	32.2
	Total	**640**	**100.0**

The respondents were drawn from the senior classes of the school. Student respondents from class IX comprised of 17 per cent of the total sample followed by 19.2 per cent drawn from class X. The number of respondents was higher in the XI and XII classes as students from the different streams were taken. 31.6 per cent comprised of class XI and 32.2 per cent from class XII.

The sample for the present study was drawn from school students of senior classes of IX to XII. The classes X and XII were considered more important and have the board examinations that are conducted by an external board in Delhi. The final examinations of classes IX and XI are conducted by the school itself, while for the classes X and XII examinations were conducted by the Central Board of Secondary Examination. The researcher regrouped the respondents into two groups, the board classes (the tenth and twelfth) and the non-board classes (the ninth and the eleventh). This regrouping helped in further statistical analysis to examine the effect of board examination on the students.

Table 4.5: Classification of students on type of examination they were approaching

No.	*Type of examination*	*Number*	*Per cent*
1.	Non-Board Examination	311	48.6
2.	Board Examination	329	51.4
	Total	**640**	**100.0**

The students appearing for board examination (X and XII) constituted 51.4 per cent of the sample while 48.6 per cent constituted the non-board classes (IX and XI).

Table 4.6 : Difference between board and non-board class students on test anxiety

No.	*Class*	*Mean*	*Standard Deviation*	*T*	*P*	*Inference*
1.	Ninth and Eleventh	44.4	11.8	4.045	0.000	S
2.	Tenth and Twelfth	48.2	11.5			

The respondents in the board classes (X and XII) reported a higher test anxiety mean score of 48.2, while the non-board classes (IX and XI) reported a mean test anxiety score of 44.4. The null hypothesis stated that there was no difference on the test anxiety scores based on the class of the respondents. It was observed that the t value was significant at $p < 0.05$. Hence the null hypothesis was rejected and the alternate hypothesis accepted. This reinforced that the students in the board classes have higher stress levels. Their test anxiety scores are higher mainly due to the pressures of board examination and the importance given to board examination by parents, peers, teachers, schools and the larger society.

The students of the board classes X and XII and the non-board classes IX and XI were observed on the component of worry subscales (tai-w) of text anxiety.

Difference between board and non-board class students on worry

It was reported that the mean of worry score among students in the non-board IX and XI classes was 17.59 and the mean score of worry among board classes X and XII was 19.32. The value of $t = 4.35$ was significant at $p<0.000$ significance level. The null hypothesis stating that there is no difference in worry of students in the board classes and non-board classes was rejected. It was observed that students in the board classes worried more about examinations than students in the non-board classes. This shows that the students see the board examination as more threatening situation. They worry about their performance and results more than the non-board classes.

Emotionality on account of examinations of board and non-board class students was also measured.

Difference between board and non-board class students on emotionality

It was reported that the mean score of emotionality among students in the non-board classes was 17.39 and the mean of emotionality among board classes was 18.94. The value of t = 3.58 was significant at p <0.000 level of significance. Hence, the null hypothesis stating no difference in emotionality in the board classes and non-board classes was rejected. It was observed that the emotionality mean score among the board class students was higher than the non-board class students indicating that students in board classes were more emotional during examinations. Due to extra pressure to perform well students often get emotionally very involved in the whole process and the feelings towards the board examinations are intense. The students believe that their whole life depends on the board examination, thus emotions run high.

Type of schools

Schools in this study are classified according to the management into government schools, independent schools and Kendriya Vidyalayas. The data was collected from students from these schools. There were many differences between the types of schools in terms of the school building, the infrastructure available, the facilities, the socioeconomic background of the students, the fee structure, the curriculum, the extra curricular activities and the like. Students from the different types of schools were taken in order to observe the association between test anxiety and the type of school they studied.

Table 4.7: Type of school

No.	*Type of School*	*Number*	*Per cent*
1.	Government	299	46.7
2.	Independent	259	40.5
3.	Kendriya Vidyalaya	82	12.8
	Total	**640**	**100**

There were 299 (46.7 per cent) students from government schools, 259 (40.5 per cent) from independent schools and 82 (12.8 per cent) from Kendriya Vidyalayas. The schools selected were in the ratio of 6:4:1 (government schools: independent schools: Kendriya Vidyalayas). But due to the difference in the strength of the students in each class in the three types of schools the respondents' ratio was 4.7:4.0:1.3. It was observed that the strength of students in selected classes of the government schools were 35-40, while the strength in the classes of the independent schools and Kendriya Vidyalayas were comparatively more ranging from 50-57 students. Another reason to the difference in student ratio in the three different types of schools was due to the streams offered in the XI and XII classes. Most schools offered two streams viz., humanities and commerce. Only one school in the independent type and the Kendriya Vidyalaya offered three streams viz., humanities, commerce and science.

The respondents drawn from three different types of schools i.e. government school, Kendriya Vidyalaya and independent schools were compared on the test anxiety scores. The mean test anxiety scores showed a difference among students in the different type of schools.

Table 4.8: Difference of test anxiety of students according to the type of school

No.	*Type of School*	*Mean*	*SD*	*Df*	*F*	*Sig.*	*Inference*
1.	Government	44.38	11.55	2	11.951	0.000	S
2.	Independent	47.14	12.00	637			
3.	Kendriya Vidyalaya	51.21	11.13				

The mean test anxiety of government school students was 44.38, that of independent schools students was 47.14 and the mean test anxiety of Kendriya Vidyalaya students was 51.21. The null hypothesis stated that there was no difference in test anxiety of students based on the type of school in which they study. The ANOVA test result (F value =11.951, p = 0.000) indicated that there is significant difference in the test anxiety of students in three types of school of the study. Hence, the null hypothesis is rejected and the alternate hypothesis accepted.

It was observed that the students have lower test anxiety in government schools, which could be due to lower expectations on these students from their parents, teachers and the schools. In the independent schools the expectation of parents, teachers and schools are higher which gets transferred to the students pressurizing them to perform better. The students of Kendriya Vidyalaya mainly come from the middle-income classes of the society. There was greater pressure on them to perform well in studies and get into a good career or profession, thus their test anxiety score was the highest. The results of this study were similar to Chatrath (2004) study that also recorded high stress levels among public school students (another name for independent schools) in Delhi. But the result of the present study is divergent to the results of the study by Grover (1996) who reported high scores of test anxiety among government and aided school students. Kendriya Vidyalaya students were observed with average test anxiety and public school students recorded low scores of test anxiety.

Difference in level of worry of students according to the type of school

The subscale of Test Anxiety Inventory –Worry (tai-w) was examined in the different type of schools. It was observed that the mean Test Anxiety Inventory –Worry varied in the different school. Kendriya Vidyalaya reported the mean worry score as 21.26 that of government school students as 17.61 and that of independent school students as 18.59. The analysis of variance to study the test of significance shows (F =17.55, p =0.000) that there is difference in Test Anxiety Inventory –Worry (tai-w) between students of different types of schools. Students of Kendriya Vidyalaya were found to be the most worrying followed by those of independent schools. Government schools students scored lowest on the worry component.

An examination into the Test Anxiety Inventory subscale Test Anxiety Inventory – Emotionality (tai-e) and type of school was made to find if there was difference in the emotionality of the students because of the type of school.

Difference in emotionality of students according to the type of school

It was observed that the mean score on Test Anxiety Inventory – Emotionality (tai-e) varied among students of different types of schools. Students of Kendriya Vidyalaya reported the mean TAI-E score of 20.43, government school students reported a mean TAI-E score of 16.76 and independent school students a mean score of 19.12. The ANOVA test of significance shows ($F = 21.82$, $p = 0.000$) that there is significant difference in the emotionality level of students based on the type of schools they study in. Students of Kendriya Vidyalaya reported higher mean TAI-E followed by independent schools and the lowest by government schools. Thus, students of Kendriya Vidyalaya, and independent schools are higher on emotionality dimension of stress than the students of government schools. This could be attributed to the difference of the socioeconomic background of the students in these different types of schools.

Percentage of marks in the last examination

Academic performance is an important indicator of the respondents' scholastic achievements. A lot of emphasis is given to the academic performance of the students. The true value of education is the overall development of the child, through gaining knowledge and skills. Examinations and its results are just a medium to judge how much the student has gained in the learning process. The schooling process is more important. Students undergo stress as they are constantly pressurised to perform their level best. But the conventional examination system is emotionally charged and stressful. Examinations are not justified for the simple reason that the students are examined for the whole year in just what they do in a three-hours examination (Kumar, 2005).

The results declared by CBSE for 2004-05 in Delhi Schools will throw light on the general trend of the academic performance of secondary examination in the different types of schools. The pass percentage of secondary examination in government schools was 48.03 per cent while the public school was 86.36 per cent. At the Senior

Secondary examination the pass percentage in government school was 76.44 per cent and public school was 89.46 per cent (Directorate of Education, 2006).

In the present study, the respondents were asked the actual percentage of marks they obtained in their last examination. The range of marks was 64 per cent, with a minimum of 31 per cent and a maximum of 95 per cent. The mean percentage of marks was 57.93. The standard deviation was 16.20.

The students were regrouped to examine their academic performance based on division obtained. The pass percentage is 33 per cent; it was found that 34 (5.3 per cent) respondents obtained less than the pass percentage. Third division (33 to 49 per cent) was obtained by little less than 189 (30 per cent) of the respondents. Almost equal to this 199 (31 per cent) respondents obtained II division (50 to 59 per cent). One-third of the respondents secured first division (above 60 per cent marks). 10.3 per cent students secured 75-84 per cent; another 11.4 per cent of students had done very well and secured a high percentage of 85 per cent and above.

An analysis of academic performance and type of school highlights indicated a positive correlation. An analysis of academic performance and type of school showed that the product moment correlation = + 0.306. It was observed that 25 (73.6 per cent) students who got below passing marks came from the government schools. Majority of the government school students 241 (80.6 per cent) had between 40 to 59 per cent per centage of marks and only 33 (11 per cent) respondents obtained a first division. Academic performance of respondents in independent schools was better in comparison to the other schools. Only 3 (1.2 per cent) students have percentage of marks below the passing percentage and majority of the respondents 163 (62.9 per cent) had first division. Academic performance of students of Kendriya Vidyalaya was average, as 54 (65.9 per cent) respondents procured II and III division and only 22 (26.8 per cent) students had got first division.

Association between test anxiety and academic performance of the students was ascertained. It was observed that students with below passing marks had a mean test anxiety of 47.5. Students with marks between 33 to 49 per cent reported mean test anxiety of 51.3. That was followed by students with marks between 60 to 74 per cent who had mean test anxiety of 44.0. The mean test anxiety scores reduced to 36.0 for students with marks of 85 per cent and more. ANOVA test was applied to find out the difference in the test anxiety scores and academic performance.

Table 4.9: Difference in text anxiety based on level of academic performance

No.	*Academic Performance*	*Mean*	*SD*	*Df*	*F*	*Sig.*	*Inference*
1.	32 & below	47.5	10.5	5	22.94	0.000	S
2.	33-49	51.3	12.2	634			
3.	50-59	47.2	12.2				
4.	60-74	44.0	8.4				
5.	75-84	41.3	8.7				
6.	85 & above	36.0	7.8				

Based on the above findings the null hypothesis was rejected and alternate hypothesis that stated there is significant difference in test anxiety based on level of academic performance was accepted. The test anxiety scores reduced as the academic performance of the students improved. Students with low marks, with just pass marks reported of mean test anxiety score of 51.3 and students with good marks 85 per cent and above reported of mean test anxiety of 36.0, showing students with good marks were more confident, well prepared for examination and experienced lower test anxiety. Students with just pass marks were not prepared and have the fear of failure thus have high-test anxiety.

The students were examined on Test Anxiety Inventory-Worry (tai-w) subscale and the academic performance of their last examination.

Table 4.10: Difference in level of worry based on level of academic performance

No.	Marks	Mean	SD	df	F	Sig.
1.	32 & below	18.55	5.01	5	25.36	0.000
2.	33-49	20.61	5.04	634		
3.	50-59	18.99	5.26			
4.	60-74	17.68	3.62			
5.	75-84	16.96	4.06			
6.	85 & above	13.73	2.87			

The mean of Test Anxiety Inventory-Worry score was different for the students who were grouped according to their performance. The students with below passing percentage obtained mean Test Anxiety Inventory-Worry of 18.55. Students with 33 per cent to 49 per cent obtained mean Test Anxiety Inventory-Worry score of 20.61 and those with 60 to 74 per cent reported mean of Test Anxiety Inventory-Worry score of 17.68. Students falling in the highest percentage group reported mean of Test Anxiety Inventory-Worry score of 13.73. The analysis of variance for the test of significance indicated that the null hypothesis is rejected and the alternate hypothesis stating that there is significant difference in the Test Anxiety Inventory –Worry score of students based on level of academic performance was accepted. It was observed that students who were not able to secure good percentage of marks were more worrisome than those students who secured high percentage marks, as they were more confident and less worrying.

Table 4.11: Difference in level of emotionality based on level of academic performance of students

No.	Marks	Mean	SD	df	F	Sig.
1.	32 & below	18.97	5.21	5	9.90	0.000
2.	33-49	19.99	6.19	634		
3.	50-59	18.20	5.51			
4.	60-74	16.81	4.45			
5.	75-84	17.31	4.29			
6.	85 & above	15.38	4.06			

Test Anxiety Inventory- Emotionality (tai-e) and the academic performance of their last examination were subjected to analysis of variance test.

The mean of Test Anxiety Inventory- Emotionality (tai-e) score significantly differed for the students grouped according to their academic performance. The mean of Test Anxiety Inventory-Emotionality score of students who secured below the passing percentage was 18.97. Students with 60 to 74 per cent reported a mean of Test Anxiety Inventory- Emotionality score of 16.81 and the students with 85 per cent and above reported the mean of Test Anxiety Inventory-Emotionality score of 15.38. The ANOVA test of significance shows ($F = 9.90$, $p = 0.000$). The null hypothesis stating no difference in Test Anxiety Inventory – Emotionality among students with different levels of academic performance was rejected and the alternate hypothesis stating there was significant difference in the level of Test Anxiety Inventory – Emotionality among students based on their academic percentage was accepted. This showed that students were more emotional when they don't secure good percentage in their examinations and students who secured high percentage was more stable and in better control of their emotions.

Family details

To understand students, it is important to understand the families they come from. Family is the basic unit of the society. The key function of family is to raise its young persons in as healthy a manner as possible. Children are said to be the products of their parent's socialisation methods. Socialisation between parent and children for many years was viewed as a one-way process. But today parent-child interaction is viewed as reciprocal. Reciprocal socialisation is a socialisation process that is bi-directional; children socialise parents just as parents socialise children (Crouter and Booth, 2003; Patterson and Fisher, 2002).

Family type

Students live in different family types. Such differences influence the way parents interact with students. Zimmerman and colleagues

(1995) observed that urban African American adolescents living in either single-mother, step parents, dual parents, mother-with-extended-family (e.g., grand parents, aunt or uncle) or extended-family-only settings (e.g. only an aunt or grand parent is present), the social support provided to youth was generally the same across family types, with one exception: youth living in single-mother families were given more support than the youth in the other four family type.

Table 4.12: Type of Family

No.	*Type of Family*	*Number Respondents*	*Per cent*
1.	Single	16	02.5
2.	Joint	96	15.0
3.	Nuclear	528	82.5
	Total	**640**	**100.0**

In the present study most of the respondents 528 (82.5 per cent) came from nuclear families. 16 (02.5 per cent) respondents lived in single parent families. An investigation was made to see if type of family had any influence on the test anxiety of the students.

Table 4.13: Difference in test anxiety based on type of family

No.	*Type of Family*	*Mean*	*SD*	*Df*	*F*	*Sig.*	*Inference*
1.	Single Parent	44.33	11.23	2	1.885	0.153	NS
2.	Joint Family	45.53	11.77	637			
3.	Nuclear	46.90	11.98				

The analysis of variance result indicates that there is no significant difference in test anxiety scores of students based on the type of family. Students from joint families or nuclear families or single parent families have been observed with similar test anxiety mean scores. Thus, it was concluded that type of family of students did not influence their examination stress.

Size of the family

Average number of children in an Indian family is on the decline. The government norm of two children per family is not strictly followed but there is a decrease in the family size. The government's popular family planning programme supported sterilisation after two children and improved contraception are some of the reasons for the decrease in family size in India. In recent times a family size of one or two children is more compatible with the decision of many women to divide their energies between family and work (Berk, 2003). Smaller family size enhances parent-child interaction. Parents of fewer children can give more time to their children's activities, schoolwork and other needs. They get more of parents' attention and resources. These account to the fact that children who grow up in smaller families are healthier, have a higher intelligence test scores, do better in school, and attain higher levels of education (Grant, 1994).

Large families are usually less well off economically. Factors associated with low socio-economic status - crowded housing, inadequate nutrition, less educated and stressed parents- contribute to adverse relationship between family environment and students' well-being.

Table 4.14: Size of the Family

No.	*Size of Family*	*Number*	*Per cent*
1	Two	6	0.9
2	Three	35	5.5
3	Four	192	30.0
4	Five	213	33.3
5	Six	102	15.9
6	More than six	92	14.4
	Total	**640**	**100.0**

In this study the respondents' family size varied from two members to nine members, the mean being five members. It was observed that less than one per cent respondents were single child in a single parent family. The respondents were regrouped to divide the families into two groups. More than one-third (36.4 per cent) students came from small families with four or less than four members. Majority (63.6 per cent) of students came from large families with five or more than five members.

An enquiry was made to find out if the size of the family of the students had any effect on their test anxiety.

Table 4.15: Difference in test anxiety of students based on the size of their family

No.	*Size of Family*	*Mean*	*SD*	*t*	*Sig (2-tailed)*	*Inference*
1.	Small Family	46.1	12.4	0.312	0.755	NS
2.	Large family	46.4	11.5			

It was observed that students of small and big families had similar mean test anxiety scores. There was no significant difference of test anxiety based on size of family, as the value of *t* was not significant at an acceptable level. Hence, the null hypothesis that size of the family of students has no significant difference on the test anxiety of the students was accepted.

Siblings

Siblings are more accessible to the students and can play an important role in a student's life. Sibling relationship includes helping, sharing, and teaching, fighting and playing. Siblings are close to each other's age and can understand each other's problems and communicate more effectively than parents can, in different situations like dealing with peers, coping with difficult teachers, discussing taboo subjects as sex or even helping in examination stress. Siblings may be more influential than parents in the socialisation process. Siblings can act as emotional support, rivals and communication partners (Carlson, 1995). In some families siblings may have stronger socialising influence on the child than parents (Circirelli, 1994). On the contrary, in Baskett and Johnson (1982) observed that students interact more positively and in more varied ways with their parents than with their siblings. In some cases students follow their parent's dictates more than those of their siblings and they behave more negatively with their siblings than with their parents (Santrock, 2004). Sibling interaction differs in different countries. In more traditional societies great importance is given to the role of siblings as caregivers to the younger siblings (Circirelli, 1994).

The number of siblings in a family throws some light to the family environment of the students. Is the student the only child? Or is the first-born child? Or is a member in a large family? These cause differences in the environment of the students. Rothbart (1971) states that parents have higher expectations for first-born children than for later-born children. They put more pressure on them for achievement and responsibility. Parents also interfere more with their activities.

The popular notion is that only child in the family is a 'spoiled brat' with negative characteristics like dependency, lack of self-control and self-centred behaviour. But researchers present a more positive image of the only child, who are often achievement-oriented and display a desirable personality in comparison to children from large families (Falbo and Poston, 1993; Jiao *et al.*, 1996).

Table 4.16: Number of the siblings

No.	*Number of Siblings*	*Frequency*	*Per cent*
1.	Nil	38	5.9
2.	1	185	28.9
3.	2	188	29.4
4.	3	154	24.1
5.	Four or more	75	11.7
	Total	**640**	**100.0**

In this study, a small percentage (5.9 per cent) of respondents had no siblings; they were the only children in the family. More than one-fourth of the respondents (28.9 per cent) had only one sibling. The category with the highest respondents (29.4 per cent) was students with two siblings. While another group of (11.7 per cent) respondents had four or more siblings.

Before moving on to the details of the parents' age, education and occupation it is important to highlight that parents strongly influence their wards. Parents play a crucial role in the growth and development of their wards. Students need the security that only their own parents can give them. They need the feeling of confidence that comes from parental faith. They also need supervision, direction and firm setting of limits. As adolescents move toward independence, they experience resistance. Parents need to understand the adolescents' choice of vocation and in helping the next generation to emerge confident.

Age of parents play a role in how they socialise with their offspring. In India too, like in other countries, the age of couples on marriage is increasing. Among the middle class men and women, there is a want to be economically secure before going in for marriage and having children. It is observed when men and women are conscious of their responsibility and have a planned child; those parents bring up their children in better stimulating environment.

Table 4.17: Father's Age

No.	*Father's Age*	*Number of Respondents*	*Per cent*
1.	below 40	93	14.5
2.	41-50	365	57.0
3.	51 & above	182	28.4

In the present study more than half (57 per cent) of the respondents' fathers were in the age group of 41-50 years. While more than one-fourth (28.4 per cent) of the respondent's fathers were 51 years and above.

Table 4.18: Mother's Age

No.	*Mother's Age*	*Number of Respondents*	*Per cent*
1.	below 40	338	52.8
2.	41-50	244	38.1
3.	51 & above	58	9.1

The mothers were comparatively younger, as more than half (52.8 per cent) of the mothers were below 40 years. 38.1 per cent of the mothers were in the age group of 41-50 years. While only 9.1 per cent mothers were 51 and above.

Socio-economic status

Socio-economic status (SES) refers to the grouping of people with similar occupational educational and economic characteristics. The inequalities in the socio-economic status, produce unequal opportunities for students (Santrock, 2004). The families, schools and neighbourhood of students have socio-economic characteristics. Some students' parents have great deal of money and prestigious occupations. These students live in comfortable houses and neighbourhoods, and go to school in which other students also come from middle and upper socio-economic background. The other students have parents who do not have much money, and occupied with less prestigious occupations. These students do not live in attractive houses and neighbourhood and they attend school where other students are from lower socio-economic background. These variations in neighbourhood affect the student's adjustment (Leffert and Blyth, 1996).

Lower SES parents generally are particular that their wards conform to society's expectation, have an authoritarian parenting style, they use physical punishment to discipline their ward. These parents are more directive, less approachable and less conversational with their wards. The higher SES parents are more particular with developing their ward's initiative, create a home atmosphere in which adolescent are nearly equal participants, are less likely to use physical punishment, are less directive, more approachable, and more conversational with their wards (Santrock, 2004). As the samples in this research were taken from all types of schools, various socio-economic status groups are represented. It includes parents of respondents from the illiterate or lower educational class to highly qualified professionals.

Table 4.19: Father's educational qualification

No.	*Father's Education*	*Number of Respondents*	*Per cent*
1.	No formal schooling	43	6.7
2.	10th and below	160	25.0
3.	Upto graduation	243	38.0
4.	P. G. and above	194	30.3
	Total	**640**	**100.0**

A small per centage (6.7 per cent) of fathers' had no formal schooling and their wards were first generation school goers. One-fourth of the fathers had gone to school but dropped out before or after their secondary examination. More than one-third of the fathers (38 per cent) had gone to senior secondary school and college. Little less than one-third of the fathers (30.3 per cent) had qualification of postgraduation and above.

Table 4.20: Difference in test anxiety based on father's education

No.	*Father's Educational Qualification*	*Mean*	*SD*	*F*	*Sig.*	*Inference*
1.	No formal Schooling	45.69	13.31	1.943	0.121	NS
2.	10th Class and below	44.70	11.13			
3.	Upto Graduation	47.57	11.09			
4.	P. G. and above	46.41	12.96			

The analysis of variance result (F=1.943, p = 0.121) shows that the null hypothesis stating differences in fathers' educational level has no significant difference on the test anxiety of the respondents was accepted. There was not much difference observed in the mean test anxiety scores of students whose fathers had no formal schooling and whose father's educational status were higher. It was observed students test anxiety score did not show much difference in the various groups. Thus, fathers' educational status was found to have no significant effect on the students test anxiety.

The respondents' mother's educational levels were comparatively lower than the fathers, but like fathers the mothers of the respondents too had diverse educational backgrounds.

Table 4.21: Mother's educational qualification

No.	*Mother's Education*	*Number of Respondents*	*Per cent*
1.	No formal schooling	146	22.8
2.	10th and below	181	28.3
3.	Upto graduation	189	29.5
4.	P.G. and above	124	19.4
	Total	**640**	**100.0**

More than one-fifth of the respondent's mothers (22.8 per cent) had no formal schooling while 28.3 per cent mothers had studied till 10th or below. Almost half (48.9 per cent) of the mothers had attended college and above. An attempt was made to find out if the respondents' test anxiety was affected by their mother's educational background.

The mothers of the respondents came from different educational levels. Some mothers had not gone to school at all, while some were postgraduates and above.

Table 4.22 : Difference in test anxiety based on mother's education

No.	*Mother's Education Qualification*	*Mean*	*SD*	*F*	*Sig.*	*Inference*
1.	No formal Schooling	46.45	11.80	5.062	0.002	S
2.	10th Class and below	47.46	11.72			
3.	Upto Graduation	43.79	11.09			
4.	P. G. and above	48.63	12.96			

It was observed that the mean test anxiety score of students whose mothers had no formal schooling was 46.4. The mothers who were 10th class and below their children reported mean test anxiety score of 47.4. Students of mothers with postgraduation and above recorded mean test anxiety score of 48.6. The analysis of variance result (F=5.062 and p=0.002) indicated that the null hypothesis is rejected and the alternative hypothesis stating there is significant difference in the test anxiety level of students and their mothers educational qualification is accepted.

Students whose mothers were low in educational status and those who were highly qualified reported mean test anxiety of 47.46 and 48.63 respectively. While students whose mother's educational status was moderate i.e. with higher secondary education to graduation, the mean test anxiety was low 43.79. Thus, it was observed that mothers with low educational status were not able to lower their ward's test anxiety levels. The mothers with higher education were also not able to control the test anxiety of their wards. While mothers with average educational status helped their children and their children scored low on the test anxiety scores. Another reason for high test anxiety among students could be that mothers with low educational background had low expectations from their wards and mothers with high educational qualifications had very high expectations from their ward.

In recent times there is a change in pattern of parents' involvement with the child. LaRossa (1998) reported that blue collar fathers had actually changed more in terms of their involvement in home-making and childcare than have middle class fathers (including professionals) when their wives were employed away from home. Since it is not in men's personal self-interest to initiate greater involvement in home-making and childcare, any change must be initiated by women. It is observed that if women are to be empowered to get greater involvement of spouse and children, they must understand themselves and be understood by family as sharing the breadwinner role. This was more so in the lower income families where the need for the wives income was more (Pitzer, 2001).

Table 4.23: Father's occupation

No.	*Father's Occupation*	*Number of Respondents*	*Per cent*
1.	Daily wage earner	68	10.6
2.	Business	202	31.6
3.	Service non-professional	211	33.0
4.	Service professional	159	24.8
	Total	**640**	**100.0**

Fathers of the respondents were involved in different occupations. A small number of fathers (10.6 per cent) were daily wage earners. In this group of daily wagers, 95.6 per cent of their wards mainly went to government school. Out of the 31.6 per cent respondents' fathers engaged in business, almost half (49 per cent) of the respondents were from the independent schools. One-third (33 per cent) of the respondents' fathers were in the non-professional service sector. Most of the fathers (61 per cent) of the Kendriya Vidyalaya respondents belonged to the service non-professional category. Almost one-fourth (24.8 per cent) of the respondents' fathers were professionals in service sector. More than half (53.5 per cent) of the students whose fathers who were professionally qualified and in the service class belonged to the independent schools.

The respondents' fathers were daily wagers, pulling rickshaw or doing unskilled work, others were into business and service sector as professionals/non-professionals. An enquiry into fathers' occupation and students test anxiety scores yielded the following results.

Table 4.24: Difference in test anxiety based on father's occupation

No.	*Father's Occupation*	*Mean*	*SD*	*F*	*Sig.*	*Inference*
1.	Daily wage earner	43.17	11.34	13.844	0.000	S
2.	Business	42.86	10.31			
3.	Service (Non-professional)	48.75	11.21			
4.	Service (Professional)	49.05	13.38			

It was observed that students whose fathers were daily wagers and whose fathers were businessmen had lower mean test anxiety of 43.17 and 42.86 respectively. The students whose parents were in service as professionals or non-professionals had high mean test anxiety of 49.05 and 48.75 respectively. The ANOVA test showed father's occupation had an effect on the test anxiety of their children (F value=13.84 and p=0.000). Hence, the null hypothesis was rejected and the alternate hypothesis stating that there is significant difference between test anxiety of the students and their father's occupation was accepted. Daily wager parents may have low aspiration and expectations of their wards and hence their ward experienced low test anxiety. It was further observed that there was a positive correlation (product moment correlation =0.23) between fathers' occupation and parents' aspirations from their wards in respect to academic performance or marks obtained. Two-third of fathers' who were daily wagers wanted their wards to achieve comparatively lower marks (upto 60 per cent marks). Students whose fathers were in service sector have higher expectations from their wards and so the test anxiety of their wards was higher. Students whose fathers' were professionals their wards mean test anxiety was higher (49.0). Here it was again observed that 60.2 per cent of fathers who were professionals had higher aspirations and wanted their wards to secure marks above 75 per cent. The test anxiety scores were low among students whose fathers were daily wagers. Thus, higher the parents occupational status, higher the parents aspirations resulting in higher test anxiety among their wards.

Mother's occupation

Table 4.25: Mother's occupation

No.	Mother's Occupation	Number of Respondents	Per cent
1.	Housewife	329	51.4
2.	Daily wage earner	17	2.7
3.	Business	16	2.5
4.	Service (non-professional)	181	28.3
5.	Service (professional)	97	15.2
	Total	**640**	**100.0**

More than half of the respondents' mothers (51.4 per cent) were housewives. Among the respondent's mothers who were employed, a small group (2.7 per cent) constituted daily wage earners. Of the 2.5 per cent mothers who were into business, their wards were equally distributed in government and independent schools. The largest number of employed mothers (58.1 per cent) is engaged in non-professional jobs in the service sector. Another group (15.2 per cent) of mothers was engaged as professionals in service sector.

More than half of the respondents' mothers were housewives, while the other half was engaged in different occupations.

Table 4.26: Difference in test anxiety based on mother's occupation

No.	Mother's Occupation	Mean	SD	F	Sig.	Inference
1.	Housewife	46.01	11.01	1.873	0.113	NS
2.	Daily wage earner	44.05	12.88			
3.	Business	44.93	9.51			
4.	Service Non-professional	45.81	12.57			
	Service Professional	46.37	13.27			

The mean test anxiety scores of the students were similar for the various occupational groups of mothers. The analysis of variance shows that F value =1.873, Sig.= 0.113, p>0.05. The null hypothesis is accepted that there is no significant difference in mothers' occupational background and the students test anxiety.

Family income

Family income is an important variable that reflects of SES of the respondents. The respondents in the study come from different income groups. The family income ranges from below Rs 5000 monthly to maximum family income in the group of Rs 25000 and above.

Table 4.27: Family Income

No.	*Family Income*	*Number of Respondents*	*Per cent*
1.	5000 & below	100	15.6
2.	5001-10000	169	26.4
3.	10001-15000	106	16.6
4.	15001-20000	53	8.3
5.	20001-25000	62	9.7
6.	25001 & above	150	23.4
	Total	**640**	**100.0**

One-third of the parents (33.1 per cent) of students in government schools were daily wage earners with low income. It was observed that 48.8 per cent of the daily wage earner fathers have a monthly income of below Rs 5000. A small group (1.1 per cent) of these respondents mentioned that many a times there fathers would not get work as they were rickshaw pullers and they would have no money at home. A low per cent 15.6 per cent respondent had a family income of Rs 5000 and below. One-fourth 169 (26.4 per cent) of the respondents family income was Rs 5001 to 10000 of which 85.2 per cent attended government schools. Little less than one-fourth (23.4 per cent) of the respondents' family income was as high as Rs 25001 and above of which most of the respondents (99.3 per cent) attended independent schools. There were 3 (0.46 per cent) of the respondents who specifically mentioned their monthly family income was above rupees one lakh.

An examination into the test anxiety scores was done to find if there was any difference in test anxiety of students in the different family income group.

Table 4.28: Difference in test anxiety based on family income

No.	Family Income	Mean	df	F	Sig.	Inference
1.	5000 & below	45.06	634	3.329	.006	S
2.	5001-10000	44.82				
3.	10001-15000	50.37				
4.	15001-20000	46.75				
5.	20001-25000	45.79				
6.	25001 & above	46.29				

Students from the different income groups reported of different mean test anxiety scores. Students in the lower family income groups scored mean test anxiety of around 45.06. Students in the middle family income group (10001 to 15000) reported mean test anxiety score of 50.37, while students in the higher family income groups reported low mean test anxiety equal to that of low income group. The ANOVA test results indicated (F = 3.329, p = 0.006) that the null hypothesis stating no difference in test anxiety scores due to student's family income was rejected and the alternate hypothesis stating that there is significant difference in test anxiety scores in students of different family income was accepted.

Family environment

Separate room

Physical space for students is very important for them to study, relax, and introspect. A place they can call their own, where they keep their belonging like books, stationary. This space teaches them to keep their belonging in a place. Parents can insist to keep their place clean and in order. Directly and indirectly they learn organisational skills, how to take care of their belongings. These responsibilities are a learning process. The students can concentrate, spend time in this space, going through their work, and keeping out other distractions.

Table 4.29: Separate room

No.	Separate Room	No. of Respondents	Per cent
1.	Yes	307	48.0
2.	No	333	52.0
	Total	**640**	**100.0**

In the present study 48 per cent of the respondents reported of having a separate room or a place in the house for study, while 52 per cent of the respondents had no separate room or place to study. A negative correlation observed in the academic performance of the student and the facility of students having a separate room. It was found that a high group (87.7 per cent) of students getting 85 per cent and above marks had a separate room or place for study. Another large group (85.3 per cent) of respondents' who had no separate room to study performed very low and did not pass in the examination. Students need to get away from the various distractions caused by family, friends, TV, to organise and plan their study and to concentrate in their work. Students must have a place in the house to their own to study.

Distractions to the students

There are changes in the lives of students due to technological advancement. These changes are likely to continue (Santrock, 2004). The present day student has access to a number of activities, TV viewing, computer, movies, electronic games apart from the activities which used to keep them busy in earlier times like friends, hobbies, play, family and neighbourhood. Thus, in the same 24 hours of a day, there are a variety of activities they can engage in. The student may not be able to keep a balance between all these activities and the increasing academic pressure. Over exposure to any of these activities will reduce the students' time for the other activities and also reduce time for academic work.

Table 4.30: Distractions of students

No.	*Distractions*	*Often*	*Sometimes*	*Rarely*	*Never*
1.	Music	13.1	32.7	31.7	22.5
2.	TV/VCD	25.2	49.7	16.8	8.3
3.	Computer	8.9	16.7	10.0	64.0
4.	Friends	15.0	40.0	29.2	15.8
5.	Neighbours	13.3	28.3	26.9	31.6
6.	Guests	12.8	44.1	26.1	17.0

Music has its benefits, it is good for relaxing and coping with stress but if students spend more time on this, their homework would suffer. Only a small group of respondents (13.1 per cent) were often distracted by music. Moreover, more than half (54.2 per cent) were not distracted by music. Many students spend more time in front of the television set than they do with their parents. Television is only one of the many mass media that affect children's behaviour, but it is the most influential one (Kotler *et. al*, 2001). Television may have an adverse influence on students development by keeping them away from homework, making them passive learners, teaching them stereotypes, providing them with violent models of aggression, and presenting them with unrealistic views of the work (Wilson, 2003). Television also has a positive influence on student's development by presenting motivating educational programmes, increasing student's information about the world and broadening their understanding of the outside world (Clifford *et al.*, 1995). In the present study a large per cent (73.9 per cent) of respondents admitted that they are distracted by television and other associated electronic gadgets. Many television channels and a variety of programmes is a big temptation for students.

Culture involves change, and everywhere this change is increased by technological revolution. Even today's students are experiencing this revolution due to the increased use of computer and internet. For students to be prepared well for tomorrow's jobs, technology needs to become an important part of their lives (Sharp, 1999). The sample in the present study has been drawn from lower, middle and higher economic groups with monthly income ranging from below Rs 5000 to above Rs 25000. Computer is still a luxury electronic gadget, which is not accessible to lower and sometimes even middle economic groups of our country. Thus, it is assumed that not all respondents have access to computers as high as 64.4 per cent of respondents have admitted that computers never distracting them. Only a small group of 8.9 per cent of the respondents was often being distracted by computers.

Friends have often been the cause of distraction for only 15 per cent of the respondents, while 69.2 per cent of the respondents were sometimes distracted by their friends. Music, TV, computer and friends as distraction can directly be controlled by the students. The students with skills in time management and organising their daily schedule can control these distractions while to control distractions from neighbours and guests they have to be helped by their parents. Almost the same percentage of respondents, (13.3 per cent and 12.8 per cent) are distracted by neighbours and guests respectively.

While examining what were the major sources of distraction experienced by the respondents it was found that television was the cause of highest distraction reported by one-fourth (25.2 per cent) of the respondents.

Help in household work

The respondents come from different socio-economic status. The students have different duties and responsibility in their house.

Table 4.31: Help in household work

No.	*Help in Household Work*	*Frequency*	*Per cent*
1	Often	254	39.7
2	Sometimes	259	40.5
3	Rarely	100	15.6
4	Never	27	4.2
	Total	**640**	**100.0**

It was observed that more than one-third (38.7 per cent) of the respondents often helped in the household work and another 40 per cent of the respondents sometime help in the household chores. Only a small group of 27 (4.2 per cent) do not do any household work in their house. Different kinds of help that the respondents do in their house are as given below.

Table 4.32: Household duties

No.	*Household Duties*	*Often*	*Sometimes*	*Rarely*	*Never*
1.	Buying milk/vegetables/ grocery etc.	22.0	36.1	17.0	22.8
2.	Helping in the kitchen	13.9	40.5	28.3	17.3
3.	Cleaning house/dusting	13.0	34.4	25.9	26.7
4.	Sibling/elderly care	13.6	27.7	19.8	38.9

More than one-fifth of the respondents (22 per cent) often had the duty to buy milk or vegetable and groceries. Findings show that equal number of respondents helped in the kitchen and helped in cleaning the house and took care of siblings or the elderly in the family. Irrespective of gender, majority of respondents (82.7 per cent) helped in the kitchen. Less than one-fourth of the respondents helped in the household work by buying milk and groceries. Most of respondents did some or the other household work.

Modification of home environment during examinations

Parents concerned about the students academic performance brings in changes in the home environment close to students' examinations. Certain modifications were made in the homes of the respondents by their parents to facilitate an environment of study.

Table 4.33 : Modifications done at home to suit studies

No.	*Modifications done at home*	*Often*	*Sometimes*	*Rarely*	*Never*
1.	Stop watching TV	32.2	43.6	12.2	12.0
2.	Disconnecting cable	21.6	22.8	18.9	36.7
3.	Transferring your roles to others	13.9	22.3	42.0	21.0
4.	Not allowing children to play outside	42.2	33.5	8.9	15.4

It was found that among the student respondents, almost one-third (32.2 per cent) of the families often stopped watching TV in the house and a high of 43.6 per cent respondents' controlled TV viewing sometimes. This controls the temptation and distraction of students towards TV. A high of 63.3 per cent respondents reported that during examinations parents removed the cable connection to the home television, which brings in a variety of TV channels. Removing the cable connection are parents ways of reducing their wards distraction. TV viewing attracts students keeping them away from books and schoolwork. Critics argue that TV trains students to become passive learners (Santrock, 2004). In order to reduce the household burden on students parents also transfer their roles in household duties to other family members. More than three-fourth (78.2 per cent) of respondents reported that their duties and responsibilities of going to the market, cleaning the house, helping in the kitchen were transferred to the younger siblings or other family members during the examination times. It was noted that large number of students (42.2 per cent) were not allowed to go out to play during examination time. Some modifications help in distressing the students during examination time like reducing distractions at home, relieving from household chaos. While some modifications like not allowing the students to do their daily activities like not permitting students to go out and play or watch TV could in fact increase the stress on the students?

Parental help and support

An examination was made into the parental help and support that was extended to the students. Ten different kinds of help were listed and the respondents' responses of often, sometimes, rarely, never were given scores. The scores were valued as, often was valued as '3', sometimes was '2', rarely was '1' and '0' score to never. The different kinds of parental help available to the students during examination time were investigated to find out what were the most forthcoming help to the students by their parents.

Table 4.34: Help from parents

No.	*Help from parents*	*Often*	*Sometimes*	*Rarely*	*Never*	*Total*	*Rating*
1.	Relieve you of household work	987	346	108	0	1441	1
2.	Whenever needed give guidance, suggestions	1011	304	97	0	1412	2
3.	Keep away distractions like TV/outing	763	314	148	0	1230	3
4.	Organise your books/ study material/room	657	292	194	0	1143	4
5.	Avoid guests/parties / get-togethers	528	372	163	0	1063	5
6.	Make special food	501	322	154	0	977	6
7.	Teach you	402	334	141	0	877	7
8.	Accompany you to school/ tuitions	264	230	140	0	634	8
9.	Stay awake with you at nights	258	234	170	0	662	9
10.	Take leave from work during examination	186	206	161	0	553	10

The responses on each type of parental help were multiplied by its scores and the value of each item was calculated by adding all the multiplied response. For the first item- Parents relieve you of household work respondents 'often' response was multiplied by its score '3' (329 x 3 = 987). Similarly all 'sometimes' response were multiplied by its score '2' (173 x 2 =346), and all 'rarely' response were multiplied by its scores '1' (108 x 1= 108). The total values were obtained by adding values of often, sometimes, and rarely (987+346+108=1441). Thus, the total score of the first item was 1441. The total values of all the helps were calculated in this manner. These total values of each parental help were listed out in descending order. Out of them the highest value was parents relieving students of household work. This item was the most forthcoming parental support followed by parental guidance and suggestion to the respondents. The third most forthcoming help listed was parental assistance in keeping distractions away like television and other outings. This was followed by parents organising books/ study material and room. Fifth most forthcoming help was parents avoiding guests/parties/get-to-gathers. Followed by the parental help of special attention given to students in the form of special food made for them. The seventh parental help listed was parents teaching students, next parental help was parents accompanying students to school/ tuitions. The ninth parental help was parents staying awake at night with the students. The least forthcoming help was parents taking leave from their work and staying at home during examinations.

The researcher further found out how much parental help was made available to student respondents by their parents. Nature of parental helps was put together for individual respondents. The response valued as often was '3', sometime '2', rarely '1' and never '0'. These values of all parental help were totalled for each respondent. The computed value of parental help was a minimum of 0 and a maximum of 30 score for all the 10 forms of parental help to each respondents. The calculated mean of the responses of all the respondents were 15.61 and a standard deviation of 6.58. Higher the scores, higher the parental help provided by the respondents parents.

Table 4.35 : Levels of parental help

No.	*Level of Parental Help*	*Number of Respondents*	*Percentage*
1.	Low	224	35.0
2.	Average	227	35.5
3.	High	189	29.5
	Total	**640**	**100**

Taking the 33.3 per cent and the 66.6 per cent position the parental help was divided into three groups. The low parental help group had scores less than 12, this comprised 35 per cent of the respondents. More than one-third of the respondent's parental help was low. The high parental help group comprised of respondents scoring 20 and above. More than one-fourth 29.5 per cent of respondents' parents provided high parental help. While the average parental help group was placed between scores13 to 19, parent of 35.5 per cent respondents provided average parental help.

Thus, it was observed that parents help students in many ways including the environmental changes made by parents to stimulate them to study. One of these is to keep away distractions, so that the students perform well. Such efforts were put together in 10 statements. Scores were assigned to these statements. To find out what is the level of parental help and support given to the students. These statement scores were totalled. These totalled scores were grouped into high parental support with higher scores and low parental support with lower score taking the percentiles. An examination was further made to find the difference in test anxiety of students due to the parental help.

Table 4.36: Difference in test anxiety based on the level of parental help

No.	*Parental Help*	*Mean*	*SD*	*F*	*Sig.*	*Inference*
1.	Low	47.7	12.0	6.092	.002	S
2.	Medium	47.0	11.9			
3.	High	43.9	11.2			

Respondents with low parental support had mean test anxiety of 47.7 and those with high parental support had low mean test anxiety of 43.9. Respondents with medium parental support reported mean test anxiety of 47.0. To understand the effect of parental help on the respondent's test anxiety scores, the ANOVA values were calculated. The value ($F=6.092$, $p=0.002$) indicated that there is significant difference in test anxiety of respondents and parental help. The parental help and support was important to keep away examination stress and was in line with the results of other studies (Nijhawan, 1972; Jemmott *et al.*, 1988).

Parental expectation

Expectations of parents can be very useful but it is important that the expectations are set according to the capacities of the students. The parents must communicate with the child, find out their interest and suggest options according to their interest for their future goal setting. Students should be helped to set goals and it is also important to encourage them to plan how they will reach their goals. A good planner needs to manage time effectively, set priority and get organised. A number of psychological and motivational factors influence student's achievement. Most important of these is the students' ability to adapt to new academic and social pressures, others being achievement motivation, intrinsic motivation, goal setting, planning and self-regulation (Pintrich and Schunk, 2002).

Table 4.37: Parents' communicated their expectation

No.	*Parent Communicated*	*Number of Respondents*	*Per cent*
1.	Yes	486	75.9
2.	No	154	24.1
	Total	**640**	**100.0**

In the present study it was observed that majority (75.9 per cent) of the parents have communicated their expectations to their children of what they wanted of their wards to become. This has both advantages and disadvantages too. Advantage is that if expectations are in consultations with the wards and according to his capacities then the students take these expectations as their goals, and work towards realising them. But if expectations are too high and not in tune to the students' interest then the students will defy these expectations or submit to them without any motivations.

Table 4.38: Parents' expectation from their children

No.	*Parents' Expectation*	*Number of Respondents*	*Per cent*
1.	Doctor	120	18.8
2.	MBA	23	3.6
3.	Scientist	4	0.6
4.	Engineer	87	13.6
5.	Civil Service	31	4.8
6.	Hotel Mgmt	5	0.8
7.	Teacher	46	7.2
8.	Good Job	241	37.7
9.	Don't Know	83	13.0
	Total	**640**	**100.0**

Parents have high expectations from the wards. Less than half of the (49.1 per cent) parents were specific and wanted their wards to become doctor, engineer, scientist or teacher. Again the highest parental expectation is for the traditionally popular careers. 18.8 per cent of the parents wanted their children to become doctors, 13.6 per cent desired their wards to become engineers and 7.2 per cent parents wanted their children to become teachers. While more than one-third (37.7 per cent) of parents were open to any profession, only condition being that it should be a good job. Most of the parents had communicated there openness towards the respondents choice of profession.

Parents had a variety of expectations from their children including what career they wanted their wards to take up. Half of the parents had fixed concrete expectations, and wanted their wards to be doctor, engineer, teacher, scientist, manager, civil servant and the like. While some parents were more flexible and wanted their wards to get into a good job of their choice another group of parents had not conveyed any expectation from their wards.

Table 4.39: Difference in test anxiety based on the nature of parental expectations

No.	Parental Expectation	Mean	SD	F	Sig.	Inference
1.	Doctor	50.8	13.3	4.4	0.000	S
2.	MBA	46.5	7.3			
3.	Scientist	48.7	14.6			
4.	Engineer	46.1	11.9			
5.	Civil Service	44.8	11.5			
6.	Hotel Mgmt.	55.6	11.2			
7.	Teacher	48.6	13.9			
8.	Good job of children's choice	43.7	10.2			
9.	Don't know	46.3	11.8			

It was observed that parents who expected their wards to become doctor had a mean test anxiety of 50.8, while parents who wanted their wards to be scientist and teacher had mean test anxiety of 48.7 and 48.6 respectively. Parents, who were not very rigid and encouraged their children to take up a career of their choice, did not impose their expectations on their children. These students had low mean test anxiety of 43.75. The analysis of variance calculated indicated that examination stress differed according to parental expectations. This indicated that parents' expectations from their wards are an important cause of test anxiety among students. Parents with rigid expectations transfer their demands to the wards, which caused high test anxiety among these children. Parents who were communicative to their wards and just wanted their wards to get a good career of the students' choice were able to relax their children, as these children scored low on test anxiety.

Parents remind the students of their expectations

Table 4.40: Parent remind students of their expectation

No.	Parent's remind	Number of Respondents	Per cent
1.	Often	302	47.2
2.	Sometimes	240	37.5
3.	Rarely	74	11.6
4.	Never	24	3.8
	Total	**640**	**100.0**

Almost half (47.2 per cent) of the parents constantly remind their wards of their expectation. Thus, there is a constant pressure on these students on the target to be achieved as they need to reach their parents expectation. 240 (37.5 per cent) of the parents do not pressurise the students by constantly reminding them of their expectations they remind sometimes. Only a small group of parents (11.6 per cent) are understanding and patient with their wards and don't put pressure by reminding of their expectations.

Parents aspiration

Every parent set aspirations for their children. This study examined the parents' desire on their wards' achievements.

Table 4.41: Parent aspiration of students academic performance

No.	*Academic Performance*	*No. of Respondents*	*Per cent*
1.	At least Pass	43	6.7
2.	At least 50 per cent	74	11.6
3.	At least 60 per cent	107	16.7
4.	At least 75 per cent	197	30.8
5.	At least 85 per cent	138	21.5
6.	At least 90 per cent	81	12.7
	Total	**640**	**100.0**

Three-fourth (75 per cent) of the parents wanted their wards to achieve a minimum of 60 per cent and above marks in their examination. While as high as 30.8 per cent wanted a distinction from the respondents and 81 (12.7 per cent) had targeted a high of more than 90 per cent marks for the respondents. Only 43 (6.7 per cent) of respondents' parents had low expectation and just wanted the students to pass the examination. Thus, the parents aimed high and wanted the student to do extremely well.

It was observed that when parents' expectation from the children was a just pass mark the mean test anxiety scores were 41.1. But when parents expected their wards to get at least a distinction (75 per cent marks) or even 90 per cent marks the mean test anxiety was higher at 48.5 and 49.6.

Table 4.42: Difference in test anxiety based on parents' aspiration

No.	*Parental Aspiration*	*Mean*	*Standard Deviation*	*F*	*Sig.*	*Inference*
1.	At least pass	41.13	9.4	6.577	0.000	S
2.	At least 50 per cent	47.47	11.8			
3.	At least 60 per cent	44.83	10.8			
4.	At least 75 per cent	48.59	11.6			
5.	At least 85 per cent	43.55	10.6			
6.	At least 90 per cent	49.60	14.6			

The analysis of variance indicated that there is significant difference between test anxiety of the respondents based on their parental aspirations. The alternate hypothesis stating that there was significant difference in parents' aspiration and test anxiety scores was accepted. It was found that parents' high aspirations resulted in student feeling pressurised and thus their test anxiety scores were higher. Parents who had low aspirations from their wards, their children reported of low test anxiety.

Incentives offered

Incentives or rewarding the student when he/she performs well is a common practice. It is important that students treat incentives not as a bribe but a reward for their hard work and good performance. Incentives and rewards are part of the extrinsic motivation, which involves doing something to obtain something else. Lepper *et al.* (1973) concluded that rewards could undermine the learning process. Students having a strong interest in art spent more time drawing without expecting a reward than students who also had a strong interest in art but knew they would be rewarded.

Table 4.43 : Incentives offered by parents

No.	*Incentives Offered*	*Percentage of respondents*
1.	Nothing specific	46.1
2.	Outing/holiday	14.7
3.	Vehicle	20.2
4.	Dress/Jewellery	13.0
5.	Mobile Phone and other gadgets	23.0

Little less than half (46.1 per cent) of the respondents mentioned that they were offered nothing specific by their parents if they performed well in their final examination. 14.7 per cent reported they were offered an outing or holiday if they got good mark in their examination. One-fifth (20.2 per cent) respondents were promised that they will be gifted with a vehicle for them. One of the respondents said "if I get 85 per cent in my XII examination, my father said he will buy me a Santro Car". Another 23 per cent of respondents were offered mobile phones, computer and other gadgets.

Parent's reaction when students don't perform well

When children do not perform well in examinations parents react differently. They either engage in negative reactions like scolding, yelling, spanking or not bothering, or in positive reactions like talking to the student and reasoning out. Research studies highlight the adverse effects of the parent's negative reactions. In earlier times corporal (physical) punishment such as spanking had been considered necessary and even desirable method of disciplining children (Greven, 1991). Gershoft (2002) study concluded that corporal punishment by parents is associated with children's high levels of aggression and lower levels of mental health. Intense punishment, like yelling, screaming or beating used by the parent is presenting the child with an out-of-control model for handling stressful situation. The children may imitate this aggressive, an out-of-control behaviour to react to difficult situations.

Child psychologists recommend reasoning with the child the best manner in handling children. Explaining the consequences of the child's actions helps reduce children's misbehaviour. Parents need to adapt to the growing children, using more talking and reasoning in the parent-child relationship (Santrock, 2004).

Table 4.44 : Parents reaction when students don't perform well

No.	*Parents reaction*	*Yes (N=640)*	*No (N=640)*
1.	Do not bother	7.7	92.3
2.	Scolding	43.9	56.1
3.	Showing displeasure in behaviour	24.4	75.6
4.	Beating	10.0	90.0
5.	Arranging for tuitions	31.3	68.8
6.	Taking assurances for better performance	49.5	50.5

Less than half (43.9 per cent) of the students mentioned that their parents scolded if they didn't perform well in examination. Another 24.4 per cent parents showed their displeasure in their behaviour towards the respondents. Another 10 per cent of the parents even resorted to beating their wards when they did not perform well in examination. A large group (80.8 per cent) of parents also responded positively. Almost one-third took steps for arranging tuitions so that their wards perform better. Half of the parents (49.5 per cent) talked to their wards and took their assurance that the student will work for better performance.

Parents compelling students to study

Table 4.45: Parents compelled students to spend more time on study

No.	*Parents Compelling*	*Number*	*Per cent*
1.	Yes	459	71.7
2.	No	181	28.3
	Total	**640**	**100.0**

Respondents felt that more than two-third of parents (71.7 per cent) compelled the students to spend more time on studies. They wanted their children to study and to do nothing else. One student mentioned that, "since I have entered my X class, my mother constantly nags me, whenever she sees me, she tells me to go and study. She wants me to stop all other activities".

Student's expectations

Students also have their own dreams. They set their own expectations from life. Researchers have found that belief that one can master a situation and produce favourable outcome and achievement can be improved when students set goals that are specific, proximal and challenging (Schunk, 2001). It is important for students to set specific concrete goals, like "I want to secure 60 per cent marks". Students can also set long-term goals. But short-term goals are vital as these are the steps towards the long-term targets. Another good planning for students is to set challenging goals. A challenging goal is a commitment by the student to himself or herself for self-improvement. Intense interest and involvement in activities are sparked by challenges.

Goals that are easy to reach do not create much interest and effort. But goals must be optional, matched to the students' skill and capacity. If goals are unrealistically high, the outcome will be repeated failure and that would lower the student's self-efficacy. It is found in research studies that high-achieving students often are self-regulatory learners (Schunk and Zimmarman, 2001). High-achieving students monitor their learning and evaluate their progress towards a goal more than low-achieving students do. Thus, encouraging students to monitor their own learning conveys the message that students are responsible for their own behaviour and learning requires active dedicated involvement by the student themselves (Pintrich, 2003).

Table 4.46: Students expectation in life

No.	*Students Expectation*	*Number of Respondents*	*Per cent*
1.	Doctor	61	9.5
2.	MBA	35	5.5
3.	Scientist	10	1.6
4.	Engineer	80	12.5
5.	Civil Service	49	7.7
6.	Business	72	11.3
7.	Hotel Mgmt	26	4.1
8.	Teacher	52	8.1
9.	Good Job	200	31.3
10.	Don't Know	55	8.6
	Total	**640**	**100.0**

Respondents had their own aspirations and career choice. The traditional profession of medicine was preferred by 9.5 per cent of the respondents. But the choice to go in for management, engineering, civil service, hotel management and teaching was higher as compared to what their parents wanted. The choice to get into business was the second highest choice after engineering. A small group (8.6 per cent) of respondents did not know what profession to choose. While 31.3 per cent were not specific and just wanted a good job, 60 per cent of the respondents had specific professional goals for themselves.

Achievement orientation

The respondent's expectation in terms of percentage of marks was also high just like their parents.

Table 4.47: Student's expectation on academic achievement

No.	*Student's Result Expectation*	*No. of Respondents*	*Per cent*
1.	At least Pass	18	2.8
2.	At least 50 per cent	43	6.7
3.	At least 60 per cent	175	27.3
4.	At least 75 per cent	130	20.3
5.	At least 85 per cent	196	30.6
6.	At least 90 per cent	78	12.2
	Total	**640**	**100.0**

Majority (90.4 per cent) of respondents aimed for at least a 1st division while 20.3 per cent respondents aimed for distinction. Another 12.2 per cent respondents' aimed as high as 90 per cent marks. Only a small group (2.8 per cent) of respondents aspired just pass marks. These findings indicate that the respondents have high aspirations. But it is also to be kept in mind that if they aspire high and do not achieve their targets it may lead to frustration, anxiety and low self esteem.

Reasons for wanting to perform well

An investigation to the students' reasons to perform well highlights what are the students own perspective or the principal reasons why they wanted to perform well in examination.

Table 4.48: Students' motivating factor to perform well in examination

No.	*Reason to perform well*	*Percentage*
1.	Get into a good career	57.2
2.	Get good marks	32.7
3.	Personal satisfaction	19.2
4.	Meet parent's expectations	32.3
5.	Meet schools/teacher's expectations	15.6
6.	Meet friend's expectation	5.6

The respondents reported different reasons for wanting to perform well in the examinations. More than half (57.2 per cent) of the respondents wanted to perform well in examination as they aspired to get into a good career. For them good performance meant getting into a good career. Almost one-third (32 per cent) wanted to perform well in examination just to secure good marks. Another one-third (32.3 per cent) of the respondents wanted to perform well in examinations in order to meet parent's expectations. While few respondents (19 per cent) wanted to perform well for their own personal satisfaction, 15.6 per cent wanted to meet the expectations of their school and teachers. One of the students mentioned that "If I get good marks in the pre-boards then only I will get the hall tickets". A small group (5.6 per cent) of respondent's reported that the principal reason for wanting to perform well is to meet friend's expectation.

It was observed that students wanted to perform well for many reasons. Most of them were very clear with their desires and felt that good performance in examination is inevitable to chase the dream of a good career. For most of the students good marks meant personal satisfaction. There were students who wanted to do well to please their parents, teachers and friends. Parents and friends play an important role in the life of students but teachers also have an important role to play. School students can find an adult friend in a teacher. Teachers may not be able to live up to their own expectation of catering to all the students in their class, as they do not feel the same for all their students, no matter how balanced and even-handed they try to be. Teacher's feeling determine how they act toward their students (Stewart *et al.*, 1985). Silberman (1971) found four distinct attitudes teachers have towards their students.

- *Attachment.* Teacher feels attachment towards students, who are a pleasure to teach. These students fulfill the teacher's personal needs and make lesser demands on the teachers' energies.
- *Concern.* Teachers feel concerned about students who are demanding yet receptive and appreciative. Teachers respond to them openly and frequently in the classroom.
- *Indifference.* Students who do not make an impression on the teacher for their ability, responsiveness, needs or misbehaviour tend to be almost invisible or forgotten.

- *Rejection.* Students more demanding who attract too much of the teachers attention with disruptive behaviour are looked as illegitimate and overwhelming. The teacher reactions are negative and unhelpful towards the rejected child.

Factors that worried students during examinations

The respondents mentioned that a variety of factors worried them during examination and lowered their performance.

Table 4.49 : Factors that worry students during examinations

No.	*Factors worry during examinations*	*Percentage of respondents*
1.	Not having separate room/place for study	31.9
2.	Not getting sufficient guidance for studying	28.3
3.	Lack of sufficient time for study	29.1
4.	Lack of adequate preparation for examination	61.6
5.	Disturbance from neighbours/own family	19.2
6.	Household chores	15.6
7.	Media (TV, serial, cricket matches, movies)	20.0
8.	Pressure of parent's expectations	18.0

The most common factor that worried respondents was lack of adequate preparation for examination. The respondents themselves felt they could not prepare for examination well so had negative thoughts about performance and this worried them. Almost, one-third (31.9 per cent) of the respondents felt that not having a separate room or place for study worried them during examination. More than one-fourth of the respondent (28.3 per cent) replied that not getting sufficient guidance for studies caused worry during examination. Another 29.1 per cent respondents felt they lacked sufficient time for study and that worried them.

Time spent on sleep

Time spent on sleep in normal times and after the examination schedule was declared was compared. The sleep timing was recorded of individual respondents before examination period, during the normal school days. The respondents reported a minimum of four hours and a maximum of nine hours of sleep, the mean being 6.79 hours and a standard deviation of 0.86.

Table 4.50: Time spent on sleep

No.	Time Spent on Sleep	Before examination dates declared	After examination dates declared
1.	Minimum Hours	4	3
2.	Maximum Hours	9	8
3.	Mean	6.79	5.94
4.	Standard Deviation	0.86	0.94

The sleep time was also recorded of the respondents once the examination comes close and the examination schedule is declared. It was observed that respondents sleep timing reduced significantly during the examinations. Now the minimum sleep hours became three hours and a maximum of eight hours. The mean sleep time reduces to 5.94 just before the examination.

Help for better performance

An attempt has been made in this research to understand students' problems; this understanding will help to solve those problems better. Thus, the students were asked to reply, according to them, what kind of help is required for them to perform better in examination.

Table 4.51: Help to perform better in examination

No.	Help to perform better	Often	Some-times	Rarely	Never	Total	Rating
1.	Help in better understanding of subject	1590	192	14	0	1796	1
2.	Organising study (schedule)	1260	410	11	0	1681	2
3.	More help from teachers	909	524	70	0	1503	3
4.	Better conditions at home	927	498	64	0	1489	4
5.	Supportive parents	873	546	56	0	1475	5
6.	Tuitions	540	642	87	0	1269	6

The responses were given scores of often '3', sometimes '2', rarely '1' and never '0'. The individual response of the students was multiplied by their score values to arrive at a total value of each kind of help. Comparing the values of each kind of help required, gives an understanding of how respondents prioritise what according to them is the most needed help. Results showed that the respondents valued better understanding of the subjects as the most important help required by them. Because they were not able to understand the subject content of their studies, they were not able to perform well. The second most important help was assistance in organising their study. Respondents felt they were unable to manage all their activities in the daily schedule. School, home, studies, friends, recreation activities, extra curricular activities were difficult to be managed within the 24 hours of the day. Most of the time, the evening play time gets extended, or time just gets utilised at home or the study time consumes the play time, to manage all the study subjects together gets difficult. If the respondents can manage to organise their studies better, they would be able to perform better in examinations. The help from teachers was rated third in the list of help required. If teachers are more cooperative, helpful it will help them understand their subject better, give them confidence in the class, and they will be able to clear their doubts and performance level will increase. Better conditions in the house and parents support scored the fourth and fifth position. The students felt that home environment and parents are also very important in helping them perform better in examination. Surprisingly tuition scored only the sixth position. Most parents resort to tuitions when they observe their wards are not performing well. It was observed in the study that tuition is not the best help that the students have opted for to help them perform better. Hence it is essential that before providing any kind of help the student must be consulted and provided help accordingly.

Students want to perform well, for which the most important help according to the students are better understanding in the subject. Teachers can play a very important role in shaping the lives of students. Students are likely to develop into competent human being when they feel cared for. Teachers need to get to know students fairly well. This is difficult in large schools with large number of students in each class. Thus, it is important to maintain a favourable teacher-student ratio. Researchers have stated that students who feel they have supportive, helpful and caring teachers are more strongly motivated to get involved in academic work in comparison to students with unsupportive, unhelpful and uncaring teachers (Ryan and Deci, 2000).

Time distribution in different study activity

To examine the time distribution of the respondents in studies, the respondents were asked, the manner in which they study. Do they study themselves/self study? Do they go for tuition? Do they study with the guidance and help of their tutors? It is a practice that some students in the senior classes, mainly in XI and XII and sometimes from IX, X, starts preparing for the medical and engineering entrance test which is scheduled after the XII class examinations. These examinations are highly competitive and lakhs of students appear for these exams, the seats in medical and engineering colleges are much lesser in number. The All India Engineering Entrance Examination (AIEEE) held on May 2003 all over the country conducted by CBSE had 2,98,490 candidates who appeared for the test to fill 12,000 seats in 109 institutions (CBSE, 2003). The students go in for coaching for preparation of entrance examinations by privately-run tutorials.

Table 4.52 : Time spent in different activities

No.	*Time Spent on Different Activities*	*Nil*	*< 1 Hour*	*<1 – 2 Hour*	*> 2 Hours*
1.	Self study	26.9	10.6	28.6	33.9
2.	Tuition	38.4	24.2	27.7	9.7
3.	Preparing for PMT, PET (entrance exams)	70.2	11.6	9.4	8.9

It was observed that more than one-fourth respondents do not study on their own; they are guided by tutors or their parents. One-third respondents spend more than two hours on self-study. Over one-third (38.4 per cent) of respondents reported they don't go for tuitions, but the remaining 61.6 per cent of the respondents go for tuitions from less than an hour to even more than two hours.

Preparing for engineering and medical examinations is an extra load for the students. The syllabus for these entrance examinations are from the XII class syllabus itself and these examinations are held after the XII board. The students start the preparation for these examinations a year before or even before sometimes. It was found that 70 per cent respondents are not involved in preparing for these examinations.

The reason being that the sample is drawn from class IX to XII and from all streams (including arts and commerce) of subjects. Another 29.9 per cent respondents are spending time on the preparation for these examinations that may increase the pressure on the students.

Time spent on studies

Students reported that they study a minimum of one hour to maximum of 12 hours a day, with a range of 11 hours. The mean hours of study is 4.66 hours of study time daily by students excluding their school hours.

Study habits

A study habit is the study practices followed by students. The study habits scale measure the study habits of the students. There were ten items in the scale out of which seven were positively worded and three were negatively worded. This scale quantifies the study habits so that respondents study behaviour can be measured and analysed. The score for the positive items are often '4', sometimes '3', rarely '2', and never '1'. The scores were reversed for the negative items often '1', sometimes '2', rarely '3' and never '4' the scores of all items were totalled of individual respondents. The minimum totalled score was 10 and maximum was 40.

Table 4.53 : Study habits

No.	*Study habits*	*Frequency*	*Percentage*
1.	Poor	245	38.3
2.	Average	213	33.3
3.	Organised/Good	182	28.4
	Total	**640**	**100**

The respondents were divided into three groups by taking the 33.3 per cent and 66.6 per cent positions as the dividing point for creating three groups. The first group of students with less than 28 were classified as students with poor study habits. The scores between 29 and 32 were respondents with average study habits and the group with high scores of 33 and above was respondents with organised/ good study habits. Higher the totalled scores better the study habits.

It was observed that most respondents (38.3 per cent) appeared in the poor study habits with low scores on the study habit scale. One-third respondents were in the average study habit group and the lowest (28.4 per cent) number of respondents had high scores thus good study habits.

The respondents study habits were examined on the test anxiety scale to understand whether test anxiety was influenced by the study habits.

Table 4.54: Difference in test anxiety based on study habits

No.	*Study Habits*	*Mean*	*SD*	*F*	*Sig.*	*Inference*
1.	Poor	49.8	11.4	22.4	.000	S
2.	Average	45.6	12.2			
3.	Organised/Good	42.4	10.5			

It was observed that respondents with poor study habits scored high on the test anxiety inventory with mean test anxiety of 49.8 and respondents who were regular and organised with their study habits were more confident with their examination and scored lower on test anxiety, the mean test anxiety was 42.4.

The ANOVA test on study habits and the test anxiety of the respondents were calculated. The F value (F=22.504, p= 0.000) indicated that there is significant difference in test anxiety of students based on their study habits. Students who were organised with their study had lower levels of test anxiety. The students that had poor study habits were unorganised this resulted in higher test anxiety among these students. The results of this study were similar to the results of Culler and Holahan (1980); Benjamin *et al.* (1981); Tobias (1985); Dendato and Diener (1986) that had also observed that students with poor study habits reported high test anxiety.

Conclusion

This chapter elaborates on the background information of the student respondents. The extent of examination stress was measured among the students from the three different type of schools. An investigation was made into the variation in examination stress due to gender difference, class difference, type of school difference and difference in the socioeconomic background of the respondents. The factors contributing to the students examination stress were studied in detail like parental expectation, study habits, home environment. This chapter highlights on the different kinds of parental help that are provided to the students. This chapter also gives insight on various factors that worry students during examination and the different factors that help students to perform better in examination.

Thus, this chapter is very beneficial to understand student's socio-economic and academic background and the extent of examination stress. The student's views have been studied in detail on various issues of examination stress.

Chapter V

Manifestations and Coping Strategies for Examination Stress

This chapter deals with the behavioural manifestations observed in the students during the examinations and the coping strategies that the students reported of practicing when experiencing examination stress. The scales developed to measure the behavioural manifestations and the coping strategies were administered on the school students. The behavioural manifestations and the coping strategies have been analysed and cross-examined by the gender, class and type of school to examine if there is any relationship between them.

Behavioural manifestations

The respondents were examined on the behaviour manifestation scale. The scale was constructed with two domains, the physiological manifestations like physical tiredness, overeating, headaches, stomach upsets, increased heart beat, trembling, breathlessness and problem with sleep. While the second domain consisted of psychological manifestations like easy mood swings, low self-esteem, mental tension, irritability, crying easily, helplessness, confusion, mental exhaustion, lack concentration and inferiority complex. The researcher has analysed the 'often' response of the respondents to understand the intensity of the different behaviour manifestations reported by each student respondents.

Table 5.1 : Behaviour manifestations of students before examination

No.	*Behavior Manifestations*	*Often*	*Some-times*	*Rarely*	*Never*
1.	Easy mood swings	5.6	15.6	48.6	30.2
2.	Low self esteem	15.9	33.9	40.3	9.8
3.	Mental tension	14.5	30.5	28.9	26.1
4.	Irritability	10.6	22.7	33.1	33.6
5.	Crying Spells	23.1	36.6	23.3	17.0
6.	Feeling Helpless	25.2	25.8	39.5	9.5
7.	Getting upset easily	16.3	24.5	42.2	17.0
8.	Uneasiness	12.3	26.4	47.5	13.8
9.	Uncontrolled negative thoughts	22.3	17.0	38.1	22.5
10.	Feeling confused	14.8	32.3	33.1	19.7
11.	Feeling of Helplessness	28.9	25.9	31.1	14.1
12.	Mental Exhaustion	19.1	35.8	25.8	19.4
13.	Nightmares	34.8	43.3	14.4	7.5
14.	Inferiority Feelings	34.5	28.1	29.5	7.8
15.	Worries	13.4	41.1	24.4	21.1
16.	Pessimism	30.3	29.5	28.3	11.9
17.	Poor concentration	14.5	36.9	33.9	14.7
18.	Forgetfulness	18.8	38.9	28.8	13.6
19.	Lack of interest in studies	19.5	30.5	34.8	15.2
20.	Tiredness	17.3	33.8	38.1	10.8
21.	Overeating	49.1	32.7	10.9	7.3
22.	Loss of Appetite	45.6	19.1	26.6	8.8
23.	Headaches	32.0	30.2	24.4	13.4
24.	Stomach upsets	39.7	22.3	32.0	5.9
25.	Fall sick	43.3	33.0	14.2	9.5
26.	Palpitations	40.0	22.5	24.2	13.3
27.	Tremors	47.0	25.2	20.0	7.8
28.	Breathless	61.1	24.5	8.4	5.9
29.	Sleep Problems	29.1	24.1	28.3	18.6

The above table shows all the problems reported by the students while preparing and before appearing for examinations. It was observed that all students exhibited behaviour manifestations in different intensities. Among the psychological manifestations it was observed that frightening dreams was the highest reported

(34.8 per cent) symptom by the students, closely followed by feeling of inferiority by more that one-third (34.4 per cent) of the students. 30.3 per cent students have mentioned that they think getting along in life is difficult, showing that they find the examination stress difficult to face. Students have reported that they find the situation helpless (28.9 per cent), and they also (25.2 per cent) feel helpless. Higher per cent of students reported physiological manifestations. Among them 61.1 per cent of students get breathlessness. Most students exhibit eating disorders, in which 49.1 per cent students found they eat more due to examination stress, while 45.6 per cent reported of lack of appetite at examination times. Forty seven per cent students experienced trembling and 40.0 per cent reported increased heartbeat. 43.3 per cent students also complained of often falling sick. 39.7 per cent and 32.0 per cent of students reported of stomach upsets and headaches.

The items 'often', 'sometimes', 'rarely' and 'never' were given a score of '4' '3' '2' '1'. The items 1 to 19 were to measure the psychological manifestations and their totals for individual respondents indicated the individual score of psychological manifestations to examination stress. The minimum score observed was 22 and maximum was 76. The calculated mean was 46.9. The respondents were grouped to low, medium and high scores of psychological manifestation.

Table 5.2 : Psychological manifestations of students classified

No.	*Psychological Manifestation*	*Number of Respondents*	*Percentage*
1.	Low	215	33.6
2.	Medium	196	30.6
3.	High	329	35.8
	Total	**740**	**100**

The lowest one-third fell below the score 42 and this was taken for the low level manifestation cut-off point. While the high psychological manifestations group was taken at the 66.6 per cent position and with a score value of 52. Respondents with score 52 and above were grouped as students with high psychological manifestation. The scores in between 43-51 was the medium group with medium psychological manifestation. It was observed that one-third respondents 215 (33.6 per cent) had low level psychological manifestations and little more than one-third (35.8 per cent) had high psychological manifestations.

The respondents with physiological manifestations were measured from items 20 to 29. The response scores were totalled for the 10 items. The maximum score of physiological manifestation was 40 and a minimum score was 10. The mean score was 20.2 with a standard deviation of 5.7.

Table 5.3 : Physiological manifestations of students classified

No.	*Physiological Manifestation*	*Number of Respondents*	*Percentage*
1.	Low	251	39.2
2.	Medium	150	23.4
3.	High	239	37.3
	Total	**640**	**100**

To group the respondents into three groups on their physiological manifestations the 33.3 per cent score position was 18 and the 66.6 per cent position was 22. Thus, score of 18 and below comprised the respondents with low physiological manifestation and score of 22 and above group comprised respondents with high physiological manifestation. The medium group had scores between 19 and 21. Respondents manifesting low physiological difficulties were 39.2 per cent while 37.3 per cent respondents manifested high physiological problems before examination.

The behavioural manifestation is the total of all the items, physiological items and psychological items. The respondents' behavioural manifestations were calculated by totalling all the scores of all 29 items. The minimum scores obtained were 32 and the maximum scores were 116. The calculated mean score was 67.25 with a standard deviation of 15.05.

Table 5.4 : Behavioral manifestations of students classified

No.	*Behavioral Manifestation*	*Number of Respondents*	*Percentage*
1	Low	222	34.7
2	Medium	208	32.5
3	High	210	32.8
	Total	**640**	**100**

The respondents were grouped into low, medium and high groups of behavioural manifestations. By dividing the distribution into three groups, the two cut off scores were the 33.3 per cent and 66.6 per cent position. The 33.3 per cent position was 61 score. Thus, respondents with 61 and below score were considered to have low behaviour manifestations. The 66.6 per cent position was 75 score, thus respondents with 75 and more had high behaviour manifestation while medium behavioural manifestation was between 62–74 scores. It was found that the respondents with low behaviour manifestation were 222 (34.7 per cent) and high behaviour manifestations were 210 (32.8 per cent).

Students showed various behaviour manifestations during examination time. To find out if there were any variations in the behaviour manifestations due to the difference in gender further analysis were made. Cross tabulation was done to find percentages of females and males reporting each of the behaviour manifestations. To facilitate this comparison the 'Often' and 'Sometimes' response were combined and 'Rarely' and 'Never' response were combined and comparisons made on gender.

Table 5.5 : Psychological behaviour manifestations and gender of students

No.	*Psychological Manifestation*	*Female Respondents*		*Male Respondents*	
		Often/ Sometimes	*Rarely/ Never*	*Often/ Sometimes*	*Rarely/ Never*
1.	Easy mood swings	18.9	81.1	23.7	76.3
2.	Low self esteem	49.5	50.5	50.2	49.8
3.	Mental tension	54.5	45.5	35.3	64.7
4.	Irritability	37.2	62.8	29.3	70.7

Contd...

5.	Crying Spells	67.8	32.2	51.4	48.6
6.	Feeling Helpless	52.3	47.7	49.5	50.5
7.	Getting upset easily	45.2	54.8	36.3	63.7
8.	Uneasiness	40.2	59.8	37.2	62.8
9.	Uncontrolled negative thoughts	40.2	59.8	38.5	61.5
10.	Feeling confused	50.2	49.8	44.2	55.8
11.	Feeling of Helplessness	50.2	49.8	59.6	40.4
12.	Mental Exhaustion	57.6	42.4	52.1	47.9
13.	Nightmares	80.2	19.8	76.0	24.0
14.	Inferiority Feelings	61.3	38.7	64.0	36.0
15.	Worries	56.0	44.0	53.0	47.0
16.	Pessimism	61.3	38.7	58.4	41.6
17.	Poor concentration	50.2	49.8	52.7	47.3
18.	Forgetfulness	56.7	43.3	58.7	41.3
19.	Lack of interest in studies	53.6	46.4	46.4	53.6

It was observed that on the various items of the psychological dimensions, more females reported (54.5 per cent) mental tension, they get angry easily (37.2 per cent). More than two-third (67.8 per cent) of female respondents felt like crying, feel helpless (52.3 per cent), get upset easily (45.2 per cent), feel uneasy (40.2 per cent), suffer uncontrolled negative thoughts (40.2 per cent), feel confused (50.2 per cent) feel mentally exhausted (57.6 per cent). A high percentage of 80.2 per cent females students experience frightening dreams, worry about their performance (56.0 per cent). 61.3 per cent of females also reported getting along in life was difficult. More than half (53.6 per cent) of females reported that they lacked interest in studies.

An examination into the psychological items of behaviour manifestation in which more percentage of male students respondents reported high as compared to their female counterpart were mood swing (23.7 per cent). More than half of the males (50.2 per cent) reported low self esteem, feel they are in a helpless situation (59.6 per cent), have problem in concentration (52.7 per cent) and lack recalling power (58.7 per cent). Almost two-third (64.0 per cent) of males reported feeling of inferiority.

An investigation was made to find out whether there was significant difference in psychological dimensions of behaviour manifestations of the students and the gender of the students.

Table 5.6: Psychological manifestations and gender

No.	*Gender*	*Mean*	*SD*	*t*	*df*	*Sig.*	*Inference*
1.	Female	47.73	10.22	1.736	638	0.083	NS
2.	Male	46.26	11.14				

The mean score of female students on the psychological dimensions of behaviour manifestations was 47.73 and the mean score of male students was 46.26. The value of $t = 1.736$, Sig. 2 (tailed) = 0.083, $P > 0.05$. The null hypothesis was accepted saying that there was no significant difference in psychological behaviour manifestations and gender difference. Male and female students do not differ much on psychological manifestations.

A comparison was made on the physiological behaviour manifestation and the gender of the respondents to find out which were the physiological behaviour manifestation items in which female students reported more as compared to male students. Cross tabulation was done and found that 70.0 per cent of females lacked appetite, 74.0 per cent reported headaches, 63.5 per cent female respondents had increased heart beat. A high of 86.1 per cent female respondents reported breathlessness and more than half (54.2 per cent) female students had difficulty to initiate and maintain sleep.

Table 5.7 : Physiological behaviour manifestations

No	*Physiological Behaviour Manifestation*	*Female Respondents*		*Male Respondents*	
		Often/ Sometimes per cent	*Rarely/ Never per cent*	*Often/ Sometimes per cent*	*Rarely/ Never per cent*
1.	Tiredness	50.2	49.8	52.1	47.9
2.	Overeating	78.6	21.4	87.9	15.1
3.	Loss of Appetite	70.0	30.0	59.3	40.7
4.	Headaches	74.0	26.0	50.2	49.8
5.	Stomach upsets	63.8	36.2	60.3	39.7

Contd...

6.	Fall sick	74.3	25.7	78.2	21.8
7.	Palpitations	63.5	36.5	61.5	38.5
8.	Tremors	71.8	28.2	72.6	27.4
9.	Breathless	86.1	13.9	85.2	14.8
10.	Sleep Problems	54.2	45.8	52.1	14.9

Results showed that the items of physiological behaviour manifestation that were reported higher by male student respondents as compared to female respondents were 52.1 per cent of male respondents were reported feeling physically tired. A high of 84.9 per cent reported over eating before and during examinations. 78.2 per cent male respondents often remained sick and 72.6 per cent of male respondents' complaint of trembling.

On eating habits it has been observed that the situation being the same, examination time 84.9 per cent of male students due to examination stress reported overeating while 70.0 per cent female students reported lack of appetite. Thus, it is observed that male students overeat in examination stress and female students' loss appetite.

An analysis into the difference in physiological manifestations and the gender of the respondents showed that the mean score of female respondents of physiological behaviour manifestation was 20.65 and for male respondents the mean score was 19.85. To examine the significance of difference in physiological behaviour manifestations and gender the *t*-test analysis was done.

Table 5.8: Physiological behaviour manifestations and gender of the students

No.	*Gender*	*Mean*	*SD*	*t*	*df*	*Sig.*	*Inference*
1.	Female	20.65	5.72	1.806	638	0.071	NS
2.	Male	19.85	5.68				

The values obtained were $t = 1.806$, Sig (2 tailed) = 0.071, $p > 0.05$.

The null hypothesis stating no difference in the physiological behaviour manifestations and gender was accepted. As there was no significant difference observed in female and male respondents on their physiological behaviour manifestation due to examination stress.

The psychological manifestation and the physiological manifestation put together were called the behaviour manifestations of examination stress. These behaviour manifestations were analysed on the bases of gender. Does the difference in gender cause difference in the behaviour manifestation of the respondents?

Table 5.9: Behaviour manifestations and gender

No.	*Gender*	*Mean*	*SD*	*t*	*df*	*Sig.*	*Inference*
1.	Female	68.40	14.73	1.923	638	0.056	NS
2.	Male	66.12	15.29				

It was observed that the mean score of behaviour manifestations of female students were 68.40 and of the male students were 66.12, $t = 1.923$, Sig. (2 tailed) = 0.056, $p > 0.05$, there was difference in the mean score of females and male, females reported higher mean score on the behavioural manifestation, the null hypothesis was accepted as the value of Sig. (2 tailed) = 0.056, the difference between the gender and behaviour manifestations was not very significant. Females manifest only slightly more behaviour problems than male students.

The study also examined the behaviour manifestation exhibited by the students of the different type of school. To examine this difference in behaviour manifestations among the students of government school, independent school and Kendriya Vidyalayas the ANOVA test was applied.

Table 5.10: Behaviour manifestations and types of school

No.	*Type of School*	*Mean*	*SD*	*df*	*F*	*Sig.*	*Inference*
1.	Government	65.61	13.09	637	3.365	0.035	S
2.	Independent	68.76	17.35				
3.	Kendriya Vidyalaya	68.46	13.33				

It was observed that government school students mean score on behaviour manifestations were 65.61, students of independent school were 68.76 and students of Kendriya Vidyalaya were 68.46 per cent. The analysis of variance shows F = 3.365, Sig. = 0.035, $p = <0.05$. The null hypothesis stating there was no difference in behaviour manifestations of students from different types of school was rejected and the alternate hypothesis that there was difference in behaviour manifestation of students from different types of school was accepted. As the results show, that government school students exhibit low behaviour manifestations. While the students of independent schools and Kendriya Vidyalaya exhibited similar mean scores of behaviour manifestations that were higher than the government school students.

An analysis into the psychological items of behaviour manifestations among students of the different type of schools showed that the mean score of the government school students' psychological manifestations were 45.40. The mean score of students of independent schools were 48.20 and the students of Kendriya Vidyalaya reported mean scores of 48.98 on psychological manifestations.

Table 5.11: Psychological manifestations and types of school

No.	*Types of School*	*Mean*	*SD*	*df*	*F*	*Sig.*	*Inference*
1.	Government	45.40	9.44	637	6.467	0.002	S
2.	Independent	48.20	12.04				
3.	Kendriya Vidyalaya	48.98	9.89				

The analysis of variance showed F = 6.467, Sig. = 0.002, $p < 0.05$. Thus the null hypothesis stating no difference in psychological behaviour manifestation of students from the different type of schools was rejected. The alternate hypothesis stating there was difference in the psychological behaviour manifestations among students of the different types of school was accepted. As the results showed, that government school students exhibited lower psychological behaviour manifestation, while students of independent schools and Kendriya Vidyalaya had more psychological behaviour manifestation. Proving again that there was more pressure on students of independent schools and Kendriya Vidyalaya, that was observed in their higher psychological behaviour manifestations.

An examination was also made to observe the difference in physiological behaviour manifestation of the students from the different types of school.

Table 5.12: Physiological manifestations and types of school

No.	*Types of School*	*Mean*	*SD*	*df*	*F*	*Sig.*	*Inference*
1.	Government	20.21	5.08	637	1.141	0.320	NS
2.	Independent	20.56	6.53				
3.	Kendriya Vidyalaya	19.48	5.06				

It was observed that students of government schools scored a mean of 20.21 on the physiological manifestation, the independent school students mean physiological manifestation was 20.56 and students of Kendriya Vidyalaya score were 19.48. ANOVA test results showed F = 1.141, Sig. = 0.320, $p < 0.05$. The null hypothesis stating no significant difference in the physiological manifestations of students from the different types of school was accepted. As the mean scores shows there was no much difference among the physiological manifestation of the three different types of schools. The student of government school, independent school and Kendriya Vidyalaya exhibited similar physiological manifestations.

An analysis was also made into the behaviour manifestation of the students to find if it differed in the students of different classes of the school. The classes were classified as non-board classes including IX and XI and the board classes including X and XII.

Table 5.13: Behaviour Manifestations and the class of the students

No.	*Class of the students*	*Mean*	*SD*	*t*	*df*	*Sig.*	*Inference*
1.	Non-board Classes	67.97	15.15	1.150	638	0.251	NS
2.	Board Classes	66.58	14.94				

It was found that the students of the non-board classes scored 67.97 mean behaviour manifestation and the board classes mean behaviour manifestation was 66.58. The value of $t = 1.150$, Sig. (2 tailed) = 0.251, $p > 0.5$. The null hypothesis stating there was no significant difference in the behaviour manifestation due to the difference in the classes was accepted. The mean behaviour manifestation of the non-board classes was similar to the mean of board classes. Students from all senior classes manifested behavioural problem and proved the presence of examination stress among all senior class students.

The students' psychological behaviour manifestations were examined in the different classes. Here too the classes were classified into non-board classes and board classes.

Table 5.14: Psychological manifestations and the class of the students

No.	*Class of the students*	*Mean*	*SD*	*t*	*df*	*Sig.*	*Inference*
1.	Non-Board Classes	47.64	10.81	1.492	638	0.136	NS
2.	Board Classes	46.38	10.60				

It was observed that the mean of non-board classes was 47.64 and board classes were 46.38. The value of t = 1.492, Sig. (2 tailed) = 0.136, $p > 0.05$. The null hypothesis was accepted that there was no significant difference in psychological behaviour manifestation of students in the different class. Students in the senior classes irrespective of board class or non-board class experience psychological behaviour manifestations.

The students' physiological behaviour manifestations were also examined of the different classes to find out if difference in classes has an effect on the physiological behaviour manifestations of the students.

Table 5.15: Physiological manifestations and class of students

No.	*Class of Respondents*	*Mean*	*SD*	*t*	*df*	*Sig.*	*Inference*
1	Non-Board Classes	20.31	5.73	0.233	368	0.816	NS
2	Board Classes	20.21	5.71				

It was observed that students classified in the non-board classes had a mean physiological behaviour manifestation score of 20.31 and the board classes mean score was 20.21. The value of t = 0.233, Sig (2 tailed) = 0.816, $p > 0.05$. The null hypothesis stating no significant difference in physiological manifestation due to the difference in class of the respondents was accepted. The mean score of physiological behaviour manifestation was similar in both the non-board classes and the board classes. Thus, this highlights that students in the senior classes of board classes and non-board classes experience physiological behaviour manifestation, thus proving again the presence of examination stress among the senior classes irrespective of board examinations.

Coping with examination stress

The student's way to handle tensions and problematic situation due to examination are their coping mechanism. For many years the focus of research had been on what stress and test anxiety do to people, but now there has been a shift to how to build up competencies to help students cope to the examination stress.

Examination failure reports have a deleterious affects on the subsequent performance of highly test-anxious individuals (Sarason, 1960). One effect is that failure arouses self pre-occupying thoughts about the consequences of failure, self-depreciation, and loss of status. These cognitive activities interfere with task-relevant activities and further lower post-failure performance. These task-irrelevant cognitive activities can be replaced by more adaptive coping mechanism (Sarason, 1972).

Individuals cannot remain in a continuous state of tension. Even if a conscious strategy is not adopted to deal with stress, some or the other strategy is adopted. Some try to leave the conflicts and stress and to take care of themselves. This is the avoidance coping strategy. Lazarus (1966) explained coping has two connotations in stress literature. Coping has been used to denote the way of dealing with stress or the effort to 'master' conditions of harm, threat or challenge when the automatic response is not readily available. Pestonjee (1999) states that a person's coping style or disposition is typically assessed by personality tests, not by actual observation of what the person says or does in a particular stress situation. A multidimensional interaction model of stress, anxiety and coping processes were proposed by Endler (1997). Coping means the typical approach of individuals when faced with a stressful situation and how they deal with it. So coping is a person-situation approach. In the examination situation specific coping behaviours are more effective and required than other behaviours like problem-focused situation rather than an emotion-focused. Persons may have preferred coping style but situational demands may "override". There are three personality styles: task-oriented (or problem-focused) coping, emotion-oriented coping and avoidance-oriented coping. Task-oriented coping is concerned with purposeful task-oriented efforts focusing on solving the problem, cognitively restructuring it, or attempting to change the situation. Emotion-oriented coping is concerned with self-oriented emotion reactions. The goal is to reduce stress, but this is not always accomplished. Responses include emotional reactions, self-preoccupation, and fantasizing. Emotion-oriented coping may increase stress. Avoidance-oriented coping involves activities and cognitive changes concerned with avoiding the stressful situation, which means distractions and social diversion. Task-oriented coping is most effective in a controllable situation, while emotion-oriented coping is most effective in an uncontrollable situation. While avoidance-oriented coping may be appropriate at the initial stage as a reaction to stress. But ultimately task-oriented coping is most effective. The coping strategies are also classified as adaptive coping strategies and maladaptive coping strategies. The adaptive coping strategies include those positive coping mannerisms which help the students to face the situation better. The maladaptive coping strategies are the negative coping ways that do not help in solving the problem and sometimes are even adverse for health (substance abuse).

Table 5.16 : Adaptive coping strategies of students to examination stress

No.	*Adaptive coping strategies*	*Often*	*Sometimes*	*Rarely*	*Never*
1.	Practice yoga/relaxation technique	28.6	32.3	22.3	16.7
2.	Meditation	6.4	17.3	39.1	37.2
3.	Prayer for courage to face difficulties	42.0	25.3	16.9	15.8
4.	Visit temples/other religious places	16.9	25.3	36.3	21.6
5.	Sharing problems with friends/ family/relatives	27.0	31.3	26.1	15.6
6.	Involve in recreational activities like TV/Music/movies	8.4	25.0	40.6	25.9
7.	Physical exercise/walking/jogging	19.2	37.0	26.9	16.9
8.	Pursuing hobbies (reading, music, instrumental, dancing, painting, etc.)	13.6	33.1	26.4	26.9
9.	Try to organise studies better	12.0	26.6	24.8	36.3
10.	Think that examination is part of life.	8.1	29.8	23.9	38.1
11.	Take examination as stepping stone for success	7.2	18.0	26.6	48.3
12.	Think of possible better outcomes	8.4	22.7	23.8	45.2
13.	Ask for guidance from others	7.2	34.1	31.9	26.9

Students cope with stress in there own ways. Some of these coping are adaptive, the adaptive coping help the students manage and deal with the difficult situation, relaxing them and helping them work out ways to meet the crisis, like practice yoga, relaxation techniques, meditation, sharing problems with friends, family, relatives, physical exercise, pursuing hobbies or organising studies. While some coping are maladaptive like sleeping off, taking medicine, substance abuse, or believing in destiny these do not help students to improve the situation, this just distract the students from the situation and lowers their confidence level and they are unable to face the crisis. If an analysis is done on the 'often' response of the respondents, it is observed that most common (42.0 per cent) coping to stress among students is praying for courage to face the difficulties of examination. Followed by 27.0 per cent of respondents share their problems with friends/family/ relatives. Another 12.0 per cent of students try to organise study better and 7.2 per cent ask for guidance from others to help cope with examination stress. It is observed that lower percentage of students have reported of adopting adaptive coping strategies. It is important to introduce task-oriented coping strategies to students and help them to adopt the strategies so that they are able to cope better to the examination situations.

Table 5.17: Maladaptive coping strategies of students to examination stress

No.	*Maladaptive coping strategies*	*Often*	*Some-times*	*Rarely*	*Never*
1.	Sleeping	10.6	35.0	36.6	17.8
2.	Take medicines to get rid of problems like headaches, stomach upset etc.	14.5	10.6	20.0	54.8
3.	Take medicines to improve concentration, reduce sleep, anti-depressant	3.9	8.3	11.3	76.6
4.	Indulge in smoking/drinking/ substance abuse	2.2	5.2	6.4	86.3
5.	Believe in destiny	15.9	19.8	31.7	32.5

Among the maladaptive coping strategies, it was observed that there are a significant number of students (14.5 per cent) that take in medicines to get rid of problems like headaches and stomach upsets. A small percentage of students (3.9 per cent) also take medicines to improve concentration, reduce sleep and anti-depressant for examination stress. Another small group (2.2 per cent) of students are of concern as they indulge in substance abuse as coping mechanisms before examinations.

The respondents response on the adaptive coping items were given scores, often was given score of '4', sometimes '3', rarely '2' and never '1'. These were items 1, 2, 3, 4, 5, 6, 7, 8, 10, 14, 15, 16, 17. The adaptive coping items were totalled. The mean score of adaptive coping strategies was 35, minimum score was 20 and maximum 49.

Table 5.18: Adaptive coping strategies of students classified

No.	*Adaptive Coping Strategies*	*No. of Respondents*	*Percentage*
1.	Low	321	50.2
2.	High	319	49.8
	Total	**640**	**100**

The distribution was divided into two groups by the mean. The low adaptive coping was score 35 and below. Half of the respondents 321 (50.2 per cent) had low adaptive coping while scores of high adaptive coping were 36 and above. 319 (49.8 per cent) respondents were in this group. The students are low with their coping strategies so they are more prone to stress. Students unable to manage the examination stress also resorted to maladaptive coping techniques. Item 9, 11, 12, 13, 18 are maladaptive. Their scores were often '1', sometime '2', rarely '3' and '4' to never. The scores on these items for each respondent were totalled. The mean was 15.9. The minimum score observed being 8 eigth and maximum 20 score.

Table 5.19 : Maladaptive coping strategies of students classified

No.	*Maladaptive Coping Strategies*	*Number of Respondents*	*Percentage*
1.	Low	338	52.8
2.	High	302	47.2
	Total	**640**	**100**

The scores were grouped into two with the mean as the cut-off point. The group with scores of 16 and below was respondents with high maladaptive coping techniques. There were 302 (47.2 per cent) respondents who to reduce stress relied on maladaptive coping technique. With the score 17 and above respondents were grouped to low maladaptive coping. There were 338 (52.8 per cent) respondents with low maladaptive coping.

Thus, we observe that the respondents get involved with comparatively lower adaptive strategies and are also involved with maladaptive strategies for coping to examination stress. This shows lack of direction to students in our schools. They are ill-equipped to deal and manage examination stress.

Table 5.20: Test anxiety and adaptive coping

No.	*Adaptive Coping*	*Mean*	*SD*	*t*	*Sig(2-tailed)*
1.	Low	50.7	11.9	10.107	0.000
2.	High	41.9	10.0		

An investigation into adaptive coping strategies and test anxiety scores found that students who had adopted low adaptive coping strategies reported mean test anxiety of 50.7. Students who had adopted high adaptive coping strategies reported mean test anxiety of 41.9. To find the difference *t*-test was done and found t=10.107, Sig (2-tailed)=.000, $p<0.05$. This explains that the null hypothesis stating no difference in adaptive coping strategies and test anxiety was rejected and the alternative hypothesis was accepted that there was significant difference in test anxiety and adaptive coping strategies. Students with low adaptive coping were not able to adjust to the demanding situation of examinations so had higher test anxiety, and students with higher adaptive coping strategies were able to adapt so reported lower test anxiety.

Table 5.21 : Test anxiety and maladaptive coping strategies

No.	*Maladaptive Coping*	*Mean*	*SD*	*t*	*Sig (2-tailed)*
1.	High	47.1	12.1	1.83	.068
2.	Low	45.4	11.5		

The students test anxiety scores and the students maladaptive coping strategies were analysed, it was observed that students who had adopted more maladaptive coping strategies there mean test anxiety was 47.1 and students who had adopted lesser maladaptive coping strategies their mean test anxiety were 45.4. The t=1.83, Sig (2-tailed) =0.068, p>0.05. The null hypothesis stating that there was no significant difference in test anxiety and maladaptive coping strategies was accepted.

An examination was done to find out the coping strategies of the female and male students. Was there any difference in coping strategies due to gender differences or were female and male students similar in their coping strategies? To make this comparison cross tabulations were made of the female and male respondents on the coping strategies. The 'often' and 'sometime' responses were combined into one group and the 'rarely' and 'never' responses were combined into another group.

The coping strategies have been taken separately the adaptive and maladaptive strategies. Adaptive strategies were helpful and resulted in positive coping. Some coping strategies help to relax and use up pent up energy and help face the difficult situation like yoga, praying to God, sharing problems with friends, physical exercise, involve in recreational activities. Some adaptive coping strategies help in resolving the problem by planning tasks to overcome the difficult situation like organising studies, asking for guidance.

Table 5.22: Adaptive coping strategies and gender

No.	*Adaptive Coping Strategies*	*Female Respondents*		*Male Respondents*	
		Often/ Sometimes (per cent)	*Rarely/ Never (per cent)*	*Often/ Sometimes (per cent)*	*Rarely/ Never (per cent)*
1.	Practice yoga/relaxation technique	65.0	35.0	56.8	43.2
2.	Meditation	33.7	66.3	13.6	86.4
3.	Prayer for courage to face difficulties	72.8	27.2	61.8	38.2
4.	Visit temples/other religious places	45.8	54.2	38.5	61.5

Contd...

5.	Sharing problems with friends/ family/ relatives	61.3	38.7	55.2	44.8
6.	Involve in recreational activities like TV/Music/ movies	39.3	60.7	27.4	72.6
7.	Physical exercise/ walking/jogging	49.2	50.8	63.4	36.6
8.	Pursuing hobbies (reading, music, instrumental, dancing, painting, etc.)	51.1	48.9	42.3	57.7
9.	Try to organise studies better	45.5	54.5	32.2	67.8
10.	Think that examination is part of life	39.9	60.1	36.0	64.0
11.	Take examination as stepping stone for success	28.2	71.8	22.1	77.9
12.	Think of possible better outcomes	38.4	61.6	23.7	76.3
13.	Ask for guidance from others	46.1	53.9	36.3	63.7

It was observed that higher percentage of female students were involved in yoga (65.0 per cent), prayed for courage to face the problem (72.8 per cent), visited temple or other religious places (45.8 per cent), practiced meditation (33.7 per cent), involved in recreational activities (39.3 per cent), shared their problems with friends/family/relatives (61.3 per cent). Over half of the female students (51.1 per cent) pursue hobbies to cope to examination stress. And in the task-oriented coping strategies also the female students respondents reported higher than the male respondents, 45.5 per cent of female students organise studies, 46.1 per cent ask for guidance and cope better for examination stress. More than one-third (39.9 per cent) of the female students think examinations are part of the life. Another 28.2 per cent female respondents take examination as stepping stone for success and over one-third (38.4 per cent) of female students think of possible better outcomes of examinations. Male student respondents had higher percentage than female respondents only on physical exercise, 63.4 per cent of males student respondents engaged in physical exercise.

Students also engaged in maladaptive coping strategies to relieve them of the examination stress but these maladaptive coping strategies instead of doing good are negative in their effect on the respondents.

Table 5.23: Maladaptive coping strategies and gender

No.	Maladaptive Coping Strategies	Female Respondents		Male Respondents	
		Often/ Sometimes (per cent)	Rare/ Never (per cent)	Often/ Sometimes (per cent)	Rare/ Never (per cent)
1.	Sleeping	52.3	47.7	38.8	61.2
2.	Take medicines to get rid of problems like headaches, stomach upset etc.	24.5	75.5	25.9	74.1
3.	Take medicines to improve concentration, reduce sleep, anti-depressant	12.1	87.9	12.3	87.7
4.	Indulge in smoking/ drinking/ substance abuse	2.8	97.2	11.8	88.2
5.	Believe in destiny	33.1	66.9	38.5	61.5

Out of the five items listed in the maladaptive coping, only on the item of sleeping the female respondents' scored higher than the male respondents. More than half (52.3 per cent) of the female respondents avoided the examination stress by sleeping off. While 38.5 per cent of the male students respondent believed in destiny, they felt that examinations and their results are because of individuals destiny there was nothing much to do in it, thus these adopted avoidance to examination as their coping strategies in times of examination stress.

The other maladaptive coping strategies, which were also negative to students' health and academic performance, were scored higher by the male respondents. One-fourth (25.9 per cent) of male respondents take medicines to get rid of the physical ailments like headache, stomach upset, stress, depression. Another 12.3 per cent of male respondents consume medicine to improve concentration, reduce sleep to study more and perform better, followed closely by 11.8 per cent of male student respondents indulging in substance abuse. Thus, schools need to cater to these students who indulge in these malpractices especially seen among the male students, an increase in awareness against the ill-effect of maladaptive coping strategies especially substance abuse and medicines over the counter will prevent students from trying out what is available in the market.

The student respondents were examined to find if there was any difference in adaptive coping strategies due to the difference in gender of the respondents.

Table 5.24: Adaptive coping strategies and gender differences

No.	*Gender*	*Mean*	*SD*	*t*	*df*	*Sig.*	*Inference*
1.	Female	36.09	5.99	4.088	638	0.000	S
2.	Male	33.97	7.06				

It was observed that female student respondents had a mean score of 36.09 on adaptive coping strategies and male student respondents had a mean score of 33.97. The value of $t = 4.088$, Sig. (2 tailed) = 0.000, $p < 0.05$. The null hypothesis stated no difference in adaptive coping strategies due to gender was rejected and the alternate hypothesis stating that there was difference in adaptive coping strategies due to gender difference was accepted. Female student respondents were more engaged in adaptive coping strategies compared to the male student respondents.

An analysis of maladaptive coping strategies and gender difference showed that the female student respondents mean score on maladaptive coping strategy was 15.79 and the male students scored 16.10.

Table 5.25: Maladaptive coping strategies and gender differences

No.	*Gender*	*Mean*	*SD*	*t*	*df*	*Sig.*	*Inference*
1.	Female	15.79	2.32	1.732	638	0.000	S
2.	Male	16.10	2.21				

The value of $t = 1.732$, Sig (2 tailed) = 0.000, $p < 0.05$. The null hypothesis was rejected that there was no difference in maladaptive coping strategies due to the gender of the respondents. The alternate hypothesis was accepted that there was significant difference in maladaptive coping strategies in female and male student respondents. The female respondents scored lower on the maladaptive coping strategies showing that lesser female respondents adopt maladaptive coping strategies. While male respondents reported higher mean scores on maladaptive coping strategies showing more male respondents adopt maladaptive coping strategies to adapt to examination pressures than the female students.

The adaptive coping strategies were examined to find if there was any difference in adaptive coping strategies due to the difference in the class of the respondents.

Table 5.26: Adaptive coping strategies and class of respondents

No.	*Class of Respondents*	*Mean*	*SD*	*t*	*df*	*Sig.*	*Inference*
1.	Non-Board Classes	35.28	6.43	0.956	638	0.339	NS
2.	Board Classes	34.78	6.82				

It was found that students of the non-board classes scored a mean adaptive coping of 35.28 and the board class student had a mean of 34.78. The value of $t = 0.956$, Sig. (2 tailed) = 0.339, $p > 0.05$. The null hypothesis was accepted stating there was no significant difference in the adaptive coping strategies of the students in different classes. Students of the non-board classes and board class respond to examination stress in a similar manner, thus their mean was not much different. The slightly lower mean in the board classes students may be due to the students being constantly supervised by their parents, so they get little time to engage in any of the activities which would have helped them to relax or unwind to reduce and cope to the examination stress.

An examination into the maladaptive coping strategies in the different classes was also done, to examine if there was any difference in maladaptive coping strategies adopted by students in the different classes in the senior school.

Table 5.27: Maladaptive coping strategies and class of respondents

No.	*Class of Respondents*	*Mean*	*SD*	*t*	*df*	*Sig.*	*Inference*
1.	Non-Board Classes	16.16	2.26	2.388	638	0.017	S
2.	Board Classes	15.73	2.27				

Results show that the mean score of maladaptive coping in non-board classes was 16.16 and the students in board classes scored 15.73, $t = 2.388$, Sig. (2 tailed) = 0.017, $p < 0.05$. The null hypothesis stating no difference in maladaptive coping in the different classes was rejected and the alternate hypothesis that there was significant difference in maladaptive coping in the different classes was accepted. It was observed that students of the non-board classes had adopted higher maladaptive coping strategies than the board classes. The reason could be that the students in the board classes are more conscious, serious and hardworking and they have a tight schedule of homework and tuitions. The parents' vigil over them, giving them less scope to engage in maladaptive coping strategies. The board students are hard pressed for time as compared to the non-board class students; this could also be another reason for the non-board class students scoring higher on the maladaptive coping strategies.

An investigation into the adaptive coping strategies of the students in the different type of school highlighted the difference in coping strategies score of students varied due to the difference in type of school.

Table 5.28: Adaptive coping strategies and types of school

No.	*Types of School*	*Mean*	*SD*	*df*	*F*	*Sig.*	*Inference*
1.	Government	37.37	6.10	637	47.057	0.001	S
2.	Independent	33.68	6.42				
3.	Kendriya Vidyalaya	30.73	5.87				

It was observed that government school student mean adaptive coping scores were 37.37. The independent school students scored 33.68 and the Kendriya Vidyalaya students mean score was 30.73. The ANOVA test result shows $F = 47.05$, Sig = 0.001, $p < 0.05$. The null hypothesis stating no difference in adaptive coping strategies in the students of different type of schools was rejected and the alternative hypothesis accepted stating there was difference in adaptive coping strategies of students in different type of schools. Results show that the students of government school were highest in adopting adaptive coping strategies, followed by independent school students. Kendriya Vidyalaya students were lowest in adopting adaptive coping strategies.

This also reconfirms the test anxiety results, which showed government school students are least anxious, it could be as they adopted highest adaptive coping strategies. Followed by independent school students scoring second in test anxiety and Kendriya Vidyalaya students were found to be highest in test anxiety and lowest in adopting adaptive coping strategies.

The maladaptive coping strategies were observed in students of the different type of schools. The results showed that the mean of maladaptive coping strategies in government school students was 15.57. The mean score of independent school students was 16.26 followed by Kendriya Vidyalaya students was 16.30.

Table 5.29: Maladaptive coping strategies and types of school

No.	*Types of School*	*Mean*	*SD*	*df*	*F*	*Sig.*	*Inference*
1.	Govt.	15.57	2.31	637	7.633	0.001	S
2.	Independent	16.26	2.22				
3.	Kendriya Vidyalaya	16.30	2.13				

The ANOVA test results indicated (F = 7.633, Sig. = 0.001, $p < 0.05$) difference in maladaptive coping strategies in students of the different types of schools. The alternate hypothesis was accepted stating that there was significant difference in maladaptive coping among students of the different type of school. Results showed that government school students scored lowest on the maladaptive coping strategies. The students of Kendriya Vidyalaya scored high on maladaptive coping strategies.

This chapter dealt with the data from the student respondents on their behaviour manifestations and the coping strategies adopted by them to face examination stress. The detailed investigation into the different behavioural manifestations of the students at examination time will help students, parents, peers, teachers and practitioners understand the problems students undergo when faced by examination stress. The coping strategies adopted by students have also given a better picture of what needs to be done to help students build up their adaptive coping strategies so that they are better equipped to cope to the pressures of examinations.

Chapter VI

Social Work Intervention

Examination stress has in recent years emerged as a phenomenon upsetting the students and affecting their efficiency. More and more students year after year are reporting of behavioural and stress-related problems that they are unable to handle around examination times. Society at large is aware of the problem. The officials at the Directorate of Education, Government of India, Central Board of Secondary Education (CBSE), National Council of Educational Research and Training (NCERT), World Health Organisation, School Authorities and Non Government Organisations, have examination stress as an important agenda in their scheme of activities. In recent years, there has been a change in their orientation and steps have been taken to control the ill-effects of this problem. Various government, non-government organisations have developed their own methods to face and deal with the problem.

Initiatives by the government organisations

Delhi is India's first city to introduce a state-run, toll-free help-line for teachers and students of government school. The proposed help-line is designed to tackle day-to-day educational crises in schools, including pressure from examination. As part of this scheme telephone sets would be installed in each of the 940 schools of the Delhi Government and New Delhi Municipal Council (NDMC) in the first phase and in the1800 schools run by the Municipal Corporation of Delhi (MCD) in the second phase. These would be directly connected to the help-line. Students can also call the toll-free help-line from outside the school to ensure confidentiality. For attending calls on helplines, the government has identified NGOs that in turn would identify and train volunteers from NGOs and specialists from the field of education, child development and mental health. However, it would be a huge challenge to identify, recruit and train counsellors to cater to a vast number of students and teachers.

The Directorate of Education, Government of NCT of Delhi for the first time has launched YUVA — a life skills programme for adolescent children in NDMC and MCD schools in Delhi. The Department of Education, Delhi Government, in association with Delhi State Aids Control Society (DSACS), has launched this programme in 2006. This programme is reaching out to principals, teachers and students in the Delhi schools. Counsellors and senior practitioners in the area of mental health have been roped in to train teachers and students covering areas such as scholastic improvement, career planning, body image, nutrition, gender equity, mental health, substance abuse, adolescent sexual and reproductive health, HIV/AIDS, and coping with stress and tension. The component of coping with stress and tension in this YUVA Programme would help students develop skills to deal with examination stress also. The schools have been directed to dedicate one period every week for students to take up the various issues of concern under the YUVA project.

In India, the Council of Boards of School Education (COBSE) comprising of representatives of examination boards across the country have reached a consensus in bringing reforms in the examination system to control examination stress among school students. The stress busting measures that the Council of Boards of School Education (COBSE) has recommended in May 2005 will be followed by the different examination boards in the country to remove the pressure on the school students. CBSE the examination board has brought in important changes to ease the tensions in board examination.

- Since March 2006, the CBSE has introduced a system of providing an extra 15 minutes before the start of any examination so that the students can thoroughly read the question paper, compose themselves, get over their jitters, help fight the examination stress and then start the examination.

- Question papers of some subjects would be made easier. The length of the papers would be aimed so that students can finish their papers half-an-hour early and get time to revise what they have written. In due course of time all the subjects will follow the same pattern.
- Internal assessment has been introduced in Mathematics, Sciences and Social Science based on projects and assignments. This will promote holistic learning inside the classroom rather than the student's future being decided through just one examination. This will again reduce the examination stress on the final examinations.
- CBSE has already de-linked the syllabi of classes IX and X as also XI and XII. Thus, the final examination is set on the class X and class XII syllabi rather than on what is taught over two years.
- In 2010-11, CBSE introduced the Continuous and Comprehensive Evaluation (CCE) and grade point system in IX and X standard. Board examination was made optional in X standard. These initiatives have greatly distressed the students. Now in 2015 the government in the centre is again rethinking of starting the X standard Board examination for all students. Five years have passed with the new X optional board examination. Government must interact with all stakeholders, collect empirical data and then take a decision whether to make Board examination compulsory for all at X standard. Education and examination must remain stress free. Education system must also keep up with the need of the time.
- CBSE has been providing telephone-counselling service since 1998 realising that students face examination stress, especially those in the board classes X and XII. The helpline is provided twice a year once at the time of examinations and again at the time of declaration of results. CBSE has felt the need and importance of round the year counselling. This has led to the

recommendation of a counsellor as a requirement for affiliation of schools to the board. (CBSE, 2003).

National Council of Educational Research and Training (NCERT) has also recognised the need for counselling for students to combat stress and tension. Teachers are like counsellors and if equipped with skills can build up relations with students based on trust, security and safety. This is the key to the teacher-learning process and is essential for encouraging students to share their intimate problems with teachers. Based on this NCERT has started six-month diploma in guidance and counselling for teachers. Teachers from all over the country and neighbouring countries have attended these courses.

The Department of Psychiatric Social Work, National Institute of Mental Health and Neuro Sciences, Bangalore has prepared materials to help students in schools. The materials have laid down strategies to help student to read, study and to help students prepare for examinations. The material also elaborates specific techniques to be followed on the day of examination.

Initiatives by schools

Individual schools in Delhi have responded to the psychosocial problems observed in students due to examination stress. But only 10 per cent of the schools in Delhi have qualified persons (school social worker/counsellor/psychologist) who can help students (Nagpal, 2005). Schools in Delhi, in their attempt to combat the problem are involved in counselling, organising talks with experts on stress management, career counselling and other related issues. Schools do respond to the concerns and problems of students like examination stress, along with other mental health issues. But these efforts are just a drop in the ocean.

The National Education Policy (1986) and National Mental Health Programme (1982) have talked about the need to prevent children from the stresses of the environment and promote mental health. Children need to be prevented from the stresses of the environment. Children need to be protected and supported by their family, school and community. Schools can play an important role in identifying mental health problems among children and the early interventions can arrest the problem from affecting the child's personality. World Health Organisation in 1987 proposed that schools, with the support of families and communities, would be the best place to develop mental health programmes for children, which will be effective in improving scholastic achievements, mental well-being and in curbing mental disorders (WHO, 1987 cited in Joseph, 2002).

Mostly, school mental health programmes are sporadic and not well organised. The school that have a sensitive principal/management and who have enterprising, dedicated school social workers/counsellors plan out effective programmes for the students year after year, batch after batch but in most of the school little is done towards the mental well-being of its students. One of the school social worker, during interview, reported that "This year I have not been able to do much as the principal is insensitive to the psychosocial needs of the students. He thinks these programmes are just a waste of time and the school must concentrate on academic achievements of the students". In another school, a counsellor reported that "my interaction with the students is not included in the time table of the school. I am able to visit students in classroom only if their scheduled subject teacher is absent. I am involved in cultural activities of the school and my counselling room is in one corner of the school building". School social worker/ counsellors have to carve a place for themselves in the school among school management, teachers, students and parents.

One counsellor in the interview reported that she had an enthusiastic Director in the school so she had various programmes with the school students on adjustment, stress management, life skill education, examination stress and other related issues. She also commented that she is so busy with counselling and group interactions that she feels that there should be a counsellor for each level in the school at primary, middle and senior level.

Initiatives by other organisations

The National Progressive School Conference (NPSC), an organisation comprising of 100 popular schools in Delhi, have formulated programmes in their schools to combat stress and tension. This also covers examination stress among the school students.

Ms Usha Ram, principal of Laxman Public School, currently the chairperson of NPSC, considers peer counselling as the best way to create an atmosphere for students that is stress and pressure free. Peer counselling is very effective as students relate more easily to their own age group. The NPSC schools have also formulated grading system for their schools till the IX Class, which will again help to address the problem of examination stress and create an environment of healthy competition. Some school have already put this in practice, others are planning to soon implement the grading system.

Media also acknowledges the problem of examination stress and responds by telecasting and airing appropriate programmes on television and radio, bringing in experts from the areas of education, psychiatry, psychology, mental health counselling and social work who give important information to students, parents and teachers to understand and help deal with the examination stress. Print media has also dealt with the issue of examination stress. Newspapers and magazines, which are read by the general population, are flooded with information on examination stress especially around examination time, with tips to reduce stress and improve performance at examination. Nutrition experts help in planning the diet for students in examination time.

Various NGOs are also involved with prevention and management of examination stress among school students. Snehi, an NGO working for positive mental health of individuals through its two programmes, Disha and Hopeline, is providing telephonic counselling to help students appearing for examination to deal with anxieties and cope with psychological distress. Since 1994, Snehi has reached out to 46,096 students and 6,665 parents affected by examination stress. The help was provided through telephonic counseling.

'Expression' an NGO has developed programmes on life skill education and school mental health. Expression believes that schools can play an important role in the overall development of students, but, at times, they end up causing stress for children and parents. School phobia, psychosomatic complaints, emotional, and behavioural problems are manifested due to the stress in school children. Expression proposes to work at two levels. At the first level, it works with junior students till 12 years. At the second level it works with the adolescents from 13 to 18 years. With the junior students it is mainly working with teachers, parents and counsellors in primary and middle school sections. With adolescents, it disseminates life skill education involving school counsellors, interested teachers, peer trainers and to all the students depending on the interest shown by the schools. Expression had conducted 240 workshops in different schools of Delhi. One of the main components of these workshops is how to face examination stress.

Max health clinic is also involved with school mental health. They organise seminars in schools with students, teachers and parents dealing with the issue of examination stress. This organisation also trains counsellors with skills like study skills, examination skills, life skills and others. They are also working on media awareness, sensitising them to the issues and problems of the general population, helping them deal with stress and tension.VIMHANS has also developed programmes for mental health needs among children and adolescents in schools.

Views of professionals from the area of student welfare

To prepare a social work intervention model for school students, the researcher interviewed four groups of professionals who are working with students and/or in student welfare. These included teachers/ principals of schools, school social workers/counsellors, NGO professionals, psychologists/psychiatrists, and social work educators. Four professionals were interviewed from each group. Thus, a total of 16 professionals were interviewed in all.

The findings from the data collected are as given below:

Majority of the respondents (75 per cent) stated that the aim of social work intervention should be to reduce and prevent students from experiencing stress by minimising the effect of factors that cause stress, by improving the school and home environment. The remaining 25 per cent of the respondents reported that by strengthening the student's academic standards and by increasing the students' self-confidence and self-esteem, the students would be able to tackle the challenges of their examination.

Eleven respondents (68.7 per cent) maintained that the students could be addressed at two levels — the general students can be made aware of examination stress at the preventive level and the students prone to the problem can be involved in the stress reduction level. All students in the senior classes from VIII class must be included in the prevention phase, as reported by (87.5 per cent) respondents. 12.5 per cent respondents felt that the junior class students must also be covered.

The **students** can be prevented from examination stress by group work. Many problems of students can be well resolved in a group setting. Two-third of the respondents (68.75 per cent) observed that group work could handle the various issues and problems of students' well. There are various techniques that can be taken up in the group session, some are delineated below:

1. Talks and discussion on issues like
   - Developing balanced personality, with self-confidence and self-esteem.
   - Improving study skills, examination taking skills.
   - Organising study and time management
   - Developing leadership qualities
2. Recreational and play therapy
   - Learning better adjustment within group members through recreational activities and play activities.
3. Role play and role modelling
   - Giving students space for self-expression.
   - Positive reinforcement for student who were alrounder and who helped other students.
4. Encouraging "peer groups". These "peer groups" should be of five to six students of the same class living in close neighbourhood. The purpose of this group is for students to support each other. Students help each other in academics, encourage and play together or study together. The more intelligent and brighter students can be promoted to help the other students who don't perform so well and who need help.

Thus, encouraging students to be responsible for their group member's development would lead to development of the whole group.

5. Students can be helped by the school counsellor/school social workers. Students can approach them, when the students feel they need help. Casework can help students to overcome their problems.

The **teachers** can help students prevent and reduce examination stress. Fifteen (93.7 per cent) of respondents stated that teachers play a vital role in shaping the lives of the students.

According to 9 (56.25 per cent) of the respondents

1. The teachers need to be oriented and sensitised by workshops on:
   - The different learning and disciplinary techniques for students
   - Prevalent student's problems
   - Need for care and affection for students
2. All the teacher's interviewed mentioned that the teachers too need counselling as in the present stressful time they too are stressed due to the extensive syllabus to be covered and due to the pressures from the school management. The school social worker should provide a specific time for counselling to the teachers too.

All respondents agreed that **parents** have to be involved in the social work intervention programme.

1. More than three-fourth (68.7 per cent) of the respondents stated that meetings should be arranged with parents after all the parents-teachers-meeting (PTM). Parents visited school for PTM every term or once in every three months. After the PTM, the parent meeting should be held for two hours in the form of talks and discussion. The issues that were suggested to be taken up are:
   - Positive child rearing patterns.

- Study habits, organising students study, time management.
- Better communication skills to build up healthy parent-child relationship.
- Documentary movie on student's issues followed by discussion.

2. More than 80 per cent (14) of the respondents agreed to parent's counselling. Social worker need to meet the parents and discuss issues and problems of their own or pertaining to their ward. This will improve the parent-child relationship.

The social work intervention at the **reduction level** is more specific and intense. Two-third (10) of the respondents mentioned that the students identified by peer groups, teachers and parents with examination stress would be dealt with. The students suffering from examination stress are enabled to overcome stress by different ways as suggested by respondents are:

1. Supported by other students and peer group members.
2. Individual students are helped by the Caseworker.
3. Students with stress are grouped together for group therapy by the school social worker.
4. The teachers play an important role in identifying students who are poor in academic performance over a period of time, or have been deteriorating in their academic performance or are anxious students.
5. Teachers can help by giving these students extra help in the class.

Half (50 per cent) of the respondents recommended that the **parents** of students suffering from examination stress need help too. This help can be provided by:

- *Parent's counselling*: Parents can be helped to create a conducive environment for the students at home.

- *Family interventions*: Sessions with parents and the students together, this helps in solving many communication and adjustment problems within families.
- *Parents support groups*: Parents of the students in the same class and living in areas close by can form "parents support group". Parents are also under pressure thus parents can help each other to improve their parenting style and better communication skills.

Students must be carefully helped and monitored by peer groups, teachers and parents as per 10 (62.5 per cent) respondents. The help will enable the students to manage their stress and improve their mental well being. Based on the observations made by the experts and the findings of the study a model of social work intervention to deal with the problem of social work intervention is proposed.

Social work intervention model

Findings of the present study show that one in every five students has high examination stress. Students, irrespective of the type of school they study in, be it government school, independent school or Kendriya Vidyalaya, suffer examination stress. Stress because of examinations is especially prevalent among the senior classes of IX to XII. Girls are more stressed than boys due to examinations. The environment at school and at home plays an important role in inducing examination stress. Thus, to reduce stress, it is important to provide a conducive environment by parents and teachers, the important adults who come in close contact with students.

The researcher proposes a social work intervention model based on the findings emerging from the views and experiences from the student respondents and from the professionals working in the area of student welfare. The social work intervention model designed to manage examination stress will be introduced at two phases.

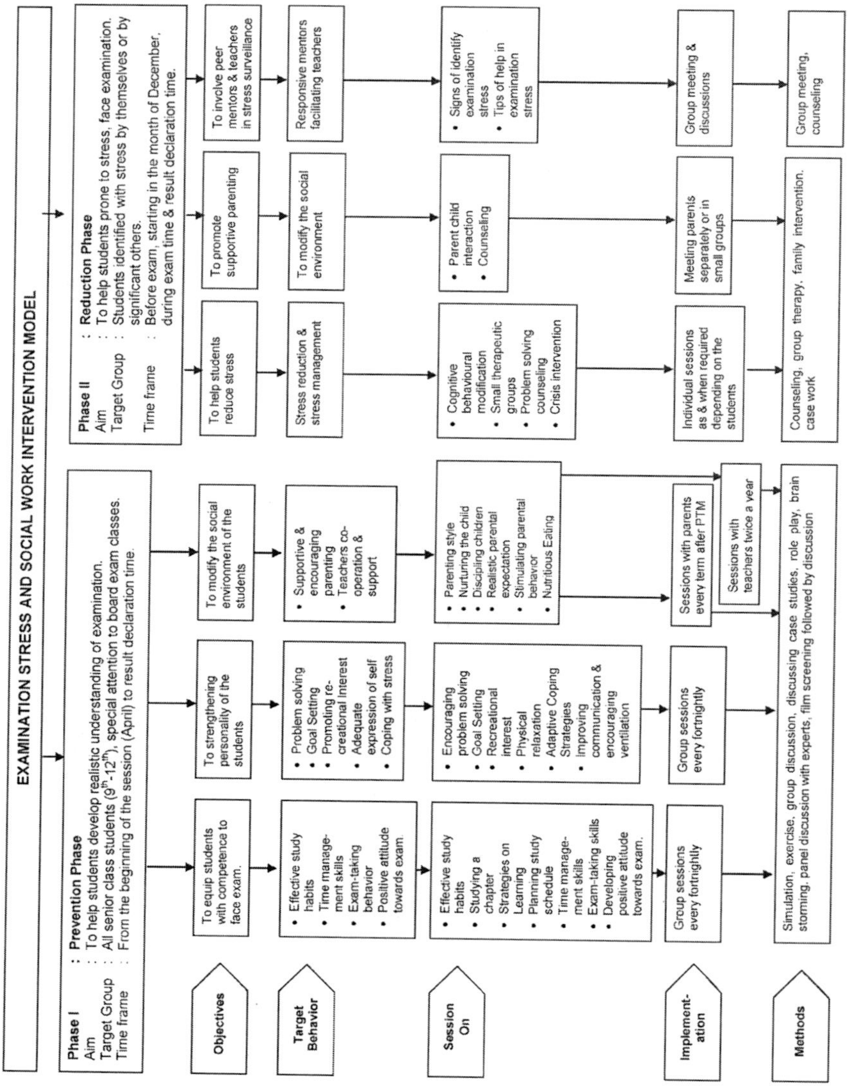
EXAMINATION STRESS AND SOCIAL WORK INTERVENTION MODEL
Phase I : Prevention Phase
Aim : To help students develop realistic understanding of examination.
Target Group : All senior class students (9th-12th), special attention to board exam classes.
Time frame : From the beginning of the session (April) to result declaration time.
Phase II : Reduction Phase
Aim : To help students prone to stress, face examination.
Target Group : Students identified with stress by themselves or by significant others.
Time frame : Before exam, starting in the month of December, during exam time & result declaration time.
Objectives
To equip students with competence to face exam.
To strengthening personality of the students
To modify the social environment of the students
To help students reduce stress
To promote supportive parenting
To involve peer mentors & teachers in stress surveillance
Target Behavior
Effective study habits
Time management skills
Exam-taking behavior
Positive attitude towards exam.
Problem solving
Goal Setting
Promoting re-creational Interest
Adequate expression of self
Coping with stress
Supportive & encouraging parenting
Teachers co-operation & support
Stress reduction & stress management
To modify the social environment
Responsive mentors facilitating teachers
Session On
Effective study habits
Studying a chapter
Strategies on Learning
Planning study schedule
Time management skills
Exam-taking skills
Developing positive attitude towards exam.
Encouraging problem solving
Goal Setting
Recreational interest
Physical relaxation
Adaptive Coping Strategies
Improving communication & encouraging ventilation
Parenting style
Nurturing the child
Discipling children
Realistic parental expectation
Stimulating parental behavior
Nutritious Eating
Cognitive behavioural modification
Small therapeutic groups
Problem solving counseling
Crisis intervention
Parent child interaction
Counseling
Signs of identify examination stress
Tips of help in examination stress
Implementation
Group sessions every fortnightly
Group sessions every fortnightly
Sessions with parents every term after PTM
Sessions with teachers twice a year
Individual sessions as & when required depending on the students
Meeting parents separately or in small groups
Group meeting & discussions
Methods
Simulation, exercise, group discussion, discussing case studies, role play, brain storming, panel discussion with experts, film screening followed by discussion
Counseling, group therapy, family intervention, case work
Group meeting, counseling

I. Prevention phase

The first phase of this model would be called the prevention phase. The **main aim** of this phase of social work intervention is to help students develop realistic understanding of examination so that students are able to adjust to the demanding situation of examination. The first phase is the primary prevention intervention that promotes healthy behaviour, and reduces the risk of psychosocial disorders because of examination stress.

The **target group** for the prevention phase would be all the students in the senior classes from class IX to XII with special emphasis given to the board classes X and XII. The students would attend the sessions in groups that comprise their class itself. So the group would vary in size from 35 to 55 according to the size of their class.

The **time frame** in this intervention phase would be from the beginning of the academic year, that is, April till the end of the session. The students will meet every fortnightly for sessions that will last for two periods.

The **specific objectives** of the prevention phase are

- To equip students with competence to face examination.
- To strengthen the personality of the students.
- To modify the social environment of the students.

The first objective of this phase is **to equip students with competence to face examination** so as to build up the capacities of the students and equip them with the competence required to face their examinations. Students lack confidence, doubt their capacities, and are deficit in skills needed for examination. Thus, it is important that they are prepared for the examination not just with the subject content but also with a positive mental framework. The **target behaviour** expected from students from this objective are:

Effective study habits

Time management skills

Exam-taking behaviour

Positive attitude towards examination

Session 1

Effective study habits: The first target behaviour of the model under this particular phase is improving study habits. The session is aimed at helping the students to introspect at their own study habits and understand healthy, effective and adaptive study habits and practices. Efforts should be made to identify how they study and then to find out deficiencies in their study habits that will help them to achieve the highest scholastic performance. Students will be introduced to scientific methods of studying. Students should be flexible in their study behaviour so that they find study interesting. Studying means to learn the subject matter and prepare for evaluation. The student needs to organise study material, formulate ideas and prepare assignments. Study habits are the combination of ways in which study is done. It includes the pattern of reading, learning and note making.

Session 2

Studying a chapter: A popular study habit for reading is the SQ3R technique (NIMHANS study material cited in Joseph 2002, STRIDE 2002). The SQ3R technique for preparing a chapter for students would include Survey, Question, Read, Recall and Review. *Survey* would mean the students should glance through the chapter, encourage the *questions* that arise when one reads through. *Read* through the text by applying the mind with its critical skills, drawing inferences and reading it again. *Recall* is retention of what is read. Recall is to improve the learning by better concentration, chance to remedy misinterpretation by loss through memory kept active by summarising in students own words. Make notes by writing down key points to remember. *Review* is to remember correctly, viewing again. To go through survey, question, read and recall again.

Session 3

Strategies on learning can be developed by students on how to learn, in the group sessions. Students should be introduced to various strategies of learning and through group activity; students must select a mechanism for themselves.

- Mental Imagery while reading helps to relate new learning to visual images.

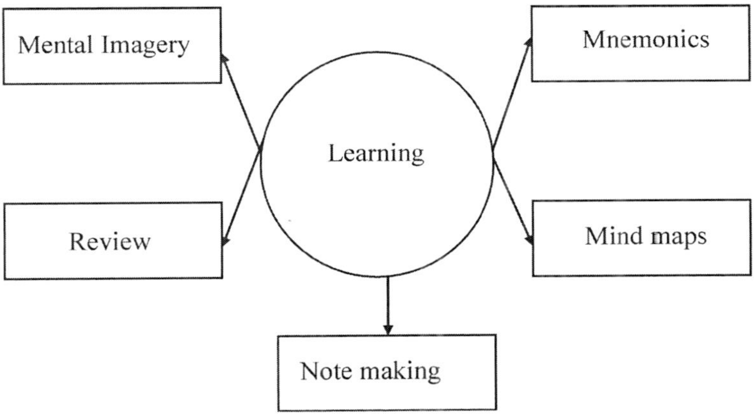

Figure 6.2: Strategies of learning.

- Mnemonics can be used to remember new terms and concepts. Mnemonics are words made up of the first letter of the words of the concepts students are learning.
- Making notes is beneficial. Note making helps to keep active while learning, thus helping concentration. Note making helps in keeping records what was learned.
- Mind maps can be developed by diagram to remember complex concepts.
- Review can help in remembering what is learnt. Review after regular short period, daily, weekly or month is beneficial. This help to transfer learning of short-term memory to long-term memory.

Session 4

Planning study schedule: Study schedule is organising studies, for example, a student has five important subjects in the X class. When he prepares these subjects, the general tendency is to start with the simpler subjects and move on to the difficult. But it is important to organise subjects in a way that the schedule starts with the most difficult subjects first as concentration is highest in the beginning followed by the easier one. The student should not sit for studies at a stretch for long times but give breaks in between studies. It is important to be flexible in studies so as to improve concentration. These sessions will be conducted by the school social worker/counsellor in a group sitting. The students will be simulated to plan out, study habits appropriate of themselves by group discussions and role play.

The second target behaviour is **time management skills.**

Sessions 5

Time management: Time is a precious commodity. Individuals have a variety of activities lined up for the day. Everything is important and cannot be left out. In time management students have to learn to balance their time between studies, play, friends and entertainment. In today's world there are more distractions for the students. Students need to bargain the time schedule according to the importance of the activity. Individual students can manage time by following these steps.

- *Look into their daily time schedule:* An hour to hour record will help students find out, how time can be distributed to the daily activities.
- *Organise their time:* Make a list of tasks according to its priority; tasks can be listed as most important, important and routine. It is important that the list is looked at the end of the day to find out how the day was spent.
- *Set daily timetable with hourly time distribution:* So every hour is given its due importance.
- *Breaks are important:* Students should be able to fix leisure activities to unwind between work times.
- *Organise their place:* Keep things in their respective place to be organised. Clean up their place.
- *Avoid unnecessary activities:* Learn to say no to useless works.
- *Schedule time for emergency:* Distribute daily work schedule.

Overcoming procrastination by managing time and getting the work done. Procrastination is putting off important tasks over and over again. Most individual procrastinate but for some this affects achievements and disrupts their careers. If students are systematic, organised and punctual in their work they will surely do well in their tasks. Students can plan for longer time frame; say six months or a year too.

Time management skills help to set up practical goals, be organised and systematic, take short breaks to relax and rejuvenate and avoid unnecessary activities. The session on time management would be conducted in-group setting through simple planning exercise, so that students at the end of the session have prepared a daily timetable for themselves.

The third target behaviour is **examination taking behaviour.** The session would be held to improve examination-taking skills so that students understand questions and answer writing skills. Students need to prepare for examinations, by studying and learning we understand the subject but now the students need to prepare for answering questions on the subject, then they need to prepare for writing the answer to the questions. Examination patterns need to be understood, time management is important. Thus, the students need to spend time on these essentials, which are not considered important but are important for a good performance in the examination.

Session 6

Examination-taking skills: Some students do very well in class but when it comes to examination they don't perform well. This is one of the reasons for examination stress. Students need to develop examination-taking skills. Examination-taking skills can be divided into preparation for examination and examination techniques. Examination preparation is a slow, consistent and a conscious effort made by students. Students need to develop individual timetables for revision covering all subjects and topic. Giving importance to revision, discussion with others, to look up previous question papers to understand the trend and type of questions, plan out answers and to prepare a sketch answer keeping in mind the marks allotment and time management for each question.

Points to be kept in mind on the day of examination

- Don't discuss answers with friends just before examination.

- Read the question paper properly before attempting the answer.
- Plan your answers.
- Attempt examination paper with simple language and legible handwriting.
- Check through the answers before submitting answer scripts.

The session would be conducted by a talk with an expert from the field of education/social work/psychiatry/psychology. The talk would be followed by question and answer session. Students would be encouraged to ask questions, from the expert for their own personal problems.

The fourth target behaviour is **positive attitude towards examination**. Students have constant fear of examinations. Examination is considered as a punishment for the students. The image of examination painted to the students by parents, teachers and school are always very negative. Thus, the students too never feels good about examinations, as one of the student expressed in the course of data collection, "I feel that examination is not to examine what the students knows but to evaluate, what the student does not know".

Session 7

Developing positive attitude towards examination: Students need to understand the purpose of examination. Students need to understand that examinations are held to find out how much the students have learned. Examination evaluates the students in the learning process. Examination thus is a tool to judge and promote students to the next level.

This session would be put forth, by screening a film highlighting the purpose of examination to develop a positive attitude towards examination. Examples can be shared of famous people, like Albert Einstein, Bill Gates, Tom Cruise, Henry Ford, A R Rahman, Sachin Tendulkar who have achieved great success in their lives, have left a mark in the world by their excellence in the field despite the fact they didn't perform well in school.

The second objective of the prevention phase is **to strengthen the personality of the students.** Students' personality also contributes to the adverse affects of examination stress. So it is important to build up on the students' personality so that they are equipped to face the stress and strains of life.

The **target behaviours** at this phase are

1. Problem solving skills
2. Goal setting
3. Promoting recreational interests
4. Adequate expression of self
5. Coping with stress

To achieve these expected target behaviour, session will be held with students to instill confidence and balanced personality trends.

Session 1

Encouraging problem-solving skills: Understanding complex, complicated situations and managing them require good problem-solving skills. Problems may seem very difficult, large and overwhelming. Problems make us move back, stop us from progressing. If students just give up, they lose the chance to move ahead in life. Thus, it is important for students to have a problem-solving nature.

Students will be encouraged to adopt techniques that help analyse the problem, brings student face to face with the problem. Steps to be followed in problem-solving are:

- *Identify the problem.* Write down on a piece of paper the problem faced. This can be elaborated by putting in details like who is involved, when and where does the problem occur.
- Put down the contributory factors to the problem on the paper using lines.
- *Analyse the whole picture.* See the problem its contributory factors, and look for all possible solutions. Solution is the ability to look for strategies to face the problem, adapt and change the situation.

- Weigh the pros and cons of each solution and select the most suitable one.

In this session the methods to be used are simulation, group discussion and role play. Students in smaller groups can take up discussions on problems that they face and work out a solution systematically.

Session 2

Goal setting: The steps student plans to take to achieve the goals strengthen the student's personality. This session will be to help students set realistic goals and work for accomplishing those goals. The process of setting goals by students helps them choose where they want to go in life. By knowing where to go, students can concentrate efforts to reach the goals. Realistic and reasonable goals can be motivating and the habits of setting and achieving goals, builds up self-confidence of the students. Students in this session are helped to set goals, follow the SMART method of setting goals. A useful way of setting goals is to use the SMART Mnemonic. Goals should be

S Specific

M Measurable

A Attainable

R Relevant

T Time-bound

This makes the goal meaningful, appropriate and students will be motivated to achieve them.

In this session, students are motivated to look ahead, plan their life, and move ahead. This session will be activity-based interaction within the group. Students are encouraged to set up their own goals. For many students this session will make them think of what are their opportunity and how they could plan to reach the goals set by them.

Session 3

Recreational interest: Recreation is very important for students; as it gives opportunity for self-expression, an enjoyment, and an entertainment for them. It was reported that students are deprived of recreational activities in school and at home, in the senior classes especially the board classes. The school converts the students' sports, dramatic and extra-curricular periods to study classes. The students are not given the time to relax and to recreate. Even at home parents cut off their hobbies, friends, playtime and television time.

In this **session** students are allowed to externalise their interests. Through the method of play, students relax, laugh and enjoy. Play activities are organised.

The fourth target behaviour for students is **coping strategies**. Sessions with students will be held to help students cope with stress.

Session 4

Physical relaxation techniques are introduced to students. These are effective in reducing stress. Simple physical relaxation technique of deep breathing and progressive muscular relaxation will help students reduce stress. **Deep breathing** is a simple, effective method of relaxation. Take a number of deep breaths and relax your body, with each breath feel the body unwind and relax more and more. Continue this for two-five minutes and observe the body relax. **Progressive muscular relaxation** is useful for relaxing the body when the muscles are tense. In the progressive muscular relaxation a group of muscles are tensed up tightly, contracted, held in this state of extreme tension for a few seconds. Then, the muscles are relaxed to the normal position; again consciously relax the same muscles even further. Follow this with the different limbs, neck, shoulder and abdomen. Slowly the individual's body is relaxed.

Session 5

Coping strategies can be of two kinds, task-oriented and emotion-oriented. Task-oriented are those in which the problem in the environment or the situation causing the stress is planned for change. The Emotion-Oriented strategies are those in which it is difficult to change the situation/environment so stress is managed by changing the interpretation of the situation and how students feel about it.

The students are helped in examination stress by task-oriented coping strategies as organising study, improving examination-taking skills, as these will help them cope to the difficult situations. Emotion-oriented coping strategies will help students manage the stress during examination time with these efforts. Now students have to relax and perform in examination without fearing about the result. Coping with stress is to acknowledge stress in our lives, and to consciously control the stress by adopting coping strategies.

This **session** would be conducted by panel discussion with experts giving tips on relaxing, followed by question and answer session. So students are helped with individual problems.

Session 6

Improving communication and **encouraging ventilation:** Students need to express their opinions, desires, needs and fears verbally and non-verbally. This could also include clarifying their doubts and asking for advice and help. It is important that students have communicable relationship with friend, parents and teachers. Free flow of information, opinions and views is necessary for the development of a healthy personality.

The target behaviour of student is the adequate expression of self. Session will be held to help students improve their communication skills. Student should be encouraged to talk out their feelings, views and experiences. This **ventilation** in the presence of an empathic listener is therapeutic. The listener could be the school social worker/counsellor/ teacher or peer. There is a need for an attentive listener with concern and care. Ventilation can be very beneficial to reduce examination stress like an old saying "a problem shared is a problem halved". This ventilation session can be conducted by group simulation, group discussion and sharing. The students can improve communication and ventilate pent up feeling among their classmates.

The third objective of the Prevention Phase is **to modify the social environment**. Students have attributed examination stress to their parents' behaviour, expectation and the family environment. Teachers also contribute to examination stress by their behaviour and expectation. To prevent student from examination stress it is important to modify the surrounding of the students. Parents play an important role in the life of students. Parenting is a challenging task. To be an effective parent, parenting should be based on security and attachment, which incorporates attitudes, emphasising on playfulness, acceptance, curiosity and empathy. There should never be room for coercion, threat, intimidation and the use of power to force submission.

Supportive and encouraging parenting: Parents target behaviour towards students must be supportive and encouraging for this the parents must be involved into the social work intervention model. Most parents are interested in the betterment of their child. To make parents effective, sessions need to be held with parents. Session should cover issues of parenting style and its effect on the children, discipline children, nurturing children with help and support.

Session 1

Parenting style: Session on parenting styles would be very beneficial for the parents. There are generally four styles of parenting: authoritarian, permissive, neglectful and authoritative. Most parents do not fall solely into one of the category but are in the middle, have some features of the different style. Some parents also change styles with changes in age, experience, and maturity level of the child.

The authoritarian parenting style practice features like parents value obedience and expect the children will be obedient too. Parents want to follow tradition and order in the family. Parents don't hesitate to use physical punishment to control children and they don't allow choices or freedom of expression from their children. The possible outcomes of this parenting style are children become followers due to the parents' pressure on them. The children lean on others to make their decision, develop low self-esteem and sometimes-even children become aggressive or defiant.

The permissive parenting style follows patterns in which parents' sets only few rules and regulations provide no structure to the children, so the parents do not enforce limits on the children. This results in children having low self-control and lack ability to manage stress, as they are adapted to a very relaxed home environment. Children remain immature and have difficulty accepting responsibility.

The neglectful parenting style is featured by parents rejects or ignores the child; the parents are not involved in the child's life and remain aloof. The parents allow the child to do, as they like. The outcome of this neglectful behaviour is that children face many challenges in their relationship with others; they always feel unwanted in life and keep looking for assurance from others. Children develop difficulty with skill development, doubting others and their own self-esteem.

The authoritative parenting style is characterised by parents setting appropriate rules and regulation for the children and the family also. The parents' are firm, consistent and fair in their dealing with children and to the others around them so the child see consistency in the parents' behaviour and understands what is wrong, what does not have to be done. Parents without aggression, physical punishment convey what they want out of the children. Parents have realistic expectation from their children. They acknowledge the child's independence; parents are communicative and reason out things with the child so the child is allowed choice in decision-making. This results in parents' empowering the child. The result of this parenting style is seen in the children's personality, they are responsible independent, and have self-esteem. The children are able to control aggressive outbreaks. This form of parenting style provides a balance between setting appropriate limits and granting independence to the child, the child is brought up in a warm, supportive and guided environment.

This session would help parents to improve their parenting. Teaching the parents how to behave and making them realise the result of their parenting would be very beneficial. A panel of experts from the field would conduct the session. Parents would be given detailed information on the topic followed by a question-answer sessions so that parents get a chance to discuss the problems they face and how to handle their day to day problems with children.

Session 2

Nurturing the Child: A nurturing parent is a loving, understanding and supportive parent. Children learn more from them than a harsh parent. Children of a nurturing parent are less prone to delinquency than children of rejecting parents. Nurturing parents are helpful, they convey to the children that:

- Children are valued
- Children can be believed
- Children can be trusted
- Children can handle life situation
- Children are listened to
- Children are cared for
- Children are very important to parents
- Children can tell everything to parents
- Parents are learning with children

The session of nurturing will be conducted with parents through group sharing and discussion. This session helps the parents deal with many of the blocks faced by parents like generation gap. Efforts to improve communication between parents and children would be encouraged.

Session 3

Disciplining children: Disciplining is crucial as it promotes children's self-control, teaches them responsibility, and helps them to make conscious choices. Helping children achieve self-discipline is very important. It lays the foundation for children's life-long personal and social development. Family experts say using physical force or threats can interfere with child's healthy development. Effective guidance and discipline focus on the development of the child, preserving the child's self-esteem and dignity. Actions that recognise the child's efforts and progress encourage healthy development. Some positive steps to prevent misbehaviour:

- Set clear consistent rules
- Show interest in child's activities
- Provide engaging playthings
- Provide simulating environment

- Encourage self-control by meaningful choices
- Focus on desired behaviour, rather than the one to be avoided
- Expect the best from the child
- Say 'yes' whenever possible
- Take action before situation is out of control
- Encourage children
- Give clear directions, one at a time
- Encourage physical activities or hobbies even in examination time

This session with parents would be held by discussing case studies and group discussion on methods of enabling children.

Session 4

Realistic parental expectation: The target behaviour of the parents must be realistic parental expectations from their children. It is quite natural for parents to expect the best for their children but it is difficult for the children to live up to their parental expectations if the demands are too high. Parents must have expectation from their children that are equal to their capacities. Parents must not aim very high. There should be a two-ways communication between parents and children on the expectations from both sides to strike balance.

Session should be organised with parents on delinking parental expectation and aspirations with the results. Parents must not be too demanding of their children. Parents must delink the expectation with the results. Goals should be set children should be encouraged, supported to meet these goal but too much of emphasis on academic result will pressurise the child and cause examination stress. If the parents' expectations are too high, unreachable the child would just abandon it. If the expectations are attainable the child will work hard for meeting them. So to avoid the ill-effects of examination stress, parents must be realistic in their parental expectations.

Session 5

Stimulating parental behaviour: The target behaviour of the parents must be stimulating for the child. Parents play a very important role in the achievements of the children. Parental behaviour must be stimulating to encourage the child to the right home environment so that the child can play, concentrate, work hard, keep distraction away at the same time, enjoy, relax, recreate, share his views. Parents are eager to help but need the right direction.

The democratic parenting style will help parents to understand that children need their freedom but its also important to be firm with them too, parents must be besides the children helping them out in making their own right choices. A balance between over-protectiveness and laissez-faire style of parenting needs to be maintained. It's important to create a conducive study environment for the child. The students' roles and responsibility must be shared by other family members, so that the student feels the importance of their studies.

Children can study better in an environment that is free from distractions avoid studying near a window, or in a room with television on. Children must have a place for themselves, a corner of a room where they can study, put his study materials. So that students can organise themselves. The room where the child studies must have good lighting, proper ventilation allowing fresh air, proper adequate furniture, clear desk, comfortable chair and shelves for storage.

Session on transferring roles and responsibilities to other family members and making the required changes to accommodate the child's examinations will encourage the child. Small steps taken by parents can motivate the child.

(a) *Recognise effort:* Give recognition to the child's efforts and small improvement. Be observant and praise the child.

(b) *Acknowledge strengths before weaknesses:* When praising the child's work start acknowledging his strengths before commenting on his weaknesses.

(c) *Provide practical support:* Don't ridicule or criticise the child when grades fall short of expectation. Be calm and empathise with the child finding out ways to improve.

(d) Give praises and rewards to recognise the child's efforts.

Parents can also help the child in organising their study. Work out a time table for the child, schedule study, emphasising on revision and play into his daily activities, as regular physical exercise is necessary for the child even in the examination time. Physical exercise for the student, relieve tension and helps to relax.

Sessions on stimulating parental behaviour can be conducted by filming a movie on parental behaviour followed by group sharing and discussions where parents' queries are handled. Parent have their doubts and problem, that can be helped out by discussion and listening to the parents and giving them tips on managing their behaviour and conduct with children.

Session 6

Nutritious diet during exam time

Exam time means long studying hours and high anxieties so it is very important that children have the right food. Children have a tendency at this time to crave for just the wrong food that is junk food, fried food, refined food, sweet food, aerated drinks, tea and coffee. The long study times disturbs the regular eating patterns thus parents must be careful with regular five to six small meals keeps blood sugar and energy level steady rather than heavy meals that would leave the child sleepy and lethargic.

- The diet of the children should include a heavy breakfast, rich in protein like skimmed milk, oats, upma, idli, egg roti roll, poha, dhokla.
- Keep healthy snacks at home like roasted chanas, nuts, raisons, low-fat yogurts.
- Serve fruits and fresh salads interestingly.
- A balanced meal would comprise roti/rice, dal, vegetable, paneer/curd.
- Water is very important to keep the body hydrated, three to four liters, keep a bottle of water near the child.
- Fresh fruit juices/*chaas* or buttermilk/*nimbu pani* or lime juice/green tea are healthy.
- Almonds, walnut, pumpkin seeds, cucumber and watermelon helps improve memory and concentration.

- Children require anti-oxidants like vitamins A, C and E to reduce damage to brain cells due to stress. Foods to increase brain efficiency are eggs, fish, carrot, pumpkin, green leafy vegetables and fresh fruits. These also increase immunity of the body and keeps away illness.
- Some stress reducing foods are brown rice, nuts, eggs, fresh vegetables and fruits. They fulfill body's need for water-soluble vitamins- Vitamin B complex and C, minerals like Zinc. These help in synthesising and functioning of adrenal hormones that help fight stress.
- Some memory enhancing foods that are rich in Omega 3 fatty acid are mainly in fish like salmon or mackerel. Other sources are flax seed, pumpkin seeds, sesame seeds, soyabean oil or canola oil.

Teachers cooperation and support

Teachers are one of the significant others' that leave deep impressions on the child's mind. Teachers are in constant contact with the children and any signs of examination stress can be observed first by the teachers. Teachers are key persons who can also predict before anyone else that a particular student is showing signs of pressure and is suffering from or is liable to suffer from examination stress.

In an experimental study conducted by Joseph (2002) the researcher observed the positive impact of child mental health orientation programme on school teachers. It was found that the capacities of the school teachers could be improved by an orientation programme that helps the teachers to understand child mental health needs and issues. NIMHANS, Bangalore have also been involved since 1975 in preparing and implementing programmes in the field of school mental health and their experience shows that school teachers can be effectively sensitised in identifying emotional problems of children. Teachers can be trained in counselling skills to improve the children's competence.

Sessions with teachers on children's needs, behavioural problems in children will help teachers identify students with problems, especially examination stress. Sessions on positive disciplining of students will help the teachers handle students in the classroom setting. Sessions will also be held with teachers on stress management, so that there is an environment of mental well-being in the school.

Session with teachers twice a year by experts followed by discussion on case studies can help teachers to be sensitised to students' problem. Sessions with parents can be planned out every term on the parents-teacher-meeting (PTM) day. Parents can be brought together in the school hall or in one of the classes to hold these sessions. Parents must be involved in these sessions from the planning stage itself. Regular correspondence, taking their views will keep the parents involved and create a friendly environment in the school.

II. Stress reduction phase

The phase II of the social work intervention model is examination stress reduction phase. At phase II the social work intervention **aims** to help students who are affected by examination stress. This is specifically for students who need special attention more than the other students. The **target groups** are students identified with stress symptoms, by themselves or by the significant others. The significant others could be parents, peer or teachers. Those who are physically close to the students and who observe behavioural problems in the students. The **time frame** for the Phase II will be before the examination starts in the month of December, few months before the final examination.

These students have already been a part of the prevention phase but the students have not been able to control the stress before examination. The students need more help. The **specific objectives** of this reduction phase are:

- To help students reduce stress
- To promote supportive parenting
- To involve peer mentors and teachers in stress surveillance

The first objective is to help student reduce their stress. The school social worker/counsellor plans out stress management and reduction sessions. These sessions will reduce stress by management in an eclectic approach combining mainly behavioural, cognitive-behavioural and supportive components.

The behavioural approaches focus on change in observable behaviour or behaviour modification. These approaches are based on the concept that psychological problems occur due to learning or conditioning and can be undone by the same processes. The school social work/counsellors can help the students. Anxiety can be managed by methods of deep breathing, progressive muscle relaxation, and meditation. These help in relaxing the students. Deep breathing is an effective exercise that relaxes the individual. Followed by simple steps of taking in breath (inhaling), holding the breath inside the lungs and then exhaling. These steps of inhale, holding the breath and exhale is repeatedly done very slowly for five to ten minutes. Progressive muscle relaxation is tightening the muscles, holding it in this tightened position and then relaxing the muscle, one by one of the various parts of body, especially hands and legs. Meditation is another technique to relax the mind. In this the individual sits in a quite place, eyes closed and concentrates at a point for 20 minutes. The mind drift away from the point to various thought and the attempt is to keep on seeing or thinking of that point. Initially a difficult task slowly the mind learns to meditate. Students can also be helped by systematic desensitisation. Students that experience distress in examination times feel various emotional and physical problems. Classical conditioning can be used to relax the body in systematic desensitisation as the students are encouraged to face the exams with support. Repeated examination situation makes the students more confident in going through the process of examination.

The cognitive approaches are important in reducing examination stress as it is the students' negative perceptions towards examination and examination results that needs to be treated. These therapeutic approaches are also called cognitive restructuring. Rational-Emotive therapy of Albert Ellis is one of the earliest cognitive-restructuring approaches. This assumes that individuals have rational and irrational tendencies. The irrational thoughts prevent from reaching the goals results in inner conflict and mental tension. This causes emotional difficulties in students, this irrational thoughts cause examination stress and fear of failure. Person centred counselling helps students build up a more realistic thinking. Meichenbaum's self-instructional training is another method of the cognitive approach. Meichenbaum uses self-instructional training to help students replace their maladaptive cognitions with rational, positive thinking in an examination situation.

The Cognitive Behavioural Approach is most suited to treat examination stress as it's a combination of restructuring the cognition of the students and help in stress reduction trainings.

The target behaviour for this objective will be stress reduction by stress management and coping to the stress by adaptive coping. The sessions for this objective will be in small therapeutic groups and through individual problem-solving counselling. These groups work and case work sessions will be organised twice in a week and if need be more sessions would be conducted.

Small Therapeutic Group: The students facing examination stress problems are collected in small groups to help them out in adaptive coping strategies. The aim is to support these students to work out their own adaptive coping strategies. Group session will help them work out solutions for themselves. Here students form support groups helping out each other. Ventilating their problems to each other so that they know that there are other students too, who feel their way. There are common emotions of fear, low self-esteem in the group, which the students feel they were suffering alone so the interactions with other students would be advantageous. The group sessions will help the students support each other.

Problem-solving Counselling: Problem-solving counselling is a structured and systematic method of interaction with client to recognise the problems or the stressors in their lives and then adopt steps to tackle these problems. Problem-solving counselling is a double-headed approach that is it tackles the emotional and the practical aspects of the problem. The emotional problem is tackled first and then the client is in a better frame of mind to solve his problems for example, a students is upset and tensed (emotional problem), for the internal assessment (practical problem). The student is first helped with his lack of confidence, and low self-image (emotional problem). Then helped with the practical problem by enabling him in seeking clarification from the subject teacher in understanding what is to be done in the assignment.

Crisis intervention requires specialised skills and experience dealing with crisis. The ability to assess and intervene during emergencies is a challenging skill. Incorrect assessment, missed opportunities, unskillful behaviour and mistakes can prolong a crisis, create new problems or turn an urgent problem into a dangerous emergency. Some skills required by the school social work/counsellor are that they can be reached seven days a week and twenty-four hours a day if necessary. They are sensitive, good listeners and are prepared to give time to the students. In most circumstances, the difficulties that students face can be addressed through the usual process. However, there are circumstances when crisis situation occur in which immediate or same day intervention by counsellor is called for. Counsellors can help by providing an objective frame of reference within which the crisis can be considered, there can be a discussion of possible alternative, to promote healthy functioning and to obtain commitment from the students.

The second objective of the Stress Reduction Phase is to promote supportive parenting for students experiencing examination stress. Students were observed pressurised due to the examination situation and the results of this study also states that parent help and support was very beneficial to students. Parents have already been addressed in sessions after the PTM in the Phase I to prevent the examination stress to occur. But as examination stress has been observed among the students. Parents of those student's who face the problem, will be again met and involved in the treatment process, so that the stress condition can be controlled and reduced.

Parent-child-interaction: The parents of students will be meet in small group to discuss the parent-child relationship. Parent child interaction of students in senior classes is a fragile relationship. There is a binding between the parent-child and a lot of differences of opinion too. Most parent-child relationship has their ups and downs.

This relationship is important to us as this sometimes affect the children's personality. The sessions will be held on parent-child relationship.

Parents interact with their children in the way they think is right. They encounter avoidance, defensiveness, resistance and even hostility from their wards. Parents become confused they sometimes give up, they get frustrated in their interaction with their child, sometimes parent-child dialogue take the form of power struggles and conflict also. Parents may also begin to disagree to each other, when parents argue about what to do; children think that parents don't know what they are doing. Parents lose credibility in front of their own children.

Parents will be met in **counselling session** to understand the students problems and for family therapy so that the parent-child relationship is strengthened. Family therapy will facilitate the social worker/counsellor to identify family patterns that contribute to behavioural disorder or mental illness. This therapy helps members to break those habits that cause the problem. Family therapy involves discussion and problem-solving sessions with the family as a whole or one to one with members having the problem. Family therapy sessions will help in strengthening communication patterns within the family. Thus, address the causes of examination stress from home and parents that affect the students.

Peer mentors and teachers in examination stress surveillance: The third objective of Phase II of the social work intervention model is to involve peer mentors and teachers in examination stress surveillance. Peers are another important groups of the significant others who are directly in touch with the students.

Socialisation with friends or peer relations plays a powerful role in the lives of adolescents. In adolescent years, some of the most enjoyable moments probably are spent with peers, on the telephone, in school activities, in the neighbourhood, at dances parties, or just being together. Peer relationship is vital for adolescents. In childhood the focus of peer relation is on being accepted and liked by the friends. Being left out or not being noticed or rejected can have a damaging effect on the student's development and can be carried on to adolescence. Teenagers prefer to have smaller groups of peer relations, which are more intense and intimate (Santrock, 2004). Gottman and Parker (1987) listed six functions of friendship/peer group companionship, stimulation, physical support, ego support, social comparison and intimacy/affection. Acknowledging the importance of peer group, the model has a special role for the peer mentor.

Students who are sensitive towards children's issues and who show interest, those students will be trained as peer mentors from each class and will form a core group. The sessions that will be taken up with the volunteered peer mentors will introduce them to the phenomena of examination stress

- Signs to identify examination stress among students.
- Tips to help in time management, effective study habits, organising study and examination taking.

Peer mentor refer students to teachers/school social worker/ counsellor, when they identify students need help. The peer mentor core group will disseminate the session information to other students and thus all the senior class students are covered. Peer mentor will be on surveillance for their class, looking out for students who are having problem in studies and are tensed and worried about their performance. The responsive peer mentor, thus form a link between service providers and students who need help. The peer mentors will be in constant touch with the school social worker/counsellor. If they identify students deteriorating in studies or with strange behaviour, like high absenteeism, loneliness, these students will be brought to the notice of the school social worker/counsellor.

Teachers are in constant interaction with the students, so they will also be involved in the surveillance team. Teachers too will be sensitised to identify and help students getting stressed with examination or study pressures. Teachers will deal with the students in class and if need be, teachers will bring these students to the notice of the school social worker/counsellor if they find students unable to manage the examination stress.

Feedback session should be held at all phases with all the different groups of students and significant others. These feedback sessions should be arranged with the school social worker and general students, parents, peer mentors, teacher and with students suffering from increased examination stress. The feedback sessions would be supportive and would act as a safety net covering all the students. So that there is always help close by and there are no cases of student neglect because of increased examination stress.

This model is an attempt to prevent examination stress among all the senior school students and to reduce the examination stress that has been diagnosed among students in all type of schools. It would be favourable to introduce this model in schools to facilitate students to cope examination stress. So that all students are provided help to enhance their performance during examinations and students get assistance if they succumb to the increased examination stress. The details of the model would help school social worker/counsellors to implement this model at individual schools. In India, there are many schools that do not have professional social worker/counsellors; this model would form a basis to understand what needs to be done to help students. These schools can invite qualified persons who can take sessions to help students according to the components of this model.

Chapter VII

Summary of Findings and Suggestions

Down the ages it has been observed that human beings have suffered various dreadful diseases. There have been plagues, polio and pneumonia and many other devastating diseases that have caused many deaths in the history of mankind. These diseases were controlled by improved environmental conditions and development in medication. In the present times stress is the main cause for various psychosomatic diseases like heart diseases, diabetes, gastrointestinal, ulcers, cancer and respiratory diseases. Stress is an incomparable phenomenon, as it has no biological carrier like germs, bacteria and virus. The working of the body and the mind causes stress. Stress can be explained as a demand to adjust and cope to life changes. Momentary feelings of stress are part of every person's life. Stress is the reactions to the physical environment or social situations, which when manageable is not harmful but when the stress is uncontrollable, for longer periods of time would result in adverse mental and physical health in individuals.

Stress is a complex problem and has increased with modernisation. It becomes important for us to learn to deal with stress as it will be with us in the future too. Everyone is talking about stress; stress seems to have invaded every section of our populations. Stress-management techniques and workshops to control it, have gained importance in our present times. School students are also affected by stress. School is considered another home for students. After family school is the most important socialising agent for a child. School plays an important role in making of an intellectual, mature and independent individual. School education is concerned with developing the body and mind, acquiring skills needed to mature into a self-reliant person with the right ideas, morals, balanced character and a behaviour which gives importance to discipline and sense of duty. But schools can also be a place of stress for the students. The school environment with its discipline, syllabus, school homework, and in some cases teachers are known to cause stress for the students. There is pressure on the students by the educational system.

Students, if exposed to optimal stress, are able to procure good results, but after certain point if the stress keeps on increasing, this stress becomes 'distress'. This brings in stress-related disorders and decreased performance. If the stress continues behavioural, physical, emotional, cognitive problems may occur. Students are just like adults and are affected by stress but they are unable to comprehend stress and so are unable to control or deal with it. So they are more susceptible to the adversities of stress as what is most needed to gain control over stress is to control one's own life.

One of the most frightening events that cause stress in students is school examination. When students develop extreme apprehension of performing poorly in an examination, they experience examination related stresses. Researches have shown that examination stress is a major factor contributing to a variety of negative outcomes like psychological distress, academic under achievement and academic failure. Many students have the mental capability to do well in examinations but are unable to do so because of extreme stress. Society also exerts pressure on students expecting students to do extremely well.

Examination stress can be explained as the discomfort, hesitation or edginess and intense fear of performing badly in the examination, and has now become a widespread form of stress among school students. Students who face examination stress feel that everything is related to their performance in examination. The examination results are linked with their value of themselves and feeling wanted by their friends and family. The examination stress is manifested in students in various ways. These manifestations can be broadly classified into four categories-physical, cognitive, emotional and behavioural. Examination stress causes dejection, absentmindedness, mood swing and many other behavioural and emotional disturbances. The student in stress is always tired and is less efficient in their work. Examination stress affects the personality and performance of the students. Stress among children as a phenomenon is on the rise and can be observed by the rise in the psychological and physiological manifestations reported by students now-a-days especially before examinations.

The reasons for the rise in examination stress can be attributed to change in the educational system that highlights perfectionism in performance. Students are expected to be the best; there is constant pressure on them to get cent per cent. Every individual is different with different abilities and capacities and all cannot be at par. The race for excellent marks has its adverse effects. The importance is not on developing competency, but on the marks obtained in the examination. This brings in unhealthy competitive in the school system and causes examination stress. Parents have higher aspirations and expectations from their children. They want their children to do exceptionally well excelling in academics this increases the pressure on the children. The scenario after schooling is very difficult for the students. The seats available in professional and non-professional courses at the college level are limited. The admissions to these professional courses are difficult as competition is very tough. This again causes stress for the students. Research studies show an increase in students reporting of severe stress feeling that they are unable to handle when examinations are nearing. Media, reports of suicide among students especially around the examination time is also on the rise. Government and non-government organisations are involved with telephone counselling services to help students cope up with the examination stress. Counsellors have reported a drastic increase in the number of stressed students due to examinations. The present research is an attempt to understand the phenomenon of examination stress, which is on the rise and has serious ramifications. This study was planned to help, in the understanding of mental health needs of students and the nature and direction of social work needed to deal with examination stress. The study will be beneficial for students, parents, teachers, and school authorities as well as professionals like social workers, counsellors, psychologists, psychiatrists, school nurses and others interested in students' mental well being.

There are a number of studies that have examined examination stress cutting across national boundaries. The researcher has reviewed the available published and unpublished research studies in the form of books, articles and other reports available on the subject. These studies have been thematically reviewed under five subheadings viz., (a) extent of examination stress among students, (b) factors contributing of examination stress, (c) manifestations of examination stress, (d) strategies of coping with examination stress and (e) evidence-based interventions.

The study aims at measuring the extent of examination stress and its behavioural manifestations among students of senior classes.

The specific objectives of the study are:

- To measure the extent of examination stress experienced by students as they approach examination.
- To understand the role-played by study habits, parental expectations, family environment and aspirations of the individual students in inducing examination stress.
- To study behavioural manifestations of examination stress seen among students.
- To explore the coping strategies used by students in dealing with stress generated by examinations.
- To suggest a model of social work intervention to deal with examination stress of students.

The present study is an inquiry into the phenomenon of examination stress and its manifestations. The study also intends to describe the role played by study habits, parental expectations, family environment and aspirations of the individual students in inducing examination stress. A descriptive research design has been used for this scientific investigation. The descriptive design used in the study allows inter group comparisons, and facilitates understanding of the factors that are responsible for its causation.

The universe of the study comprises all students in senior classes (IXth to XIIth) in the National Capital Territory of Delhi. As per the Central Board of Secondary Education there are 1216 schools with secondary level education in the locale of the study. To identify the units to be studied a multistage stratified random sampling method was used. The sampling process followed was that at the first stage of the sampling, eleven schools in the universe were selected from the 1216 senior secondary schools in Delhi. For which a comprehensive list of all the schools of the National Capital Territory of Delhi was procured from Central Board of Secondary Education (CBSE). Stratification of the universe was done at the first stage of the sample based on the types of schools. One per cent of schools were selected from all the three strata using random numbers. Thus, one Kendriya Vidyalaya, six government schools, and four independent schools were selected. At the second stage of sampling from the different sections in the schools one section was randomly selected from classes IXth and Xth. For XIth and XIIth classes, one section from each of the streams offered was chosen (science, humanities, and commerce). All the three streams were included to have a better representation of all properties of the universe. At the third stage of sampling twenty per cent of students were selected on random basis from each of the selected sections in the selected schools. The total sample of students selected was 640.

The data collected from the professionals for designing a social work intervention were procured from experienced professionals, who have been working on the issue of examination stress based on purposive method of sampling. Four different areas of professionals were identified who are directly involved with students that are school social workers/counsellors, professionals and NGO representatives in the field of student welfare, social work educators and teachers/ principals. From these four different areas of professionals in the NCT of Delhi, four professionals from each category were selected. Thus, the total number of professional selected was 16.

The primary data for the study were collected from two sources, the school students and professionals working in the field of student welfare. The data was collected from the students by a questionnaire that had multiple-choice questions including the Test Anxiety Inventory (TAI) developed by Charles D. Spielberger (1980) and colleagues. In addition the researcher developed Likert type three scales for studying study habits, behavioural manifestations and coping strategies. The data from the professionals were collected with help of an interview guide.

The major findings of the study are elaborated below:

The Test Anxiety Inventory (TAI) was administered in this research to study the extent of examination stress among the respondents. It was observed that one in every five student was reported with high test anxiety. More than half of the student respondents were observed with medium test anxiety. Thus, over three-fourth of the students need help as they show signs of examination stress and would also be affected by the adversities that are resultants of examination stress.

In the present study 50.5 per cent of the respondents were female students and male students comprised 49.5 per cent of the total sample. Female students reported higher test anxiety compared to their male counterpart. The preference given to male children in the Indian families is reflected in the present study too, as female students show higher test anxiety could be because of the greater pressures on the girl child to perform well in school or to discontinue her studies.

The sample of the student respondents ranged from 13 years to 20 years, selected from IX class to XII class. Out of which 48.6 per cent were from the non-board (IX and XI) classes and 51.4 per cent of the students were from the board classes (X and XII). The respondents in the board classes X and XII were observed with higher test anxiety as compared to the non-board classes IX and XI. Students in the board classes are under more pressures due to the importance given to board examination by parents, peer, teachers, and schools and the society at large.

The sample of the student respondents were selected from the different type of schools in Delhi. Schools are classified according to the management, into government schools, independent schools and Kendriya Vidyalayas. There are many differences in these different types of school, the school building, the infrastructure available, the facilities, the socioeconomic background of the students, the fee structure, the curriculum, the extra curricular activities are just to mention a few. The student respondents comprised of 46.7 per cent students from government schools, 40.5 per cent from independent schools and 12.8 per cent from Kendriya Vidyalaya. The schools selected were in the ratio of 6:4:1 (government schools: independent schools: Kendriya Vidyalayas). Results show that the government school students have lower test anxiety, which can be attributed to lower expectations from the parents, teachers and school. The students from independent schools reported higher test anxiety. In the independent schools the expectation of parents of the students, teachers and schools were higher which gets transferred to the students so they are pressurised to perform better. The students of Kendriya Vidyalaya reported highest test anxiety these students mainly come from the middle-income classes of the society. There is greater pressure on them to perform well in studies and get into a career or profession that could be the reason for their test anxiety scores being the highest.

In this study 53.4 per cent of student respondents were preparing for the All India Board and 46.6 per cent respondents were preparing for the Delhi Board. The students that followed the All India Board were reported to have higher test anxiety. This is mainly because of the type of school that follow the two boards differ in management, school environment. Government schools follow the Delhi Board and Kendriya Vidyalayas and the independent schools mainly follow the All India Board. The syllabus in the schools following the two different boards is quite similar. Thus, it is not the difference in the examination board that is causing the difference in test anxiety but it is the difference in the type of school that attributes to the difference in test anxiety of the students.

Academic performance evaluates the student and indicates the academic standard. An examination of the respondents' scholastic achievements was done by exploring the marks of the students in the last final examinations in the last class. A lot of emphasis is given to the academic performance of the students rather than to the learning process. Students are stressed as they are constantly under pressure to perform well or even the best. The respondents' percentage of marks ranged from minimum of 31 per cent to a maximum of 95 per cent. The mean percentage of marks was 57.9 per cent. It was found that 5.3 per cent respondents had performed unsatisfactory and had obtain percentage marks less than the pass percentage. Third division was obtained by 30 per cent of the respondents. One-third of the respondents had secured first division that is 60 per cent and more marks. There were 10.3 per cent of students who got 75-84 per cent. Another 11.4 per cent of students had done well and secured a high percentage of 85 per cent and above. An analysis into percentage of marks obtained and the test anxiety shows that there was significant difference among test anxiety scores and the academic performance of the students. The test anxiety scores reduced as the academic performance of the students improved. Students with low marks, with just pass marks reported higher test anxiety and students with better marks 85 per cent and above reported of lower test anxiety. Results showed that students with good marks were confident, well prepared for examination thus had lower test anxiety. While students with just pass marks were not prepared and have the fear of failure thus have high-test anxiety.

Most of the respondents (82.5 per cent) hailed from nuclear families, while 15 per cent respondents came from joint families. A small group of respondents 2.5 per cent live in single parent families. Findings show that there was no significant difference of test anxiety among students due to the type of the family that the students come from.

In this study, the respondents' family size varied from two members to nine members, mean family size being five members. More than one-third students came from small families with four or less than four members. Majority of students (63.6 per cent) came from large families with five or more than five members. It was found that a small percentage 5.9 per cent of respondents had no siblings; they were the only child in the family. More than one-fourth of the respondents 28.9 per cent had only one sibling. 29.4 per cent of respondents reported having two siblings. A small group of (3.1 per cent) respondents had five or more than five sibling. An enquiry was made to find out if the respondents' family size had an affect on the test anxiety of the students, results showed there was no significant difference of test anxiety of students due to the size of family.

In the present study more than half of the respondents' fathers (57 per cent) were in the age group of 41-50 years. While more than one-fourth (28.4 per cent) of the respondent's father were 51 years and above. The mothers were comparatively younger, as more than half of the mothers (52.8 per cent) were below 40 years. Also, 38.1 per cent of the mothers were in the age group of 41-50 years and only 9.1 per cent of the mothers were 51 and above.

A small percentage of fathers (6.7 per cent) had no formal schooling and their wards were first generation schoolers. One-fourth of the fathers had gone to school but dropped out before or after their secondary examination. More than one-third of the fathers (38 per cent) had gone to senior secondary school and college. Little less than one-third of the fathers 30.3 per cent were postgraduate and above. There was a mixed group of fathers with varied educational levels. The analysis of variance reports no significant difference on the test anxiety of the respondents due to the difference in the students' educational qualification.

The respondents' mother's educational levels were comparatively lower than the fathers, but like fathers too the mothers of the respondents had diverse educational background. More than one-fifth of the respondent's mothers (22.8 per cent) had no formal schooling, and 28.3 per cent mothers had studied till Xth or below. Almost half (48.9 per cent) of the mothers had attended college. An exploration showed that the respondents' test anxiety was affected by their mothers' educational background. It was observed that students whose mothers were educated till graduation their wards reported lower test anxiety score than students whose mothers were less educated and the highly educated. As mothers with low educational background had low expectations from their wards and mothers with high educational qualification had very high expectations from their ward. One of the causes for examination stress among students is due to very high and very low expectations of the mothers.

The fathers of the respondent were involved in different types of occupation. A small number of fathers (10.6 per cent) were daily wagers. Almost one-third (31.6 per cent) of respondents' fathers were into business, another 33 per cent were in the non-professional service sector and 24.8 per cent in service sector. Results show that students whose fathers were occupied as daily wagers and students whose fathers were into business both these groups of students had lower test anxiety, while students whose parents were into service as professionals and non-professionals had high test anxiety. Students whose fathers were daily wager may have low aspiration and expectations thus their wards test anxiety scores were low. Business fathers also pressurised their wards less so the students reported lower test anxiety. Students whose fathers were in service sector professional and non-professionals have higher expectation from their wards thus the test anxiety of their wards was higher.

More than half of the respondents' mothers (51.4 per cent) were housewives. Only 2.7 per cent of mothers were daily wage earners. Another small group (2.5 per cent) of mothers was into business. Among all the employed mothers more than half were engaged in non-professional jobs in the service sector. 15.2 per cent of mothers were engaged as professional in service sector. There was no significant difference observed in mothers' occupational background and the students test anxiety.

Family monthly income ranged from below Rs 5000 to maximum of Rs 25000 and above. The respondents in the study were found coming from different income groups. 15.6 per cent respondents reported of family income of Rs 5000 and below. One-fourth 169 (26.4 per cent) of the respondents family income was Rs 5001 to 10000. Little less than one-fourth 150 (23.4 per cent) of the respondents' family income was a high of Rs 25001 and above. There were three (0.46 per cent) respondents who mentioned their monthly family income was rupees one lakh. Results show a significant difference between test anxiety scores of the students of different family income groups.

Highest test anxiety was reported in the family income group of Rs 10001-15000.

The present study found that 48 per cent of respondents reported of having a separate room or a place in the house to study, while more than half 52 per cent of the respondents had no separate place to study. Students having a place exclusive for themselves is beneficial for their studies, as further analysis of coefficient correlation showed that students without a place to study reported of lower academic performance.

An enquiry into the family environment revealed that students reported that television distracted them most from studies, followed by friends, neighbours and music. Students reported least distractions from computers. It was observed that more than one-third of the respondents often helped in the household work and another 40 per cent of the respondents sometime help in the household chores. Only a small group of 4.2 per cent students do not do any household work in their house.

One-fifth of the respondents often had the duty to buy milk or vegetable and groceries. Only 13 per cent of the respondents helped often in the kitchen, helped in cleaning house and were involved in caring for the siblings or the elderly in the family. Certain modifications were made in the homes of the respondents by their parents to facilitate an environment of study during examinations. It was found that among the student respondents, almost one-third of the families often stopped watching TV in the house and a high of 43.6 per cent control TV viewing sometimes. A large number of (63.3 per cent) respondents reported that parents removed the cable connection to the home television. More than three-fourth of respondents reported that their duties and responsibilities of going to the market, cleaning the house, helping in the kitchen were transferred to the younger sibling, during the respondent's examination times.

The study examined the impact of parental help and support during examination on the anxiety of students. Results showed that the most forthcoming parental support was parents relieving students of household work followed by parental guidance and suggestion to the respondents. The third parental help was parents keeping away distractions like TV/outings, followed by parents organising books/ study material and room of the respondents. Fifth help was parents avoiding guests/parties/get-to-gathers. Sixth parental help was mothers making special food for the students. Seventh parental help was parents teaching the students. The eight scored parental help were parents accompanying students to school/tuitions. Followed by parents staying awake at night with the students. The least forthcoming help was parents taking leave from their work and staying at home for their wards.

Results showed that 35 per cent of the respondents received less parental help. Another 35 per cent respondent's fell in the medium parental help group. More than one-fourth of the respondents' parents provided high parental help. Results show that respondents with low parental support scored higher test anxiety. The respondents with higher parental support were able to handle the examination situation better and reported lower test anxiety.

In the present study it was observed that three-fourth of the parents have communicated their expectations to their children of what they wanted their wards to become.

In the study, 49.1 per cent of the parents had clear ideas and wanted their wards to become doctor, engineers, scientists or teachers. The highest number (18.8 per cent) of parents wanted their children to become doctors, 13.6 per cent desired their wards to become engineers and 7.2 per cent parents wanted their children to become teachers. More than one-third of parents wanted their ward to join any profession that would offer a good job. Results show that parents with fixed expectations and wanting their wards to become doctors or scientists had higher test anxiety. Parents, who were not very rigid and encouraged their children to take up a career of their choice, did not pressurise their children; and so these students had low mean test anxiety. Parents' expectations if high can be the cause of student's examination stress.

Parents remind the students of their expectations so that there is a constant push for the students. Almost half (47.2 per cent) of the parents constantly remind their wards of their expectation. Another 37.5 per cent of respondents' parents do not continuously remind their wards of the parental expectation but only remind occasionally. Only a small group of parents (11.6 per cent) are understanding and tolerant with their wards and don't remind the students of their expectations.

Parents' expectations from children, on the students' academic performance was reported to be high. Three-fourth of the parents wanted their wards to achieve a minimum of 60 per cent and above marks in their examination, while as high as 30.8 per cent wanted a distinction from the respondents and another group (12.7 per cent) of parents had targeted a high of more than 90 per cent marks from the respondents. The parents' expectations on students' results were the marks desired by the parents from their children. It was observed that when parents' expectation from the children was a just pass mark the mean test anxiety scores were 41.1. But when parents expected their wards to get at least a distinction (75 per cent mark) or even 90 per cent marks the mean test anxiety was higher. Results showed there was significant difference in parents' aspiration and test anxiety of the students. It was observed that parents' high aspiration resulted in student having high test anxiety. Parents who had low aspirations from their wards, their children reported low test anxiety.

More than half of the students reported that they were offered incentives. There are 23 per cent of respondents who were offered mobile phones, computer and other gadgets. One-fifth of the respondents were offered a vehicle if they performed well in the examination. 14.7 per cent students reported they were offered an outing or holiday.

Parents had mixed reactions when their wards didn't perform well in examination. Most parents scolded their wards and 24.4 per cent respondents' parents showed their displeasure in their behaviour towards the respondents. Ten per cent of parents resorted to beating their wards. One-third parent took steps for arranging tuitions so that their wards perform better in their examination. Half of the parents (49.5 per cent) talked to their wards and took their assurance that the student will work for better performance. Respondents felt that parents compelled them to study more than needed. More than two-third of students' parents compelled the students to spend more time on studies.

Respondents had their own aspirations and career choice. The profession of a doctor was preferred by 9.5 per cent of the respondents. The choice to go in for management, engineering, civil service, hotel management and teaching was also high. The choice to get into business was second highest, after engineering. A small group of (8.6 per cent) respondents did not know what profession to take up and another 31.3 per cent wanted a good job.

Students' aspirations were found to be high. 90.4 per cent of respondents aimed for at least a first division. One-fifth of the respondents aimed for distinction. 12.2 per cent respondents aimed higher, at least 90 per cent marks. Only 2.8 per cent aspired, just passing marks. Thus, the respondents have high aspirations, if they aspire high and do not achieve their targets it may lead to frustration, anxiety and low self-esteem.

The respondents reported different reasons for wanting to perform well in examination. More than half (57.2 per cent) of the respondents wanted to perform well in examination as they aspired to get into a good career. Almost one-third wanted to perform well in examination to secure good marks. Another group of one-third of the respondents wanted to perform well in the examination to meet their parent's expectations. While another group of respondents (19 per cent) wanted to perform well for their own personal satisfaction and 15.6 per cent respondents wanted to meet their schools and teachers expectation. And 5.6 per cent of respondent's reported that the principal reason for wanting to perform well is to meet friend's expectation.

Respondents reported different factors that worried students during examination. Among them the highest reported (61.6 per cent) factor that worried respondents was lack of adequate preparation for examination. Almost one-third (31.9 per cent) of the respondents felt that, not having a separate room or place for study, for their examinations during the examination days worried them. More than one-fourth of the respondents (28.3 per cent) replied that not getting sufficient guidance for studies caused worry during examination. Another 29.1 per cent respondents felt they lacked sufficient time for study so that worried them.

A comparison into the time for sleep of the respondents was made before the examination dates are declared and after the examination schedule was declared. The respondents reported a minimum of four hours and a maximum of nine hours of sleep before the examination time, with the mean sleeping time being 6.79 hours. The sleeping time of the respondents once the examination comes close and the examination schedule is declared shows a decrease. It was observed that respondents reduced their time for sleep. The minimum sleep hours became three hours and a maximum of eight hours. The mean sleep time reduced to 5.94 just before the examination.

The study gave information on the student's view of what are the help they require in performing better in examination. Results showed that the respondents valued better understanding of the subject as the most important help for better performance in examinations. The second most important help required was assistance in organising their study. Help from teachers was rated next in the list of help required. The next two helps listed were better conditions in the house and parental support. Interestingly tuition scored the last.

One-fourth of the respondents reported they do not study on their own; they have to be guided by tutors or their parents. One-third respondents spend more than two hours on self-study. Only one-third of respondents reported they don't go for tuitions, but the remaining 61.6 per cent of respondent go for tuitions. Students reported that they study a minimum of one hour to maximum of 12 hours a day. The mean study time was 4.66 hours excluding their time spend in schools.

Study habits scale examined the study habits of the students. It was observed that 38.3 per cent of the respondents were found to have poor study habits. One-third respondents were average in their study habits and only 28.4 per cent respondents had good study habits. The results on study habits and the test anxiety of the respondents show that respondents with poor study habits reported high on the test anxiety. Respondents who were regular and organised with their study practices were lower on test anxiety indicating that examination stress can be reduced if study habits are improved.

The respondents' behavioural manifestations of examination stress were examined on two domains, the physiological manifestations and the psychological manifestations. It was observed that all student respondents exhibited one or the other behaviour manifestations. Among the psychological manifestations observed were, 34.8 per cent of students reported frightening dreams, followed by more than one-third (34.4 per cent) having feeling of inferiority, 30.3 per cent students have mentioned that they think getting along in life is difficult, showing that they find the examination stress difficult to face. Students have reported that they find the situation helpless (28.9 per cent), and they also (25.2 per cent) feel helpless. Among the physiological manifestations exhibited by the students, 61.1 per cent of students get breathless. Most of the student's exhibit eating disorders, in which 49.1 per cent students found they eat more due to examination stress, while 45.6 per cent reported of lack of appetite at examination times. 47.0 per cent students experienced trembling and 40.0 per cent reported increased heartbeat. 43.3 per cent students also complained of often remaining sick. More than one-third of students reported of stomach upsets, another 32.0 suffered from headaches.

It was observed that one-third respondents (33.6 per cent) had low psychological manifestations and little more than one-third (35.8 per cent) had high psychological manifestations. Another 39.2 per cent of the respondents manifested low physiological manifestations, while 37.3 per cent respondents manifested high physiological problems before examination. It was observed that 34.7 per cent of the respondents reported low behaviour manifestation and 32.8 per cent exhibited high behaviour manifestations.

Variations were found in the percentages of females and males reporting each of the behaviour manifestations. It was observed that on the various items of the psychological dimensions, more females as compared to male students reported (54.5 per cent) mental tension, female students get angry easily (37.2 per cent). More than one-third (67.8 per cent) of female respondents felt like crying, felt helpless (52.3 per cent), get upset easily (45.2 per cent), feel uneasy (40.2 per cent,) suffer uncontrolled negative thoughts (40.2 per cent), feel confused (50.2 per cent), feel mentally exhausted (57.6 per cent). A high percentage of 80.2 per cent females students experience frightening dreams, worry about their performance (56.0 per cent). 61.3 per cent of females also reported getting along in life was difficult. More than half (53.6 per cent) of females reported that they lacked interest in studies.

More male students reported mood swing (23.7 per cent). More than half of the males (50.2 per cent) reported low self esteem, feel they are in a helpless situation (59.6 per cent) have problem in concentration (52.7 per cent) and lack recalling power (58.7 per cent). Almost two-third (64.0 per cent) of males reported feeling of inferiority. Though variations were found there was no significant difference in psychological dimensions of behaviour manifestations of the students and the gender of the students.

A comparison on the physiological behaviour manifestation and the gender of the respondents was found by cross-tabulation and found that females reported higher on behaviour manifestations like poor appetite, headaches, and increased heart beat. A high of 86.1 per cent female respondents reported breathlessness and more than half (54.2 per cent) female students had difficulty to initiate and maintain sleep. Results showed that the items of physiological behaviour manifestation that were reported higher by male student respondents were feeling tired, over eating, falling sick and trembling. An analysis into the difference in physiological manifestations and the gender of the respondents showed that there was no significant difference between male and female respondents on physiological manifestations.

The psychological manifestation and the physiological manifestation put together were called the behaviour manifestations of examination stress. These behaviour manifestations analysed on the bases of gender found that the difference between the gender and behaviour manifestations was not statistically significant. Females manifested slightly more behaviour problems than male students.

The examination of the behavioural manifestations exhibited by the students of the different types of schools showed a significant difference. The students of independent schools and Kendriya Vidyalaya exhibited similar behaviour manifestations that were higher than the government school students. However, the analysis made into the behaviour manifestations of the students and the different classes of the school showed no significant difference in the behaviour manifestation due to the difference in the classes of the students.

The study also made an enquiry into the coping strategies of the students in facing examination stress. It was found that most commonly used (42.0 per cent) coping strategy is praying for courage to face the difficulties of examination followed by 27.0 per cent of respondents share their problems with friends/family/relatives. 12.0 per cent of students try to organise study better and 7.2 per cent ask for guidance from others to help cope with examination stress. It is observed that lower percentage of students have reported of adopting adaptive coping strategies. Among the maladaptive coping strategies, it was observed that there are a significant number of students (10.9 per cent) resorted to sleeping and believing in destiny (15.4 per cent) to cope to examination stress. There was another 14.5 per cent take medicines to get rid of problems like headaches and stomach upsets and stress. A small percentage of students (3.9 per cent) also take medicines to improve memory, concentration and reduce sleep.

It was observed that half (50.2 per cent) of the respondents had low adaptive coping while 49.8 per cent respondents reported high adaptive coping. Students also resorted to maladaptive coping techniques. There are 52.8 per cent respondents who relied on high maladaptive coping techniques to reduce stress and 47.2 per cent respondents reported of having low maladaptive coping techniques.

An investigation into adaptive coping strategies and test anxiety scores found that students who had adopted low adaptive coping strategies reported high test anxiety. Students who had adopted high adaptive coping strategies reported of lower test anxiety. This shows that there was a significant difference in test anxiety and adaptive coping strategies. The students test anxiety scores and maladaptive coping strategies were analysed and it was observed that no significant difference in test anxiety and maladaptive coping strategies existed.

An examination to compare the coping strategies of the female and male students showed there was significant difference in adaptive and maladaptive coping strategies of both female and male respondents. It was observed that among the adaptive coping strategies higher percentage of female students were involved in yoga (65.0 per cent), prayed for courage to face the problem (72.8 per cent), visited temple or other religious places (45.8 per cent), took meditation (33.7 per cent), involved in recreational activities (39.3 per cent), and shared their problems with friends/family/relatives (61.3 per cent). Over half of the female students (51.1 per cent) pursued hobbies to cope with examination stress. And in the task oriented coping strategies also the female students reported higher than the male respondents, 45.5 per cent of female students organise studies, 46.1 per cent ask for guidance and cope better for examination stress. 39.9 per cent of the female students think examinations are part of the life. 28.2 per cent take examination as stepping stone for success and over one-third (38.4 per cent) of female students think of possible better outcomes of examinations. Male respondents had higher percentage than female respondents only on physical exercise, 63.4 per cent of males student respondents engaged in physical exercise.

Out of the five items listed in the maladaptive coping, only on sleeping the female respondents scored higher (52.3 per cent) than the male respondents. On all the other maladaptive coping styles male students scored higher. One-third (38.5 per cent) of the male students believed in destiny. The other maladaptive coping strategies, which were also negative to students' health and academic performance, were scored higher by the male respondents. One-fourth (25.9 per cent) of male respondents took medicines to get rid of the physical ailments like headache, stomach upset, stress, depression. 12.3 per cent of male respondents consume medicine to improve concentration, reduce sleep to study more and perform better, followed closely by 11.8 per cent of male student respondents indulging in substance abuse.

It was observed that there was significant difference in adaptive coping strategies due to gender difference. Female student respondents were more engaged in adaptive coping strategies compared to the male student respondents. A comparison on maladaptive coping strategies and gender shows a significant difference in maladaptive coping strategies in female and male student respondents. The female respondent's score lower on the maladaptive coping strategies showing that lesser female respondents adopt maladaptive coping strategies.

The adaptive coping strategies were examined to find if there was any difference in adaptive coping strategies due to the difference in the class of the respondents. It was found that there was no significant difference in the adaptive coping strategies of the students in different classes. Students of the non-board classes and board classes respond to examination stress with similar adaptive coping strategies. An examination into the maladaptive coping strategies in the different classes found that there was significant difference in maladaptive coping in the different classes. It was observed that students of the non-board classes had higher maladaptive coping strategies as compared to the board classes.

An investigation into the adaptive coping strategies of the students in the different types of schools highlighted there was a significant difference in coping strategies observed of students due to the difference in type of school. Results show that the students of government school were highest in adopting adaptive coping strategies, followed by those in the independent schools. The maladaptive coping strategies were also observed in students of the different type of schools and the results showed that there was significant difference in maladaptive coping among students of the different types of schools. Government school students scored lowest on the maladaptive coping strategies, these students were least involved with maladaptive coping strategies. Kendriya Vidyalaya students scored highest followed by Independent school students.

A social work intervention model was designed combining the data of the views and experiences from the student respondents and from the professionals working in the area of student welfare. The social work intervention model prepared to manage examination stress is to be introduced at two phases. The two phases will be called the prevention phase and the reduction phase.

The first phase of this model will aim at social work intervention to help students develop realistic understanding of examination. So that students are able to adjust to the demanding situation of examination. The target group for this phase constitutes all the students in the senior classes from class IX to XII with emphasis given to the board classes X and XII. The students will attend the individual programme sessions in groups. The time frame for this intervention phase will be from the beginning of the academic year to the result declaration time. The students will meet every fortnightly for sessions that will last for two periods.

The specific objectives of the prevention phase will be to equip students with competence to face examination, to strengthen the personality of the students and to modify the social environment of the students. To meet the first objective of this phase that is to equip students with competence to face examination, sessions will be held on effective study habits, studying a book/chapter, strategies on learning, planning study schedule, time management, examination-taking skills, ad developing positive attitude towards examination.

The second objective of the prevention phase is to strengthen the personality of the students, and sessions will be held on encouraging problem-solving skills, goal setting, recreational interest, physical relaxation, coping strategies, improving communication, and encouraging ventilation.

The third objective of the prevention phase is to modify the social environment. Parents will be enabled to be supportive and encouraging to their children. Teachers will be encouraged to be cooperative and supportive. The sessions with the parents will be held on parenting style, nurturing the child, disciplining children, realistic parental expectation, and stimulating parental behaviour.

The interventions methods to be used in the first phase of the model will be group discussion, simulation activities, group exercise, role play, brain storming, panel discussion with experts, and screening of film followed by discussion.

The second phase of the social work intervention model will be the Stress Reduction Phase. In this phase the aim will be to help students who are prone to examination stress. The target group constitute students identified with stress symptoms, by themselves or by the significant others. The significant others could be parents, peer or teachers. Those persons who are close to the students and who observe behavioural problems in the students. The time frame for the Phase II will be before the examination starts in the month of December, examination time and results declaration time.

The specific objective of this phase is: to help students reduce stress, to promote supportive parenting and to involve peer mentors and teachers in stress surveillance. The first objective is to help student reduce stress to meet this objective the school social worker/counsellor plans out stress management and reduction sessions. These sessions will reduce stress management within an eclectic framework. The combinations of approaches that will be used are behavioural approaches, cognitive approaches and crisis intervention. Examination stress can be managed by methods of deep breathing, progressive muscle relaxation, and meditation. Students will also be helped by systematic desensitisation. The cognitive approaches will be used in reducing examination stress. Ellis's rational emotive therapy and Meichenbaum's self-instructional training methods will be included. The Cognitive Behavioural Approach is most suited to treat examination stress as it's a combination of restructuring the cognition of the students and help in stress reduction trainings.

The sessions for this objective will be in small therapeutic groups and through individual problem-solving counselling. Group work and casework sessions will be organised twice in a week and if need be more often too. Crisis intervention is also proposed to be taken up by the school social worker/counsellors.

The second objective of the Stress Reduction Phase is to promote enabling parenting for students experiencing examination stress. Parents of those students who are stressed will be again met and involved in the treatment process of the students, so that the stress condition can be controlled and reduced. Sessions will be held with individual parents or small group of parents on parent-child interaction. Parents will also be met in counselling session to understand the students problems and for family therapy so that the parent-child relationship is strengthened.

The third objective of Phase II of the social work intervention model is to involve peer mentors and teachers in examination stress surveillance. Peer is another important groups of the significant others who are directly in touch with the students. Two students who are sensitive to students' problems and interested in the programme will be trained as peer mentors from each class and will form a core group. The sessions that will be taken up with the volunteered peer mentors that will introduce them to the phenomena of examination stress

- Signs to identify examination stress among students.
- Tips to help in time management, effective study habits, organising study and examination taking tips.

The peer mentor core group will transfer the session information to other students and so all the senior class students are covered. Peer mentor will be on surveillance for their class, looking out for students who are having problem in studies and are tensed and worried about their performance. The responsive peer mentor thus forms a link between service providers and students who need help. The peer mentors will be in constant touch with the school social worker/counsellor. If they identify students deteriorating in studies or with strange behaviour, like high absenteeism, loneliness, these students will be brought to the notice of the school social worker/counsellor.

Teachers are in constant interaction with the students, thus will also form the surveillance team. Teachers too will be sensitised to identify and help students getting anxious with examination or study pressures. Teachers will deal with the students in class and if need be, teachers will bring these students to the notice of the school social worker/counsellor if they find students unable to manage the examination stress. Feedback sessions will be held at all phases with all the different groups of students and significant others. The feedback sessions will be arranged with the school social worker/counsellor and general students, parents, peer mentors, teacher and students suffering from increased examination stress. These feedback sessions will be helpful and will act as a safety net covering all the students. This model will create a network in individual schools to address the problem of examination stress.

Suggestions

The social work intervention model would be beneficial if introduced in all schools so that all students are provided help to enhance their academic performance and manage their stress during examinations. If not provided with help students would not be able to endure the rising stress and would succumb to the increased examination stress level. Leading to larger number of students developing psychological and physiological problems and students suicide rate could also go up.

Importance of a school social worker

A school social worker is essential in every school. Social work practice in schools is able to tackle a variety of situations for all the individuals in that system. These individuals are children, parents, teachers, non-teaching staff and others in the system and also the communities from where these children come. The nature of service is for developmental, preventive, facilitative and supportive in crisis management. These services are most aptly performed by a professionally qualified social worker. The social workers with their methods, skills and techniques can work towards making the school environment, a better place for learning, growing and working for the members within the system. But the ground realities are different; very few schools have a qualified school social worker. CBSE (2003) recommends the need for a school social worker making it a requisite for affiliation into the board, but in the implementation stage this is not practiced. The schools that have a social worker/counsellor, organise activities but their initiative are sporadic and just a drop in the ocean. School social workers need to get organised, so that they have a platform to meet, exchange ideas and draw out plans for working effectively. Most of the time school social workers work is not recognised and their initiatives die out. A forum for school social worker will be beneficial to improve this area of social work, which is still in its childhood state in India.

School mental health programme a necessity in every school

The extent of mental health problems in children highlight the need for a variety of interventions in school which is a formal set up where most children go to. Mental health awareness through the school children can reach the general households in our country. School, family and community must work hand in hand to arrest the problems of mental health in the society.

The World Health Organisation (2002) states that schools are the most appropriate place to initiate a comprehensive mental health programme for children. School mental health programmes are effective in improving learning, mental well-being, identifying mental disorder and appropriately treating it also. The Education Department or the Health Department of our country has not realised the potential schools have in reaching out to the Indian population on various issues of mental hygiene and mental well-being. Schools must lay more importance to the school mental health programme rather than only emphasising on the scholastic development of the child.

Need for involving parents in the school set up

There is a change in the scenario in the Indian society. The size of the family is shrinking but children still remain vulnerable due to many aspects like poverty, neglect in health and hygiene, child abuse and to add to this list is the stress and strain of modern life on the child. The value of life is deteriorating. The child needs to be protected from the harsh and impersonal society. It is the duty of parents to adjust with changing times, remove generation gap, and increase communication with the child. One of the main causes of examination stress observed in this study is parental expectations and aspirations. Parents need to be realistic with their child. Schools need to give a platform for more parents' involvement so that the school together with parents can closely nurture the child. Schools through the parent-teacher-association can involve the parents for the developmental needs of the child. The child in some cases is a child with a problem and school/parents individually are unable to handle them. If the school and parents can work together many issues and problems of the children can be treated. Thus, there is a need to strengthen parents-teacher-association and more involvement of parents in school.

References

Akande, A. (1990). Influence of urban-rural upbringing on Nigerian students' test anxiety. *Psychological Reports,* 67, 3(2), 1261-1262.

Albert, R., and Haber, R. N. (1960). Anxiety in academic situation. *Journal of Abnormal and Social Psychology*, 61, 207-215.

Anand, R. (2002). *A study of family environment and anxiety level of maladjusted adolescents.* Ph.D dissertation, Department of Psychology, Delhi University, New Delhi.

Antony, B. (2006). Social work in school setting. *Supplementing reading material*–1, BSWE-005, Indira Gandhi National Open University, New Delhi.

Araki, N. (1992). Test anxiety in elementary school and junior high school students in Japan. Special issue: Anxiety research in Japan. *Anxiety, Stress and Coping an International Journal,* 5, 3, 205-215.

Ayora, A. (1993). Anxiety in evaluation or examination situations in high school students from Loja (Ecuador). *Revista Latinoamericana de Psicologia*, 25, 3, 425-431.

Bartlett, D. (1998). *Stress perspective and processes.* Buckingham: Open University Press.

Baskett, L. M., and Johnson, S. M. (1982). The young child's interaction with parents versus siblings. *Child Development*, 53, 643-650.

Baumrind, D., Larzelere, R. E., and Cowan, P.A. (2002). Ordinary physical punishment: Is it harmful. *Psychological Bulletin,* 128, 590-595.

Beidel, D. C. (1991). Social phobia and over anxious disorder in school-age children. *Journal of the American Academy of Child and Adolescent Psychiatry*, 545-552.

Beidel, D. C., and Turner, S. M. (1998). Co-morbidity of test anxiety and other anxiety disorders in children. *Journal of Abnormal Child Psychology*, 16, 275-287.

Benjamin, M., Mckeachie, W. J., Lin,Y., and Holinger, D. P. (1981). Test anxiety: Deficits in information processing. *Journal of Educational Psychology*, 73, 6, 816-824.

Benjamin, M. N. (1991). A comparison of training programmes intended for different types of test-anxious students: Further support for an information- processing model. *Journal of Educational Psychology*, 83, 1, 134-139.

Berk, L. E. (2003). *Child development (6th Ed.).* Delhi : Pearson Education.

Bernard, L. C., and Krupat, E. (1994). *Health psychology: Biopsychosocial factors in health and illness.* New York: Harcourt Brace College Publishers.

Besharat, M. A. (2003). Parental perfectionism and children's test anxiety. *Psychological Report*, 93, 3, 2, 1049-1055. Retrieved October 11, 2006, from http://www.ncbi.nlm.nih.gov/entrez/query.fcgi?cmd=Retrieve&db=PubMed&list_uids=1...

Bhadwal, S. C., and Panda, P. K. (1992). The composite effect of a curricular programme on the test anxiety of rural primary school students: A one-year study. *Educational Review*, 44, 2, 205-220.

Birenbaum, M., and Gutvirtz, Y. (1993). The relationship between test anxiety and seriousness of errors in algebra. *Journal of Psychoeducational Assessment*, 11, 1, 12-19.

Birenbaum, M., and Nasser, F. (1994). On the relationship between test anxiety and test performance. *Measurement and Evaluation in Counseling and Development,* 27, 1, 293-301.

Bosch, J. A., Geus, E. E. J. D., Ring, C. and Amerongen, A. V. N. (2004). Academic examination and immunity: Academic stress or examination stress ? *Psychosomatic Medicine*, 66, 625-627. Retrieved August 8, 2006, from http://www. psychosomatic medicine.org/cgi/contentabstract/66/625.

Braday, J. R. (1987). A comparison of three multimodel treatment packages for test anxiety. Doctoral Dissertation, University of Mississippi. *Dissertation Abstracts International* 48, 5, 1148A.

Brown, J. D., Schaffer, R., Vargas, L., and Romocki, L. S. (2003). Popular media culture and the promise of critical media literacy. In S.F. Hamilton, and M.A. Hamilton, (Eds.), *The youth development handbook.* Newbury Park, CA: Sage.

Brown, S. D. and Nelson, T. L. (1983). Beyond the uniformity myth: A comparison of academically successful and unsuccessful test-anxious college students. *Journal of Counseling Psychology*, 30, 3, 367-374.

Bruch, M. A., Juster, H. R. and Kaflowitz, N G. (1983). Relationships of cognitive components of test anxiety to test performance. *Journal of Counseling Psychology*, 30, 527-536.

Carlson, K. S. (1995). *Attachment in sibling relationships during adolescence: Links to other familial and peer relationships* Paper presented at the meeting of the Society for Research in Child Development, Indianapolis.

Carver, C. S., Peterson, L. M., Follansbee, D. J. and Scheier, M. F. (1983). Effects of self-directed attention on performance and persistence among persons high and low in test anxiety. *Cognitive Therapy and Research*, 7, 4, 333-353. Retrieved September 11, 2006, from http://www.springerlink.com/content/ k154n38776630367/.

Cassady, J. C., and Johnson, R. E. (2002). Cognitive test anxiety and academic performance. *Contemporary Educational Psychology*, 27, 2, 270-295. Retrieved September 11, 2006, from http://www.ingentaconnect.com/content/ap/ep/2002 /00000027/00000002/art01094.

Cates, G. L., and Rhymer, K. N. (2003). Examining the relationship between mathematics anxiety and mathematics performance: An instructional hierarchy perspective. *Journal of Behavioral Education,* 12, 1, 23-24.

CBSE (2003) *Annual Report 2003*. Central Board of Secondary Examination, New Delhi.

Chatrath, H. (2004). *Stress among school going adolescents*. Ph.D dissertation, Department of Medicine, Delhi University, New Delhi.

Chengappa, R. (2005). *Killer exams how to revamp the system*, India Today, March 28.

Circirelli, V. G. (1994). Sibling relationships in cross-cultural perspective. *Journal of Marriage and the Family*, 56, 7-20.

Clifford, B. R., Gunter, B., and McAleer, J. L. (1995). *Television and children*. Hillsdale, NJ: Erlbaum.

Coes, M. C. (1991). Test anxiety: A quantitative evaluation of its effects on the Brazilian college entrance examination. *Psicologia Teoria e Pesquisa,* 7, 2, 137-147.

Comunian, A. L. (1993). Anxiety, cognitive interference, and school performance of Italian children. *Psychological Reports*, 73, 3, 747-754.

Cornish, R. D., and Dilley, J. S. (1973). Comparison of three methods of reducing test anxiety: systematic desensitization, implosive therapy, and study counseling. *Journal of Counseling Psychology*, 20, 6, 499-503.

Crocker, L., and Schmitt, A. (1987). Improving multiple – choice test performance for examinees with different levels of test anxiety. *Journal of experimental education*, 55, 201-206.

Crouter, A. C., and Booth, A. (2003). *Children's influence on family dynamics.* Mahwah, JN: Erlbaum.

Culler, R. E, and Holahan, C. J. (1980). Test anxiety and academic performance: The effect of study-related behaviors. *Journal of Educational Psychology*, 72, 1, 16-20.

Davis, T. E. (1988). *The effects of progressive muscle relaxation on state-trait test anxiety in seventh-grade students*. Doctoral Dissertation, Drake University. Dissertation Abstracts Internationals, 48, 8, 2020A.

Deffenbacher, J. L. (1977). Relationship of worry and emotionality to performance on the miller analogies test. *Journal of Educational Psychology*, 69, 2, 191-195.

Deffenbacher, J. L. (1986). Cognitive and physiological components of test anxiety in real-life examination. *Cognitive Therapy and Research*, 10, 6, 635-644.

Deinzer, R., Kleineidam, C., Striller-Winkler, R., Idel, H., and Bachq, D. (2000). Prolonged reduction of Salivary immunoglobulin A (SlgA) after a major academic examination. *International Journal Pscyhophysiology*, 37, 3, 219-232. Retrieved August 8, 2006, http://www.ncbi.nlm.gov/entrez/querry.fegi?itool= abstractplus&pubmed &cmd =retrieve& dopt=abstract&list_uids=10858568.

Deinzer, R., and Schuller, N. (1998). Dynamics of stress-related decrease of salivary immunoglobulin A (sIgA) : Relationship to symptoms of the common cold and studying behavior. *Behavioral Medicine*, 23,161- 169.

Dendato, K. M., and Diener, D. (1986). Effectiveness of cognitive/relaxation therapy and study-skills training in reducing self-reporting anxiety and improving the academic performance of test-anxious students. *Journal of Counseling Psychology*, 33, 2,131-135.

Dienstbier, R. A. (1989). Arousal and physiological toughness: Implications for mental and physical health. *Psychological Review*, 96, 84-100.

Directorate of Education, (2006). *Annual Report 2006*. Directorate of Education, New Delhi.

Doctor, R. M. and Altman, F. (1969). Worry and emotionality as components of test anxiety : Replication and further data. *Psychological Reports*, 24, 563-568.

Duke, T., and Davidson, J. (2002). Ordinary and recurrent dream recall of active, past and non-recurrent dreamers during and after academic stress. *Dreaming: Journal of the Association for the study of dreams*, 12, 45, 185-197.

Dusek, J. B., and Dusek, J. F. (1978). Children's coping with stress in testing situations. In D. C. Spielberger, and G. I. Sarason, (Ed.), *Stress and anxiety* (pp. 377-382). Washington: Hemisphere Publishing Corpcration.

Edwards, L.A. (1957). *Techniques of attitude scale construction*. New York: Appleton- Century- Crofts, Inc.

E'Elia, V. (1998). Investigation of the impact of a cognitive behavioural intervention on high school student's academic self-concept, test anxiety and school motivation. *Dissertation Abstracts International Section B: The Sciences and Engineering*, 58, 12B, 6842.

El-Safty, M. M. (1995). Test anxiety and its relation to achievement motivation: A cross-cultural study between high school students in Egypt and Arab Emirates. *Derasat Nafseya*, 5, 1, 71-106.

El-Zahhar, E.N., and Hocevar, D. (1991). Cultural and sexual differences in test anxiety, trait anxiety and arousability Egypt, Brazil, and the United States. *Journal of cross-cultural psychology*, 22, 2, 238-249.

Eman, S., Dogar, I. A., Khalid, M. and Haider, N. (2012). Gender differences in test anxiety and examination stress. *Journal of Pakistan psychiatric society*. Volume 9. Issue 2.

Endler, N. S. (1997). Stress, anxiety and coping: the multidimensional interaction model. *Canadian Psychology*. Retrieved September 6, 2006, from htt://www.findarticles.com/p/articles/mi_qa3711/is_199708/ai_n8774699/print.

Fadia, N., and Takahashi, T. (1996). An application of confirmatory factor analysis with item parcels for testing the structure of test anxiety among Israeli-Arab high school students. Paper presentation at the annual meeting of the National Council on Measurement in Education. New York, April 9-11,1996.

Falbo, T., and Poston, D. L. (1993). The academic, personality, and physical outcoes of only children in China. *Child Development*, 64, 18-35.

Fortuyn, H. A. D., Broekhoven, F. V., Span, P. N., Backstrom, T., Zitman, F. C., and Verkes, R.J. (2004). Effect of Ph.D. examination stress on allopregnanolone and cortisol plasma levels and peripheral benzodiazepine receptor density. *Psychoneuroendocrinology*, 29, 1341-1344. Retrieved August 8, 2006, from http://www.physpharm.find.uwo.ca/undergrad/survivalweby3/s6-jobs/PHD%20 stress.pdf.

Franken, R. E. (1994). *Human motivation* (3rd ed.) Belmont, C.A: Brooks/Cole Publishing Company.

Galassi, J. P., Frierson, H. T. Jr., and Shaver, K. (1981). Behaviour of high, moderate, and low test anxious students during an actual test situation.

Clinical Psychology, 49, 1, 51-62. Retrieved June 12, 2006, from http://www. ncbi.nlm.nib.gov/entrez/queryfcgi?:cmd=retrieve&db=pubmed&list-ids=7217475 &dopt=citation.

Gandhi, A. (1990). *School social work.* New Delhi: Commonwealth Publishers.

Gershoff, E. T. (2002). Corporal punishment by parents and associated child behaviours and expriences. A meta-analysis and theoretical review. *Psychological Bulletin,* 128, 539-579.

Gevorkian, E., Daian, A. V., Adamian, T. S. I., Griogrian, S. S. and Minasian, S. M. (2003). The influence of examination stress on psychophysiological characteristics and heart rate in students. *Zh Vyssh Nerv Deiat Lm I P Pavlova*, 53, 1, 46-50. Retrieved August 8, 2006, http://www.ncbi.nlm.gov/entrez/ querry.fegi?itool=abstractplus&pubmed&cmd=retrieve&dopt=abstract&list_uids=12669503.

Gierl, M. J., and Rogers, W. T. (1996). A confirmatory factor analysis of the test anxiety inventory using Canadian high school students. *Educational and Psychological Measurement*, 56, 2, 315-324.

Gottman, J. M., and Parker, J. G. (1987). *Conversations of friends.* New York: Cambridge University Press.

Grant, J. P. (1994). *The state of the world's children 1994.* New York: Oxford University Press for UNICEF.

Greven, P. (1991). *Spare the child: The religious roots of punishment and the psychological impact of physical abuse.* New York: Knopf.

Grina, M. E. (1987). A descriptive study of community college students coping with examination stress. Ph.D dissertation, Department of Education, Oregan State University, Oregan.

Gropper, M. (2005). *Psych talk with Dr. Mike : Managing stress before it manages you.* Retrieved November 5, 2006, from http://www. jpost.com/servlet/satellite? pagename=jpost%2FIPArticle%.

Grover, P. (1996). A study of test anxiety among tenth grade school boys and girls in Delhi. Ph.D dissertation, Department of Psychology, Delhi University, New Delhi.

Gupta, A. and Sharma, S. (1991). Interactive effect of trait anxiety and intelligence on an easy task. *Journal of Personality and Clinical Studies,* 7, 1, 9-13.

Guo, G., and Van Wey, L. K. (1999). Sibship size and intellectual development: Is the relationship causal ? *American Sociological Review*, 64, 169-187.

Handbook on Social Welfare Statistics (2004). Ministry of Social Justice and Empowerment, Government of India.

Hembree, R. (1988). Correlates, causes, effects, and treatment of test anxiety. *Review of Educational Research Spring*, 58, 1, 47-77. Retrieved September 9, 2007, from http://www.../sici?sici=0034-6543% 28198821%2958%3A13ACCEATO%3e 2.0.CO% 3B2-I&size=

Hannah, E. (2006). School exam stress extreme, (April 16, 2006), *The Sydney Morning Herald*. Retrieved August 15, 2006 from http://www. smh.com.au.

Harris G., and Johnson, S. B. (1980). Comparison of individualized covert modeling self-control desensitization and study skills training for alleviation of test anxiety. *Journal of Consulting and Clinical Psychology*, 48, 2, 186-194.

Harris, M. M. (1988). Meta-analyses of test anxiety among college students. Doctoral Dissertations, Ohio State University, *Dissertation Abstracts International*, 49, 2, 543B.

Hattie, J., Biggs, J. and Purdie, N. (1996). Effects of learning skills interventions on student learning : A meta-analysis. *Review of Education Research*, 6, 2, 99-136. Retrieved September 11, 2006 from http:// links.js.../sici?sici=0034-6543(199622)66% 3A2%3C99% 3AEOLSIO%/3E2.0.CO%3B2-

Hembree, R. (1990). The nature, effects and relief of Mathematics anxiety. *Journal of Research in Mathematics Education,* 21, 1, 33-45. Retrieved September 9, 2006, from http://links..../sici=0021-8251(199001) 21%3A1%3C33%3ATNEARO %3E2. 0. CO%3B2.

Higgins, B.A. (2000). *Analysis of the effects of integrated instruction of metacognitive and study skills upon the self-efficacy and achievement of male and female students.* M.A. dissertation, Department of Education, University of Miami, Ohio.

Hollandsworth, J. G., Jr., Glazeski, R. C., Kirkland, K., Jones, G. E., and Van Norman, L. R. (1979). An analysis of the nature and effects of test anxiety. *Cognitive, Behavioral and Physiological Components, Cognitive Therapy and Research*, 3, 165-180.

Jeanell, P. (1984). The relationship of fear of success and psychosomatic symptoms in high school students. Doctoral Dissertation, University of New York. *Dissertation Abstracts International* 46, 1, 312B.

Jemmott, J. B., Borysenko, J. Z., Borysenko, M., McClelland, D. C., Chapman, R., Meyer, D., and Benson, H. (1983). Academic stress, power motivation, and decrease in secretion rate of salivary secretary immunoglobulin A. *Lancet*, 8339, 1, 1400-2. Retrieved September 9, 2006, from http://www.ncbi.nl.../ query.fcgi?cmd =retrieve and db=pubmed&list_uids=6134179&dopt=Abstrac

Jemmott, J. B., and Magloire, K. (1988). Academic stress, social and secretory immunoglobulin A. *Journal Perspective Social Psychology*, 55, 5, 803-810.

Jiao, S., Ji, G., and Jing, Q. (1996). Cognitive development of Chinese urban only children and children with siblings. *Child Development*, 67, 387-395.

Johansson, G., Laakso, M. L., Peder, M., and Karonen, S. L. (1988). Examination stress decreases plasma level of luteinizing hormone in male students. *Psychosomatic medicine*, 50, 3, 286-294. Retrieved August 8, 2006, from http://www. psychosomaticmedicine.org/cgi/content/abstract/15/3/286.

Joseph, M. V. (2002). *Mental Health in classroom*. Kalamassery: Rajagiri College of Social Science.

Juster, H. R. (1985). Components of test anxiety and examination performance: A test of three models. Doctoral Dissertation, University of New York. *Dissertation Abstracts International* 46, 2, 662B.

Kanchana, M., and Kaliappan, K.V. (2002). Effect of behaviour modification techniques in reducing test anxiety and improving study skills on academic achievement of high school girls. *Indian Journal of Applied Psychology*, 39, 39-48.

Karp, L., Weizman, A., Tyano, S., and Gavish, M. (1989). Examination stress, platelet perpheral benzodiazepine binding sites, and plasma hormone levels. *Life Sciences*, 44, 16, 1077-1082. Retrieved August 8, 2006, from http://www. ncbi.nlm. nih.gov/entrez/query.fcgi?db =PubMed&cmd=Retrieve&dopt=Citation&list-uids = 89200784.

Katyal, S., and Vasudeva, P. (2001). Gender differences in academic stress and its correlates. *Personality Study and Group Behavior*, 21, 31-38.

Kaul, A. (2005, December 27). Now, mental health programme in school curriculam. *Times of India.*

Keogh, E., Bond, F.W., French C.C., Richards A. and Davis R. E. (2004). Test anxiety, susceptibility to distraction and examination performance. *Anxiety, Stress* and *Coping*, 75, 3, 241-252. Retrieved August 8, 2006, from http://www.services.inist .fr/cgi-bin/public/view-doc

King, N. J., Mietz, A., Tinney, L., and Ollendick, T. H. (1995). Psychopathology and cognition in adolescents experiencing severe test anxiety. *Journal of Clinical Child Psychology*, 24, 49-55.

Kirschmann, K., and Rohm, A. (1991). Test anxiety, attribution and school performance with regard to sex and type of school. *Zeitschrift fur differentielle und Diagnostische Psychologie,* 12, 3, 177-184.

Kondas, O. (1982). Examination anxiety as a special mental state. *Psychological Aspect*, 62, 1149.

Kotler, J. A., Wright, J. C., and Huston, A. C. (2001). Television use in families with children. In J. Bryant, and J. A. Bryant, (Eds.), *Television and the American family.* Mahwah, NJ: Erlbaum.

Koul, L., and Bhadwal. S. C. (1991). Effect of formative evaluation on the test anxiety of high school students following programmed instruction material in general science. *Journal of Psychological Researches*, 35, 1, 34-41.

Kouzma, N. M., and Kennedy, G. A. (2004). Self-reported sources of stress in senior high school students. *Psychological Reports*, 94, 314-316.

Krishnamurthy, S. (2000). Test anxiety of higher secondary students as related to their achievement in history. *The Educational Review*, 106, 11, 194-197.

Kumar, K. (2005). Burden of exams. *Economic and Political Weekly*, 40(19), 1937-1939.

LaRossa, R. (1998). Fatherhood and social change. *Family Relations*, 37, 4, 451-457.

Lata, S., and Dwivedi, K. (2001). The effect of music on anxiety. *Psycho-Lingua,* 31, 2, 143-146.

Lazarus, R. S. (1966). *Psychological stress and the coping process.* New York: Springer.

Lazarus, R. S. (1970). *Psychological stress and the coping process*. New York: McGraw- Hill Book Company.

Lazarus, R. S., and Folkman, S. (1984). *Stress, appraisal and coping*. New York: Springer.

Lee, J. H. (1999). Test anxiety and working memory. *Journal of Experimental Education*, 67, 218-241.

Lee, M., and Larson, R. (1996). Effectiveness of coping in adolescence: The case of Korean examination. *International Journal of Behavioral Development*, 19, 4, 851-869. Retrieved August 8, 2006, from http://www.jbd.sagepub.com/cgi /content/abstract/19/4/851.

Leffert, N., and Blyth, D. A. (1996). *The effects of community contexts on early adolescents.* Paper presented at the meeting of the Society for Research on Adolescence, Boston.

Lent, R. W. and Russell, R. K. (1978). Treatment of test anxiety by cue-controlled desensitisation and study skills training. *Journal of Counselling Psychology*, 25, 3, 217-224. Retrieved August 8, 2006, from http://www.el-RecordDetails&ERICExtSearch_SearchValue_o=EJ219405&ERICEXtSearch_SearchType_O=enc_accno&objectld =09000006800a9d12.

Lepper, M., Greene, D., and Nisbett, R. (1973). Undermining children's intrinsic interest with intrinsic rewards: A test of the overjustification hypothesis. *Journal of Personality and Social Psychology*, 28, 129-137.

Lewis, L., Walter, A., and Griffith, A. (2000). Managing pre-examination stress through remote counselling using a session script from a 'sentinel subject'. *Journal of Telemedicine and tele care*, 6, 2, 43-44. Retrieved August 8, 2006, from http://www.ingentaconnect.com/content/rsm/jtt/ 2000/00000006/A002 0452/art00019.jsessionid=1aydo2ewvzfhr.alice.

Liebert, R. M., and Morris, L. W. (1967). Cognitive and emotional components of test anxiety: A distinction and some initial data. *Psychological Reports*, 20, 975-978.

Makarenko, M. V., L. Yzohub, V. S. and Iukhymenko, L. (2003). Heart rhythm in students with different individual and typological characteristics of the higher nervous activity during examination stress. *Fiziol Zh*, 49, 1, 28-33. Retrieved August 08, 2006, from http://www.ncbi.nlm.gov/ entrez/querry.fegi?itool=abstractplus&pub med&cmd=retrieve &dopt=abstract&list_uids=12669518.

Mandler, G. (1982). Stress and through processes. In L. Goldberger and S. Breznitz, (Eds.), Handbook of stress: Theoretical and clinical aspects. New York: The Free Press.

Mandler, G., and Sarason, S. B. (1952). A study of anxiety and learning. *Journal of Abnormal Social Psychology*, 47, 166-173.

Markle, J. R. (2006). Relax within. Retrived December 25, 2006, from http:/ /www. relaxwithin.com/mkinds.htm.

Marucha, P. T., Kiecolt, J. K., and Favagchi, M. (1998). Mucoral wound healing is impaired by examination stress. *Psychosomatic Medicine*, 60, 362-365. Retrieved August 8, 2006, from http://www.phi. psychiatry.ohio_ stati.edu/jkg/ JKG%20Article %20PDFS/118.pdf.

McCann, B. S., Benjamin, G. A. H., Wilkinson, C. W., Carter, J., Retzlajt, B. M., Russo, J., and Knopp, R. H. (1996). Variations in plasma lipid concentration during examination stress. *International Journal of Behavioral Medicine*, 3, 3, 251-265. Retrieved August 8, 2006, from http://www. erlbaum.com/index.htm.

McClelland, D. C., Ross, G., and Patel, V. (1985). The effect of an academic examination on salivary norepinephrine and immunoglobulin levels. *Human Stress*, 11 (2), 52-59. Retrieved September 17, 2006, from http:/ /www.ncbi.nl.../query.fcgi?cmd= retrieve&db=pubmed&list_ uids=3843108&dopt=Abstrac

McLoyd, V. C., and Smith, J. (2002). Physical discipline and behaviour problems in African American, European American, and Hispanic children: Emotional support as moderator. *Journal of Marriage and Family*, 64, 40-53.

Merton, R. K. (1957). *Social structure and anomie*. In R. K. Merton, (Ed.) Social theory and social structure, (2nd ed.) New York : Free Press.

Minor, S. W. and Gold, S. R. (1985). Worry and emotionality components of test anxiety. *Journal of Personality Assessment,* 49, 1.

Misra, G. (1991), *Psychological perspectives on stress and health.* New Delhi: Concepts Publishers.

Morris, L. W., Davis, M. A., and Hutchings, C. H. (1981). Cognitive and emotional components of anxiety: Literature review and a revised worry – emotionality scale. *Journal of Educational Psychology*, 73, 4, 541-555.

Mouton, C., Fillion, L., Tawadros, E., and Tessier, R. (1989). Salivary IgA is a weak stress marker. *Behavioral Medicines*, 15 (4), 179-185. Retrieved September 17, 2006, from http://www.ncbi.nl.../query.fcgi?cmd =retrieve&db=pubmed&list_uids= 2597782 &dopt=Abstra.

Murray, J. P. (2000). Media effects. In A. Kazdin, (Ed.), *Encyclopedia of psychology*. Washington, DC, and New York: American Psychological Association and Oxford University Press.

Musch, J., and Broder, A. (1999). Test anxiety versus academic skills: A comparison of two alternative models for predicting performance in a statistics exam. *British Journal of Educational Psychology*, 69, 105-116.

Mwamwenda, T. S. (1994). Test anxiety and academic achievement among South African university students. *Psychological Reports*, 75, 1593-1594.

Nagpal, J. (2005). Life *skills education and school MH Programme*. Paper presented at 12th National Conference of Sahodaya School Complexes, Bhubeneswar 18-19th November, 2005. Retrieved January 1, 2007, from http://www. cbse.nic.in/sahobook.pdf.

National Crime Record Bureau, (2000). Ministry of Home Affairs, Government of India.

Newbegin, I., and Owens, A. (1996). Self-esteem and anxiety in secondary school achievement. *Journal of Social Behavior and Personality*, 11, 3, 521-530.

Nijhawan, H.K. (1972). *Anxiety in school children*. New Delhi: Wiley Eastern Private Limited.

Oaten, M., and Cheng, K. (2005). Academic examination stress impairs self-control. *Journal of Clinical Psychology*, 24, 2, 254-279. Retrieved August 8, 2006, from http://www. extenza-eps.com/GPI/doi/abs/10.1521/jscp.24.2.254.62276.

Ollendick, T. H., and Meyer, J. (1984). *School phobia*. In S. M. Tumer, (Ed.) Behavioral theories and treatment of anxiety. New York: Plenum.

Onwuegbuzie, A. J., and Daley, C. E. (1996). The relative contributions of examination-taking coping strategies and study coping strategies to test anxiety: A concurrent analysis. *Cognitive Therapy and Research*, 20, 3, 287-303. Retrieved September 11, 2006, from http://www.springerlink.com/content/ u7v65r60199n7358/.

Osterhouse, R. A. (1972). Desensitization and study-skills training as treatment for two types of test-anxious students. *Journal of Counseling Psychology*, 19, 4, 301-307.

Osterhouse, R. A. (1975). Classroom anxiety and the examination performance of test-anxious students. *The Journal of Educational Research*, 68 (7), 247-250.

Palmer, T. J. (1999, July). Exam stress and the mature student. *Stress News*. Retrieved August 12, 2006, from http:// www.isma.org.uk/stressnw/examstress.htm

Parker, G., Cai, Y., Jan, S., Dear, K., Henderson, A. S., Poh, G. T., and Kwea, G. C. (2003). Examination stress in Singapore primary school children: Low compliance by subjects can impact on study results. *Acta Psychiatrica Scandinavica*, 108, 3, 239-243. Retrieved August 8, 2006, from http://www.ingentaconnect.com/ content/mksg/acp/2003/00000108/00000003 /art 00012.

Patterson, G. R., and Fisher, P. A. (2002). Recent developments in our understanding of parenting: Bidirectional effects, casual models, and the search for parsimony. In M. H. Bornstein, (Ed.), *Handbook of parenting* (2nd ed.). Mahwah, New Jersey: Erlbaum.

Paulman, R. G., and Kennelly, K. J. (1984). Test anxiety and ineffective test taking: Different names, same construct. *Journal of educational psychology*, 76, 2, 279-288.

Pearlin, L. I. (1982). *The social contexts of stress*. In L. Goldberger and S. Breznitz, eds. Handbook of stress : Theoretical and clinical aspects. New York : The Free Press.

Peleng-Popko, O. (2002). Children's test anxiety and family interaction patterns. *Anxiety, stress and coping*, 15, 1, 45-59. Retrieved August 8, 2006 from http://www. ingentaconnect.com/content/routledg/gasc/2002/ 00000015/00000001/art00004.

Pestonjee, D.M. (1999). *Stress and coping the Indian experience*. New Delhi: Sage Publications.

Pintrich, P. R. (2003). Motivation and classroom learning. In I. B. Weiner (Ed.), *Handbook of Psychology*, Vol. 7, New York: Wiley.

Pintrich, P. R., and Schunk, D. H. (2002). *Motivation in education* (2nd Ed.). Upper Saddle River, New Jersy: Prentice Hall.

Pitzer, R. L. (2001). *Children, youth and family consortium*. Retrieved October 16, 2006, from http://www.cyfc.umn.edu/family/resources/ AB1011.htm.

Posen, D. B. (1995). Stress management for patient and physician. *The Canadian Journal of Continuing Medical Education*, 1-6. Retrieved August 9, 2006, from http://www.mentalhealth.com/mag1/p51-str.html.

Post, D. (n.d.). *Case teaching notes for the 2000 meter row: A case study in performance anxiety.* Retrieved August 29, 2006, from http://www. sciencecases.org/crew_ anxiety/crew_ anxiety_notes.asp.

Pramanik, T., Ghosh, A., and Chapagain, G. (2005). Effect of examination stress on the alteration of B.P. in young normotensives clinical methods and pathophysiology. *B. P. Monitoring*, 10, 3, 149-150. Retrieved August 8, 2006, from bpmonitoring.com /pt/re/bpm/fulltext.00126097-200506000-00006.htm;jsessionid=GDYMK93J LTC7nJd.

Putwain, D. (2008). Examination stress and test anxiety. *Psychologist*. Volume 21. Issue 12.

Putwain, D.W. (2011). How is examination stress experienced by secondary students preparing for their general certificate of secondary education examinations and how can it be explained? *International Journal of Qualitative Studies in Education.* Volume 24. No. 6.

Putwain, D.W., Connors, L. and Symes, W. (2010). Do cognitive distortions mediate the test anxiety-examination performance relationship? *Educational Psychology*. Volume 30, Issue 1.

Qureshi, F., Alam, J, Khan, M. A. and Sheraz, G. (2002). Effect of examination stress on blood cell parameters of students in a Pakistani medical college. *Journal of Ayub Medical College Abottabad*, 14 (1),

20-22. Retrieved August 8, 2006, from http://www.ayubmed.edu.pk/JAMC/PAST/14-1/Faiyaz.htm.

Rajendran, R., and Kaliappan, K. V. (1991). A factorial study of sources of student academic stress. *Journal of Psychological Researches*, 35, 1, 53-57.

Ramya, N. (2002). *Coping patterns of junior college students*. M.Phil. dissertation, Department of Psychiatric Social Work, NIMHANS, Bangalore

Rao, K, Moudad, S., and Subbakrishna, D. K. (2000). Appraisal of stress and coping behaviour in college students. *Journal of the Indian Academy of Applied Psychology*, 26, 1 and 2, 5-13.

Richardson, F. C., and Suinn, R. M. (1974). Effects of two short-term desensitization methods in the treatment of test anxiety. *Journal of Counseling Psychology*, 21, 5, 457-458.

Rodgers, J. L., Cleveland, H. H., Van Den Oord, E., and Rowe, D. C. (2000). Resolving the debate over birth order, family size, and intelligence. *American Psychologist*, 55, 599-612.

Rothbart, M. K. (1971). Birth order and mother-child interaction. *Journal of personality and social psychology*, 17, 113-120.

Roy, A. M. (n.d). Course work stress in university students: Investigating problem solving coping, wishful thinking coping, anxiety and depression as predictors of coursework stress. Retrieved September 9, 2006 from http://www. gerardkeegan.co.uk/tsp/arm_project_2.pdf.

Ryan, R., and Deci, E. (2000). Self-determination theory and the facilitation of intrinsic motivation, social development, and well-being. *American Psychologist,* 55, 68-78.

Sanghvi, C. (1994). *Intervention programme in examination anxiety*. Ph.D dissertation, Department of Psychology, Delhi University, New Delhi.

Sanghvi, C. (1995). Efficacy of study skills training in managing study habits and test anxiety of high test anxious students. *Journal of the Indian Academy of Applied Psychology,* 21, 1, 71-75.

Santrock, J. W. (2004). *Child development (10th Ed.)*. Boston : McGraw Hill.

Saraladevi, K., and Devaraj, N. (2003). Effect of examination stress on total and differential count of white blood corpuscles. *Journal of Psychological Researches*, 47, 1, 9-16.

Saraladevi, (2004, October 1-3). *Influence of examination stress on enzymes among students*. Paper presented at the International Conference on Psychophysiology of Panic Attack, University of Westminster, London,

UK. Retrieved August 8, 2006, from http://www. anxiety-panic.com/ conference/c004ah.ctm.

Sarason, I. G. (1960). Empirical findings and theoretical problems in the use of anxiety scales. *Psychological Bulletin*, 57, 403-415.

Sarason, I. G. (1961). Test anxiety and the intellectual performance of college students. *Journal of Educational Psychology*, 52, 4, 201-206.

Sarason, I. G. (1972). Experimental approaches to test anxiety: Attention and the uses of information. In D. C. Spielberger, (Ed.), *Anxiety Current trends in theory and research* (pp. 381-403). New York: Academic Press.

Sarason, I. G. (1973). Test anxiety and cognitive modeling. *Journal of Personality and Social Psychology*, 28, 410-413.

Sarason, I.G. (1975). Anxiety and self-preoccupation. In I. G. Sarason and C. D. Spielberger (Eds.), *Stress and anxiety*, 2. Washington, D. C. : Hemisphere.

Sarason, I. G. (1984). Stress, anxiety, and cognitive interference: Reactions to tests. *Journal of Personality and Social Psychology*, 46, 4, 929-938.

Sarason, I. G., and Sarason, B. R. (1990). Test Anxiety. In H. Leitenberg (Ed.) *Handbook of social and evaluative anxiety* (pp. 475-496). New York : Plenum Press.

Sarason, S. B. (1972). Anxiety, intervention, and the culture of the school. In D. C. Spielberger, (Ed.), *Anxiety current trends in theory and research* pp. 469-477. New York: Academic Press.

Sarason, S. B., Davidson, K. S., Lighthall, F. F., Waite, R. R., and Ruebush, B. K. (1960). *Anxiety in elementary school children – A report of research*. New York: John Wiley & Son, Inc.

Sarason, S. B., and Mandler, G. (1952), Some correlates of test anxiety. *Journal of abnormal and social psychology* 47, 810-817.

Sarikaya, O., Civaner, M., and Kalaca, S. (2006). The anxieties of medical students related to clinical training. *International Journal Clinical Practice.* Retrieved August 8, 2006, from http://www. pubmed.gov/ entrez/query.fcgi? db=pubmed& cmd= Retrieve&dopt=AbstractPlus &list_Uids=167874382itool=iconabstr&query_hl =3&itool =pubmed_ docsum16787438.

Schmidt, L., Sieverding, M., Scheiter, F. and Obergfell, J. (2015). Predicting and explaining students' stress with the Demand–Control Model: does neuroticism also matter? *Efucational Psychology*. Volume 35. Issue 4.

Schmitt, A. P., and Crocker, L. (1982). *Measurement of test anxiety for examines, grades 6-8*. Paper presented at annual meeting of American Educational Research Association, New York.

Schunk, D. H. (2001). Social cognitive theory and self-regulated learning. In B. J. Zimmerman and D. H. Schunk (Eds.), *Self-regulated learning and achievement* (2nd Ed.). Mahwah, NJ : Erlbaum.

Schunk, D. H., and Zimmerman, B. J. (Eds.). (2001). Self-regulation and learning. In I. B. Weiner (Ed.), *Handbook of psychology*. New York: Wiley.

Selye, H. (1956). *The stress of life.* New York: McGraw Hill.

Selye, H. (1985). History and present status of the stress concept. In A. Monat and R. S. Lazarus, (Eds.), *Stress and coping*, (2nd ed.) New York: Columbia University.

Semple, C. G., Gray, C. E., Borland, W., Espie, C. A., and Beasfall, G. H. (1988). Endocrine effects of examination stress. *Clinical Science*, 74, 255-259. Retrieved August 8, 2006, from http://www. clinsci.org/cs/074/cs0740255.htm.

Sharma, S. (1978). Anxiety and academic achievement. *Indian Educational Review*, 54-73.

Sharma, S. (2002). Anxiety in students. *Psychological Studies*, 47, (1-3), 49-53.

Sharma, S., and Sud, A. (1990). Examination stress and test anxiety: A cross-cultural perspective. *Psychology and Developing Societies*, 2, 2, 183-201.

Sharp, V. (1999). *Computer education for teachers* (3rd Ed.), New York: McGraw-Hill.

Shcherbatykh, I. (2000). Effects of parameters of the higher nervous activity on stress in students during examinations. *Zn Vyssh Nerv Deiat Im IP Pavlova*, 50, 6, 959-965. Retrieved August 8, 2006, from http://www.ncbi.nlm.gov/entrez/ querry.fegi?itool=abstractplus&pubmed&cmd=retrieve&dopt=abstract&list_uids=11190095.

Shenkin, A., Salman, P., Taylor, S., and Taylor, W. (2004). Effect of micronutrient supplementation on the immune response to examination stress. *Journal of Parental and External Nutrition*. Retrieved August 8, 2006, from http://www. findarticles.com/p/articles/mi-qa3762/is_200401/ai_n9347992-28K.

Shioya, S. (1995). Relationship of test anxiety and learning behaviour to cognitive appraisals in high school students. *Japanese Journal of Educational Psychology*, 43, 2, 13-21.

Shukla, N., Verma, N. C., Tandon, S. N., Khanna, D. N., Tewari, S., Pandey, U. S., and Singh, S. K. (1993). Examination stress in medical student: A study. *Indian Journal of Medical Sciences*, 47, 2, 264-266.

Silberman, M. L. (1971). Teacher's attitudes and actions towards their students. In M. L. Silberman (Ed.). *The experiment of schooling.* New York: Holt, Rinehart & Winsteon.

Simic, N. (2006). Evaluation of examination stress based on the changes of sinus arrhythmia parameters. *Acta Med Croatica*, 60, 1, 27-33.

Singh, A., and Broota, A. (1992). Socio-personal variables and examination anxiety. *Journal of the Indian Academy of Applied Psychology*, 18, 1 and 2, 73-78.

Smith, K. L., Michael, W. B., and Hocevar, D. (1990). Performance on creativity measures with examination taking instructions intended to induce high or low levels of test anxiety.

Sood, P. (1998). Academic stress and coping strategies of high school students. *Behavioural Medicine Journal*, 1, 1, 63-71.

Son, X., and Matsubara, T. (1991). A study of junior high school students' anxiety about tests and their parents' attitudes to instruction : A comparison between China and Japan. *Japanese Journal of Counseling Science,* 24, 2, 101-110.

Soric, I. (1999). Anxiety and coping in the context of a school examination. *Social Behavior and Personality,* 27, 3, 319-330.

Spangler, G. (1997). Psychological and physiological responses during an exam and their relation to personality characteristics. *Psychoneuroendocrinology*, 22(6), 423-441. Retrieved September 19, 2006, from http://www.ncbi.nl.../query.fcgi?cmd= retrieve&db =pubmed &list_uids =9364621&dopt=Abstrac.

Spangler, G., Pekrun, R., Klaudia, K., and Hofmann, H. (2002). Students emotions, physiological reactions and coping in academic examination. *Anxiety, stress and coping*, 15, 4, 413-432. Retrieved August 14, 2006, from http://www.ww55ntdxxxzzw5vof(45)/pp/home/contribution.asp? referner= parent & backto= issue

Sparfeldt, J., Rost, D. H., Baumeister, U.M. and Christ, O. (2013). Test anxiety in written and oral examinations. *Learning and individual differences.* Volume 24.

Spiegler, M. D., Morris, L. W., and Liebert, R. M. (1968). Cognitive and emotional components of test anxiety: Temporal factors. *Psychological Reports*, 22, 451-456.

Spielberger, C.D. (1966). The effects of anxiety on complex learning and academic achievement. In D. C. Spielberger, (Ed.), *Anxiety and behaviour* (pp. 361-397). New York: Academic Press.

Spielberger, C.D. (1972). Current trends in theory and research on anxiety. In D. C. Spielberger, (Ed.), *Anxiety current trends in theory and research* (pp. 3-19). New York: Academic Press.

Spielberger, C.D. (1972). Anxiety as an emotional state. In D. C. Spielberger, (Ed.), *Anxiety current trends in theory and research* (pp. 24-49). New York: Academic Press.

Spielberger, C.D. (1972). Conceptual and methodological issues in anxiety research. In D. C. Spielberger, (Ed.), *Anxiety current trends in theory and research* (pp. 481-493). New York: Academic Press.

Spielberger, C.D., Gonzalez, P.H., Taylor, J.C., Algeze, B., and Anton, D.W. (1978). Examination stress and test anxiety. In D. C. Spielberger, and G. I. Sarason, (Ed.), *Stress and anxiety* (pp. 167-191). Washington: Hemisphere Publishing Corporation.

Spielberger, C.D., (1980). *Test anxiety inventory : Preliminary professional manual.* Palo Alto, CA : Consulting Psychologists Press.

Stanton, H. E. (1992). Using hypnotic success imagery to reduce test anxiety. *Australian Journal of Clinical and Experimental Hypnosis*, 20, 1, 31-37.

Stewart, A. C., Friedman, S., and Koch, J. (1985). *Child development a topical approach*. New York : John Wiley & Sons.

Stober, J., and Pekrun, R. (2004), Advances in test anxiety research. *Anxiety, stress and coping* 17, 3, 205-211. Retrieved March 3, 2006, from http:// taylor and francis. Metapress.com/media/n97bk9fdrl6jrv80jywv/contribution/4/e1vbteu57gig1=6.pdf

Stowell, J.R., Tumminaro, T. and Attarwala, M. (2008). Moderating effects of coping on the relationship between test anxiety and negative mood. *Stress and Health: Journal of the international society for investigation of stress.* Volume 24. Issue 4.

Strack, J. and Esteves, F. (2015). Exams? Why worry? Interpreting anxiety as facilitative and stress appraisals. *Anxiety, Stress and Coping*. Mar. Vol. 28. Issue 2.

Strelets, V. B., Samks, N. N., and Golikova, Z. V. (1998). The Physiological indices of pre-examination stress. *Zh Vyssh Nevv Deiat Im I P Pavlova*, 48, 3, 458-463. Retrieved August 8, 2006, from http://www.ncbi.nlm.gov/entrez/ querry.fegi?itool=abstractplus&pubmed&cmd=retrieve&dopt=abstract&list_uids=9700909.

STRIDE. (2002). *Effective learning : A practical guide for open distance learners*. Indira Gandhi National Open University, New Delhi.

Sud, A. (1990). A comparative study of test anxiety across Indian and Italian cultures. *Psychological Studies*, 35, 1, 69-75.

Sud, A. (1991). The educational level differences on test anxiety within Indian and US cultures. *Journal of Personality and Clinical Studies,* 7, 2, 131-136.

Sud, A. (1994). Attentional skills training/cognitive modeling: Short term therapeutic cognitive interventions for test anxiety. Directorate of Education. *Psychological Studies*, 39, 1, 1-7.

Sud, A., and Prabha, C. (2003). Academic performance in relation to perfectionism, test procrastination and test anxiety of high school children. *Psychological Studies*, 48, 3, 77-81.

Sud, A., and Prabha, I. (1995). Test anxiety and academic performance: Efficacy of cognitive/relaxation therapies. *Psychological Studies*, 40, 3, 179-186.

Tobias, S. (1985). Test anxiety: Interference, defective skills, and cognitive capacity. *Educational Psychologist*, 20, 3, 135-142. Retrieved September 11, 2006, from http://www.leaonline.com/doi/abs/10.1207/s15326985ep2003_3?journalCode=ep.

Torsheim, T., and Wold, B.(2001). School-related stress, school support, and somatic complaints: A general population study. *Journal of adolescent research*, 16, 3, 293-301.

Ursin, H. and Eriksen, H. R. (2004). The cognitive activation theory of stress. *Psychoneuroendocrinology*, 29 (5), 567-592. Retrieved August 14, 2006, from http://www.ncbi.../query.fcgi?cmd-Retrieve&db=pubmed&dopt=Abstract&list_ uids =1504108.

Volkmer, R. R., and Feather, N. T. (1991). Relations between Type A scores, internal locus of control and test anxiety. *Personality and Individual Differences,* 12, 2, 205-209.

Wachelka, D., and Katz, R. C. (1999). Reducing test anxiety and improving academic self-esteem in high school and college students with learning disabilities. *Journal of Behavior Therapy and Experimental Psychiatry,* 30, 3, 191-198.

Wessel, I., and Mersch, P. P. A. (1994). A cognitive behavioural group treatment for test anxious adolescents. *Anxiety, Stress and Coping an International Journal,* 7, 2, 149-160.

Williams, J.E. (1996). Gender related worry and emotionality test anxiety for high achieving students. *Psychology in the schools*, 33, 2, 159-162.

Williams, J. E. (1996). The relation between efficacy for self-regulated learning and domain specific academic performance, controlling for test anxiety. *Journal of research and development in Education,* 29, 2, 77-80.

Wilson, C. C. (2003). *Racism, sexism, and the media.* Newbury Park, CA: Sage.

Wittmaier, B. C. (1972). Test anxiety and study habits. *The Journal of Educational Research*, 65, 8.

Wine, J. (1971). Test anxiety and direction of attention. *Psychological Bulletin*, 76, 2, 92-104.

Wine, J. D. (1980). Cognitive-attentional theory of test anxiety. In I. G. Sarason (Ed.), *Test anxiety : Theory, research, and applications.* Hillsdale, N.J: Erlbaum

Yue, X. (1994). A comparative study of test anxiety among Chinese and American high school students. *Bulletin of the Hong Kong Psychological Society*, 32-33, 47-59.

Zeidner, M. (1996). How do high school and college students cope with test situations? *British Journal of Education Psychology*, 66, 1, 115-128.

Zeidner, M. (1998). *Test anxiety: The state of the art.* New York: Plenum Press.

Zimmerman, M., Salem, D., and Maton, K. (1995). Family structure and psychosocial correlates among urban African-American adolescent males. *Child Development*, 66, 1598-1613.

Appendix

APPENDIX –I

QUESTIONNAIRE FOR THE STUDENTS

1. Name ______________________________
2. Sex Male ☐ Female ☐
3. Age (in years) ______________________________
4. Class IX ☐ X ☐ XI ☐ XII ☐
5. School ______________________________
6. Percentage of marks obtained in the previous final examination ______________________________

FAMILY BACKGROUND

7. Type of family
   - Joint Family ☐
   - Nuclear Family ☐
   - Single Parent Family ☐
8. Size of Family ______________________________
9. No. of Siblings ______________________________
10. Father's Age / Mother's age

Father's Age		Mother's age	
Below 40 years	☐	Below 40 years	
Between 41-50	☐	Between 41-50	☐
51 & above	☐	51 & above	☐

11. Education of Parents

	Father	*Mother*
No formal schooling	☐	☐
Below 10th	☐	☐

Upto graduation ☐ ☐
Post graduation & above ☐ ☐
Any other, specify ____________________

12. Occupation of parents

Father		*Mother*	
Daily Wage Earners	☐	Housewife	☐
Business	☐	Daily Wage Earner	☐
Service (non-professional)	☐	Business	☐
Service (professional)	☐	Service (non-professional)	☐
Any other, specify________		Service (professional)	☐
		Any other specify ________	

13. Family Income (Monthly Income in Rupees)

Below 5000 ☐
5001 to 10000 ☐
10001 to 15000 ☐
15001 to 20000 ☐
20001 to 25000 ☐
25001 & above ☐
Any other, specify ____________________

FAMILY ENVIRONMENT

14. Do you have a separate room/place for study?

Yes ☐ No ☐

15. Do any of the following distract you?

No.	*Items*	*Often*	*Sometimes*	*Rarely*	*Never*
1.	Music				
2.	TV/VCD				
3.	Computer				
4.	Friends				
5.	Neighbours				
6.	Guests				
7.	Any other, specify				

16. Do you help in household work?

Often ☐ Sometimes ☐ Rarely ☐ Never ☐

17. What are the usual household duties you perform?

No.	Duties	Often	Sometimes	Rarely	Never
1.	Buying milk/vegetables/ grocery etc.				
2.	Helping in the kitchen				
3.	Cleaning house/dusting				
4.	Sibling/elderly care				
5.	Any other, specify				

18. Which of the following modifications are done at your home to suit studies?

No.	Modifications	Often	Sometimes	Rarely	Never
1.	Stop watching TV				
2.	Decabling				
3.	Transferring your roles to others				
4.	Any other, specify				

19. What help do your parents provide during your examinations?

No.	Parents help	Often	Sometimes	Rarely	Never
1.	Relieve you of household work				
2.	Organise your books/study material/ room				
3.	Teach you				
4.	Accompany you to school/tuitions				
5.	Make special food				
6.	Stay awake with you at nights				
7.	Take leave from work during examination				
8.	Avoid guests/parties/get-to-gathers				
9.	Keep away distractions like TV/outing				
10.	Whenever needed give guidance, suggestions				
11.	Any other, specify				

PATENTAL EXPECTATION

20. Have your parents clearly communicated their expectation from you?

    Yes ☐ No ☐

21. What do your parents want you to be in life?

    Doctor ☐ MBA ☐ Scientist ☐ Engineer ☐
    Civil Service ☐ Good Job ☐ I don't know ☐

    Any other, specify ____________________

22. Do your parents frequently remind you of their expectation?

    Often ☐ Sometimes ☐ Rarely ☐ Never ☐

23. What do your parents want you to achieve in this year's final examination?

    At least pass per cent ☐
    At least 50 per cent ☐
    At least 60 per cent ☐
    At least 75 per cent ☐
    At least 85 per cent ☐
    At least 90 per cent ☐
    Any other, specify ____________________

24. What incentives have your parents offered for your good performance in your final examination? If yes, specify

    Nothing specific ☐
    Outing/holiday ☐
    Vehicle ☐
    Dress/Jewellary ☐
    Mobile phone and Other gadgets ☐
    Any other, specify ____________________

25. When you couldn't perform well in examination (as per parent's expectations) what was their reaction?

    Do not bother ☐
    Scolded ☐

Showing displeasure in behaviour ☐
Beating ☐
Arranging for tuitions ☐
Taking assurances for better performance ☐
Any other, specify ____________________

26. Do you think that you are compelled to spend more time on studies by your parents?

    Yes ☐ No ☐

BEHAVIOUR AND EXPECTATIONS

27. What do you want to be in life?

    Doctor ☐ MBA ☐ Scientist ☐ Engineer ☐
    Civil Service ☐ Good Job ☐ I don't know ☐
    Any other, specify ____________________

28. What do you want to achieve in this academic year's final examination?

    At least pass per cent ☐
    At least 50 per cent ☐
    At least 60 per cent ☐
    At least 75 per cent ☐
    At least 85 per cent ☐
    At least 90 per cent ☐
    Any other, specify ____________________

29. How much time (in approximation) do you spend on sleep daily before the declaration of examination schedule?
30. While preparing for examination and during examination how much time (in approximation) do you spend on sleep?
31. What do you think is the principal reason for you wanting to perform well in examination?

    Get into a good career ☐
    Get good marks ☐
    Personal satisfaction ☐
    Meet parent's expectations ☐

Meet school/teacher's expectations ☐
Meet friend's expectations ☐
Any other, specify ____________________

32. Which of the following factors worry you most during examination?

Not having separate room/place for study ☐
Not getting sufficient guidance for studying ☐
Lack of sufficient time for study ☐
Lack of adequate preparation for examination ☐
Disturbance from neighbours/own family ☐
Household chores ☐
Media (TV, serial, cricket matches, movies) ☐
Pressure of parent's expectations ☐
Any other, specify ____________________

33. In your understanding what can help you perform better in examination?

No.	*Help to perform better*	*Often*	*Sometimes*	*Rarely*	*Never*
1.	Organising study (schedule)				
2.	Better understanding of subject				
3.	More help from teachers				
4.	Tuitions				
5.	Supportive parents				
6.	Better conditions at home				

34. When studying how much time do you spend in each of the following activities (in approximation) daily:

No.	*Activities*	*Often*	*Sometimes*	*Rarely*	*Never*
1.	Self study				
2.	Tuition				
3.	Preparing for PMT, PET (entrance exams)				

STUDY HAB ITS

35. How much time do you spend on study everyday? ________ (after school)__________

36. What are the study habits that you practice?

No.	*Activities*	*Often*	*Sometimes*	*Rarely*	*Never*
1.	I study everyday				
2.	When studying for longer time, I take rest in between				
3.	I have all the required books and study materials				
4.	I read very carefully taking down notes				
5.	I am attentive in class				
6.	I frequently remain absent from class				
7.	I cram certain things without understanding				
8.	I prepare a schedule to revise all subjects				
9.	I am not able to plan study time				
10.	I will find it useful if a guidance programme in study habits is arranged.				

37. Test Anxiety Inventory

(a) I feel confident and relaxed while taking examination.

Almost never ☐ Sometime ☐ Often ☐ Almost always ☐

(b) While taking examination I have an uneasy, upset feeling.

Almost never ☐ Sometime ☐ Often ☐ Almost always ☐

(c) Thinking about my grade in a course interferes with my work on test.

Almost never ☐ Sometime ☐ Often ☐ Almost always ☐

(d) I freeze up on important examinations.

Almost never ☐ Sometime ☐ Often ☐ Almost always ☐

(e) During examination I find myself thinking about whether I'll ever get through.

Almost never ☐ Sometime ☐ Often ☐ Almost always ☐

(f) The harder I work at taking a test the more confused I get.

Almost never ☐ Sometime ☐ Often ☐ Almost always ☐

(g) Thoughts of doing poorly interfere with my concentration on test.

Almost never ☐ Sometime ☐ Often ☐ Almost always ☐

(h) I feel jittery when taking an important examination.

Almost never ☐ Sometime ☐ Often ☐ Almost always ☐

(i) Even when I am well prepared for a test. I feel very nervous about it.

Almost never ☐ Sometime ☐ Often ☐ Almost always ☐

(j) I start feeling very uneasy just before getting test paper back.

Almost never ☐ Sometime ☐ Often ☐ Almost always ☐

(k) During test I feel very tense.

Almost never ☐ Sometime ☐ Often ☐ Almost always ☐

(l) I wish examination did not bother me so much.

Almost never ☐ Sometime ☐ Often ☐ Almost always ☐

(m) During important test I am so tense that my stomach gets upset.

Almost never ☐ Sometime ☐ Often ☐ Almost always ☐

(n) I seem to defeat myself while working on important test.

Almost never ☐ Sometime ☐ Often ☐ Almost always ☐

(o) I feel very panicky when I take an important test.

Almost never ☐ Sometime ☐ Often ☐ Almost always ☐

(p) I worry a great deal before taking an important examination.

Almost never ☐ Sometime ☐ Often ☐ Almost always ☐

(q) During test I find myself thinking about the consequences of failing.

Almost never ☐ Sometime ☐ Often ☐ Almost always ☐

(r) I feel my heart beating very fast during important test.

Almost never ☐ Sometime ☐ Often ☐ Almost always ☐

(s) After an examination is over I try to stop worrying about it but I just can't.

Almost never ☐ Sometime ☐ Often ☐ Almost always ☐

(t) During examination I get so nervous that I forget facts I really know.

Almost never ☐ Sometime ☐ Often ☐ Almost always ☐

BEHAVIOURAL MANIFESTATION

38. Following are some of the problems faced by people while facing difficulties. Read the following statements carefully and indicate whether you experience the same while preparing/appearing for examinations.

No.	***Behavioural manifestation***	***Often***	***Sometimes***	***Rarely***	***Never***
1.	I have easy mood swings				
2.	I have low self esteem				
3.	I have mental tension				
4.	I get angry very easily				
5.	I feel like crying				
6.	I feel helpless				
7.	I get upset easily				
8.	I feel uneasy				
9.	I suffer uncontrolled negative thoughts				
10.	I feel confused				
11.	I feel I am in a helpless situation				
12.	I feel mentally exhausted				
13.	I get frightening dreams				
14	I have a feeling of inferiority				
15.	I worry that I would not perform well				
16.	I think getting alone in life is difficult				
17.	I have problem in concentration				
18.	I lack recalling power				
19.	I lack interest in studies				

20. I feel physically tired
21. I overeat
22. I lack appetite
23. I have headaches
24. I have stomach upsets
25. I often remain sick
26. I have increased heart beat
27. I tremble
28. I get breathless

COPING WITH STRESS

39. When I experience any of the above mentioned difficulties I engage in the following

No.	*Coping strategies*	*Often*	*Sometimes*	*Rarely*	*Never*
1.	Practice yoga/relaxation technique				
2.	Meditation				
3.	Prayer for courage to face difficulties				
4.	Visit temples/other religious places				
5.	Sharing problems with friends/ family/relatives				
6.	Involve in recreational activities like TV/Music/ movies				
7.	Physical exercise/walking/ jogging				
8.	Pursuing hobbies (reading, music, instrumental, dancing, painting, etc.)				
9.	Sleeping				
10.	Try to organise studies better				
11.	Take medicines to get rid of problems like headaches, stomach upset, stress, anti-depressant				
12.	Take medicines to improve concentration, reduce sleep, improve memory				

13. Indulge in smoking/drinking/ substance abuse
14 Think that examination is part of life
15. Take examination as stepping stone for success
16. Think of possible better outcomes of examination
17. Ask for guidance from others
18. Believe in destiny
19. Any other, specify.

APPENDIX –II

INTERVEW GUIDE FOR PROFESSIONALS TO DESIGN A SOCIAL WORK INTERVENTION MODEL TO ADDRESS EXAMINATION STRESS

1. What will be the objective of the model?
2. What will be the components of the model?
3. What will be the approach followed?
4. What strategies should be followed?
5. What techniques should be used?
6. What will be the expected outcome/goal of the intervention model?
7. Who would be the ideal person to implement this model?

Index